# Beyond Organizational Change

## Structure, Discourse and Power in UK Financial Services

Glenn Morgan
and
Andrew Sturdy

First published in Great Britain 2000 by
**MACMILLAN PRESS LTD**
Houndmills, Basingstoke, Hampshire RG21 6XS and London
Companies and representatives throughout the world

A catalogue record for this book is available from the British Library.

ISBN 0–333–52699–6

First published in the United States of America 2000 by
**ST. MARTIN'S PRESS, INC.,**
Scholarly and Reference Division,
175 Fifth Avenue, New York, N.Y. 10010

ISBN 0–312–23188–1 (cloth)

Library of Congress Cataloging-in-Publication Data
Morgan, Glenn.
Beyond organizational change: structure, discourse and power in UK financial
services / Glenn Morgan and Andrew Sturdy.
p. cm
Includes bibliographical references and index.
ISBN 0–312–23188–1 (cloth)
1. Financial services industry—Great Britain.   2. Organizational change—
Great Britain.
I. Sturdy, Andrew.   II. Title.
HG186.G7 M63 2000
332. 1′068′4—dc21                                                     00–021165

This book is printed on paper suitable for recycling and made from fully managed and
sustained forest sources.

10   9   8   7   6   5   4   3   2   1
09   08   07   06   05   04   03   02   01   00

Printed in Great Britain

# Contents

# List of Tables

# Acknowledgements

This book is the product of many years' work since we started exploring financial services in the mid-1980s. In this time, we have conducted research projects in numerous companies and with a number of colleagues in different universities in the UK and overseas. Over that period, we have published a number of papers on aspects of financial services in the UK and elsewhere. Many of the arguments of those papers have been incorporated in this book. However, the book goes further in developing a historical and theoretical account of processes of change in financial services. Therefore, we hope that even for those familiar with our previous work, this book will provide a new perspective on the theoretical and empirical problems which we address.

This work began at the Financial Services Research Centre (FSRC) at UMIST in the late 1980s when we both spent a number of years working there. David Knights who led the FSRC has undoubtedly done more than anybody else in the UK to show that the study of retail financial services organizations can be made 'critical'. Many of the ideas in the book have arisen out of conversations, debates and arguments with David over the years. We would also like to thank other colleagues in and around the FSRC during those years for their comments and support, particularly Hugh Willmott, Helen Dean, Fergus Murray, Chris Grey and Deborah Kerfoot. Since we both left UMIST in 1992, our ideas have been influenced by confrontations and debates with other perspectives. Glenn Morgan would particularly like to thank Richard Whitley (Manchester Business School), Peer Hull Kristensen (Copenhagen Business School) and Sigrid Quack (Wissenschaftszentrum, Berlin) for their advice and support. Similarly, Andrew Sturdy is grateful to Barry Wilkinson and Stephen Fineman (Bath School of Management).

Last, but by no means least, we are grateful for the invaluable support of family and friends, Alison Morgan and Heather McCallum in particular.

GLENN MORGAN
ANDREW STURDY

# Part I
# Introduction

# 1 The Social Approach to Organizational Change

INTRODUCTION

Over the last two decades, the issue of organizational change has
assumed central importance within the study of business and management. Indeed, sometimes one might imagine that radical change is
a new experience or observation in the history of work and employment. Particular attention has been given to broad changes – the pace
of technological 'development', the internationalization of markets and
the emergence of new competitors – as well as the ways in which organizations are (re-)building their structures, strategies and cultures in
order to adapt to and shape the new circumstances. How such organizational changes are achieved and the conditions of their emergence and,
for many, 'success' have become central questions for organization and
management theory. In this introduction, we present a critical examination of some of the main approaches to these issues. We then go
on to outline a largely separate literature which has informed our own
approach and introduce how it has been developed in the analysis of
change in the UK financial services sector.

This book is designed to contribute to the *understanding* of the nature
and management of change at two levels. Firstly, we believe it offers a
distinctive and valuable approach to the study of organizational change.
Secondly we believe it offers a range of insights into the process of
change that has occurred over the last two decades within one of the
UK's major sectors – financial services. Our hope is that by the end of
the book, the reader will have been challenged to think about organizational change in new ways through an exploration of the continuing
emergence of management knowledges and practices, especially those
which have come to be associated with 'strategy'. We examine their
institutional domains and dynamics, tensions and contradictions and
subjective experience and outcomes. In doing so, we seek to go *beyond
organizational change*, as it is commonly perceived, in two senses.
Firstly, *organizations* are not our prime focus, but the institutions, discourses and identities which sustain and transform them in a particular

3

industry or 'organizational field'. Secondly, *change* is seen to be as much associated with producing order(s) as it is with transformation.

In this introduction, we set out to achieve three tasks. Firstly, we review dominant approaches to the study of organizational change and identify the bases and characteristics of our own approach. Secondly, we account for our choice of financial services as a sector within which to develop this approach. Thirdly, we briefly outline the structure of the book as a whole.

**What is organizational change?**

The first difficulty in any discussion of change is to identify the object of study. For Ford and Ford (1994), change is a phenomenon of *time* involving two elements: *identity* (what something is and becomes) and the *process* of transformation. However, change is crucially determined by one's perspective(s). For example, according to the logic of 'trialectics' (*ibid.*), there are no 'things' in the world (which change) other than change or movement – it is not so much that everything changes, but everything *is* change. People, organizations, ideas etc. are abstractions of movement – temporary, identifiable 'resting points' (*ibid.*: 766). Less abstractly, Kanter *et al.* (1992) suggest that stability is unnoticed change. While such positions rightly challenge the focus of traditional organizational theory on explaining and/or achieving stability, the question of what counts as organizational change is still meaningful. Firstly, one can debate the *extent* to which change has occurred, such as, say, the flattening of organizational hierarchies. Secondly, the *significance* of change may be contested – the same phenomena can be treated as evidence both of change and of stability or continuity depending upon the perspective which is taken (for example, see Morgan, 1986; Jacques, 1996; Gerlach, 1996). For example, for an individual employee, a new job location or work-group member may be experienced as a highly significant change. However, even organization-wide or broader changes which senior management and industry commentators feel are important may, from outside the organization, appear insignificant. For instance, the increasing attention to customer service in organizational cultures and practices may be seen as having, if anything, only a marginal effect on producers' overall power over consumers (Burton, 1994). By contrast, others, such as management consultants ('change agents') and some academics, have an interest in drawing attention to and even celebrating change as a means of promoting it. Indeed, change has become fashionable to the point of being seen as a business imperative – the world is changing so we must change with it.

Some academic studies have tried to overcome the ambiguity over the nature and extent of organizational change by distinguishing between two main types of change process (see Dunphy and Stace, 1988). The first can be referred to as the sort of ongoing change which is seen as necessary for any organization to adapt to what is going on in its own environment. March, for example, notes that 'organisations are continually changing, routinely, easily and responsively' (1981: 563). However, it is often claimed that this level of change is 'skin-deep'. The analogy here is that the organization has some sort of 'character' in a way similar to that which may be claimed of the individual subject. Surface changes, therefore, do not necessarily change what lies underneath, the 'character' of the organization. This 'character' is referred to by a variety of terms. Some authors may use the term organizational culture, the set of assumptions, norms, values and beliefs which underlie actions and structures and provide the framework within which these are constructed (see Bate, 1994, and Ott, 1989). Others have developed the argument to link aspects of organizational culture to systems and processes and prefer to analyse the totality in terms of 'configurations' or 'archetypes' (Greenwood and Hinings, 1993; Meyer *et al.*, 1993; see also Miller and Friesen, 1984). From this perspective much of the change which occurs in organizations does not fundamentally alter the culture or archetype; rather it is absorbed or dealt with by the existing patterns of arrangements; there is no fundamental break, rather a process of development (Bate, 1994).

This type of change is contrasted with what Levy calls 'second-order' change (1986) and Bate terms 'cultural transformation' (1994). This is the situation where organizations undergo a major strategic and structural change which necessitates a thoroughgoing re-examination of all facets of the system, its values and processes. Greenwood and Hinings, for example, are concerned to develop an understanding of how existing archetypes break down and organizations move from one archetype to another; they refer to this process of change in terms of movement from one design track to another (Greenwood and Hinings, 1993).

This distinction between different levels of change is important to recognize. However, it embodies two assumptions that need to be treated with some scepticism. First, it invites one to treat organizations as though they have, or should have, a strong inner unity, whether one terms that culture or archetype. Whilst authors like Bate and Greenwood and Hinings clearly recognize that this is an oversimplification, it can become implicit and unexamined in work from this perspective. It is therefore necessary to incorporate into the analysis the existence and persistence of different, shifting and often conflicting orientations, alliances, interests, identities and values in any particular organization. To do otherwise and thereby assume a dominant 'culture' may be misleading (Parker, 1995). Secondly, there is the problem of conflating the pace of change with its nature. Change may appear to be rapid when it is forced on the organization from the top-down as part of an explicit process of transformation. However, top-down programmes of change may peter out as they face resistance or indifference lower down the organization. On the other hand, gradual, slow change may eventually lead the organization to a new archetype – 'radical incrementalism' (Colville *et al.*, 1993: 563). As March has stated: 'substantial changes occur as the routine consequence of standard procedures or as the unintended consequence of ordinary adaptation' (1981: 575).

In this book, our concern is primarily with change that appears, or is claimed, to have transformed the organization. We are less concerned with top-down change projects that proclaim a rapid transformation of the organization than with the gradual but transformative processes that reshape organizations and the sectors in which they are located. From this perspective, top-down change projects are understood as the attempts of management to come to terms with and act upon the forces that are seen to be reshaping the activities of their organizations. But this is only one part of the process whereby an organization is transformed. It also occurs through changes in practices and languages which are not necessarily or exclusively articulated in top-down initiatives. Instead, these emerge as actors at various levels within the organization and beyond seek to deal with and make sense of their changing circumstances. Moreover, it is not at all clear that these actors always realize the extent and consequences of the changes which are occurring. Nor do they necessarily conceive of them in transformatory as opposed to developmental or adaptive terms. This makes it difficult to push change processes into orderly boxes and argue in terms of transformation from one archetype to another. When we study the process of organizational change, where we draw the start and finish lines is, to a degree, arbitrary. So, the story does not have a clear beginning or end, other than that which we, as observers and authors, construct for it.

## APPROACHES TO THE STUDY OF ORGANIZATIONAL CHANGE

Seeking to account for change and, by association or contradistinction, stability has a long history in ancient and modern philosophy (e.g. Taoism, Heraclitus, Hegel) and, relatedly, social, especially systems, theory. The concern in both cases is with identifying underlying, often hidden, *logics of change* or, more conventionally, single or multi-factor determinants or *motors of change*. For example, in the latter case, a range of established approaches can be identified. Cohen, for instance, critically reviews seven perspectives on the primary cause of social change: technological development; economic/materialistic (e.g. Marx); structured conflict; malintegration or incompatibility of system elements; system adaptation (e.g. functionalism); ideational (e.g. Weber), and; cultural interaction (1968). In the former case of change logics, Morgan highlights three possible metaphors of flux:

> ... as an autopoietic manifestation of our own actions [self-producing systems], as a network of mutual causality shaped by processes of positive and negative feedback [cybernetics], and as a dialectical process of unfolding contradiction. (1986: 268)

We do not concern ourselves here with replicating the detail of all these approaches which are widely documented. Rather, we shall see how to a certain extent they have been, and continue to be, applied to organizations, sometimes explicitly. For example, a recent development has been an application of 'chaos' theory from the natural sciences – the 'constrained instability' and partial unpredictability of non-linear systems such as the weather (Gleick, 1987). In organizational terms, such 'chaos' renders conventional strategic control self-defeating, mythical or a delusion (Stacey, 1992: 63). Similarly, others have sought to develop new organizational change logics such as 'trialectics' mentioned earlier (Ford and Ford, 1994) or, in recognition of the limitations of single-frame approaches, an integrative, interactive and contingency approach to basic theories of change (Van de Ven and Poole, 1995: Nadler, 1998). Indeed, while we do not seek to construct such a general theory of change, in setting out our 'social' approach to organizational change different logics and motors of change are drawn on, particularly those associated with ideational and social structural interaction and contradiction.

However, before addressing some of these issues, we turn to more conventional organizational change literature where change theories are mostly implicit. Emphasis is given to describing, classifying and prescribing change (Morgan, 1986) which tends to reflect assumptions about organizations and human behaviour more than about change. So, for example, behaviourist/rationalist, humanist and pluralist perspectives give rise respectively to restructuring, participation and conflict resolution/management as effective change approaches (see Fineman, 1991). This is evident in the following review where, recognizing heterogeneity within some perspectives and complementarity between them, we nevertheless set out three mainstream approaches to *organizational* change. The first can be labelled *managerialist* in that the framework of analysis is set by the requirements of management to achieve change and the authors are largely concerned to offer prescriptions and techniques whereby managers can and should engineer change and control. The second approach we term *political*. Here, there is a greater recognition that actors within organizations bring different sets of values and interests into any change context. Political conflict, bargaining and negotiation become the central elements of analysis and the key managerial skill is that of political manipulation. In our view, both these approaches are limited in relying too much upon the way in which managers in organizations perceive the problems and solutions of change at the expense of its social and historical constitution. In this sense, they do not problematize the way in which managers perceive change. They do not subject the categories of management thought to critical analysis and ask how and why they have developed in this particular way and what may be the implications for organizational change and actors. We would argue that there is another approach which we would wish to term the *social* approach to organizational change which does attempt to address these issues. This approach can be discerned in, and drawn from, a number of works and, sometimes conflicting, theoretical perspectives which examine how management practices and knowledges are constructed and reproduced in particular institutional and social settings. Here, rather than adopt a single factor approach to change, different economic, institutional and social logics are evident and integrated in an effort to illuminate and explain complex change processes.

**The managerialist approach to change**

If we examine recent literature on the management of change it is immediately obvious that there is a great amount of work which has as its overt goal the task of educating and helping managers to manage and even 'love' change (Peters, 1989). It broadly accepts and reproduces management's definitions of the situation or 'problem' (e.g. insufficient employee commitment, increased competition). It then seeks to stimulate action and/or advise on how best to define, and achieve the goal which management sets. It does this either through universalistic prescription or through variations of contingency theory whereby change methods and goals are dependent upon contextual variables (e.g. Dunphy and Stace, 1988; Daft, 1998; Nadler, 1998; Senior, 1998). The approach is typically based upon what might be termed an 'engineering' view of change in organizations – how does management best get from state A to state B? Often, prescriptions depart little from Lewin's much cited model from the 1950s – unfreeze; change; re-freeze (1951) – by stating that if this is where you are and this is where you want to be, here is the route map to get there (e.g. Beckhard and Harris, 1987, c.f. Weick, 1987; Kanter *et al.*, 1992). Clearly, and as intimated earlier, there is a broad and established literature on change management techniques. Indeed, in a review by Huczynski, over 350 possible methods of achieving change were identified (1987) including the varying degrees of emphasis given to change through imposition or participation (e.g. Dunphy and Stace, 1988). Nevertheless, it is possible to identify two broad approaches of this type which have developed recently which emphasise leadership and culture and organizational structure and processes.

*Leadership and cultural change approach*

As major US and other Western companies in a range of industries saw their markets eroding with foreign competition, particularly from Japan and the Far East, major problems of financial and business viability emerged which were seen to require management action on a large scale. Two associated approaches to change developed. The first was to re-emphasize the importance of leadership as distinct from management. For Kotter, for example, 'management is about coping with complexity...Leadership by contrast is about coping with change' (1990: 104). In this framework, the leader was restored to the heroic figure capable of setting the direction of change or 'vision' and motivating people to follow – organizational change could best be instituted by cultivating and/or bringing in a charismatic leader (c.f. Nadler and Tushman, 1990). Whilst this approach continues to have significant appeal, it is clearly flawed in a number of respects. Firstly, it individualizes social relations and underplays the complexities of power and context in organizations (see Knights and Morgan 1992; Thomas 1993 for reviews and critiques of this literature). Also, even if one discounts the valid contention that 'charisma' is produced through assuming leadership status rather than prior experience or inheritance, then there are simply not enough Bill Gates' or Harvey Jones' to go round!

Perhaps partly as a result of its limitations, this approach was often linked to a wider and now quite familiar perspective seemingly capable of infinite replication. This was the so-called cultural change programme. In this approach, leadership was given less significance and more attention was paid to managing meaning – the key values and norms of the organization as a whole. From a managerialist (and unitary) perspective, the operation was threefold; first, identify the current shared values and norms of the organization; second, state what the culture *should* be; third, identify the gap between the two and develop a plan to close it. The notion of what the culture *should* be was, and remains, controversial. At first, authors such as Peters and Waterman (1982) were cited in emphasizing the need for a strong culture – one in which all members of the organization were committed to its goals. However, the danger of a strong culture was that it would be resistant to change and become ossified. Gradually therefore, authors began to emphasize the need for culture to fit the environment and then more generally the need for the culture to encourage adaptiveness, continuous (or organizational) learning and change in order to meet organizational objectives (see Kotter and Heskett, 1992, for a clear statement of these changing perspectives). The writings of Peters, Kanter and their associates clearly reveal this sort of transition in the ways in which their own orientations developed from the early 1980s (Peters and Waterman, 1982; Peters and Austin, 1985; Peters, 1989; Kanter, 1985, 1989; Kanter *et al*., 1992). These arguments (reinforced by other approaches deriving from a variety of sources such as Total Quality Management) eventually developed into the ideas of organizational leaning and the 'learning organization', (see Easterby-Smith, 1997, Handy, 1989 and Garvin, 1993).

Often cultural change programmes focused on the customer and the idea that organizations had become too self-centred. They needed to get 'close to the market', to provide 'quality for the customer' and therefore 'add value for the shareholder'. These initiatives and polemics continue today in various forms (e.g. Rucci *et al*., 1998). The articulation of the vision and company mission has to be translated into a series of practical prescriptions for employees which can be seen to have an impact (Schaffer and Thomson, 1992). However, the prescriptions typically were not to act as *direct* control mechanisms so much as ways of releasing the energies of lower-level employees to act in ways which they would have been doing anyway if they had not been prevented by bureaucracy and the dead hand of middle management (Peters, 1989). Employees were to 'internalize' the goals of the company, to redefine themselves as achieving self-identity and respect through fulfilment in work and satisfying customer needs (c.f. Sturdy, 1998).

In common with many management ideas historically, a concept of leadership was not entirely absent from this approach (see Huczynski, 1993). Change programmes were heavily driven from the top of the organization, yet relied on commitment from below. Peters and Waterman referred to this as the requirement for simultaneous 'loose–tight' properties in organizations; tight in the sense that there was a central core of values to which everyone was committed but loose in that individuals lower down were free to act as they wanted so long as they were in accord with the basic values (Peters and Waterman, 1982). For senior management this approach offered a guide and continued legitimation for their power and status, yet its relevance to either middle management (sometimes made the scapegoat for organizational problems) or lower-level employees (expected to work more intensively in order to enhance their own self-worth) was not always clear (Kunda, 1991; c.f. Anthony, 1990). Even with an assumption of a unitary model of the organization, these cultural change programmes would be problematic in seeking to disrupt or 'unfreeze' taken for granted values and practices. In the complexity and contradictions of the 'real world', many of them foundered after the initial wave of enthusiasm and people found themselves dealing with the same old problems of increased competition, decreasing margins and an absence of employee commitment and communication.

Reevaluation of these types of programmes generated a series of prescriptions about how to increase the likelihood of success. Indeed, their very difficulty has come to be defined as a potential source of 'competitive advantage' in that many firms will not be able to replicate success (Boxall, 1996; Rucci *et al.*, 1998). For example, Beer and colleagues at Harvard argued that change programmes in the 1980s had not actually produced change (Beer *et al.*, 1990). In order to be successful, managers had to be much more circumspect, changing expectations and standards gradually, building support both inside and outside the organization prior to incremental change. All the time however, top management had to maintain its vision and nerve, utilizing opportunities to move its supporters into key positions (Kotter, 1990; Pascale, 1990).

These prescriptions and reevaluations introduced very little that was new into the argument. Indeed, they tended to follow the preference for incremental change and token employee participation which characterizes the 1960s, and still influential, North American tradition in Organization Development (see Dunphy and Stace, 1988). Also, while they offered a more sophisticated or cautious view of 'cultural engineering', they still looked at change in terms of management's objectives and the central ideas of leadership and culture. Many managerialist approaches to change continue to utilize this framework. However, as the changing environment became more of a focus and the 1980s boom petered out and recession began to bite more deeply, a harder edge began to reappear in management-change literature promoting more radical change and coercive practices (*ibid*.: Legge, 1995).

*Organization structure, processes and change*

The perceived limitations of large-scale and incremental cultural change programmes has contributed to and coincided with a growing managerial interest in restructuring organizational processes and activities (see also Grint, 1994). For example, there is a growing literature on what is termed business process reengineering (BPR) (Hammer and Champy, 1993) – the idea that organizations need to go right back to the drawing board and consider what they want to achieve, how they are currently achieving it and how it can be most efficiently organized, particularly with the aid of information and communication technologies. Authors in this perspective argue that there is often a huge gap between how things are currently done and how things should be done. BPR presents (re-packages) a number of practices and concepts to change or rebuild the organization in a new image. However, it has very little to say about problems of resistance, conflict and competing values. Hammer and Champy for example argue that 'the key to success lies in knowledge and ability' (1993: 200). However, when it comes to knowledge about people and their responses to change they offer little beyond common-sense managerial homilies:

Trying to please everyone is a hopeless ambition . . . the first step in managing resistance is to expect it and not to let it set the effort back ... Take longer [than twelve months] ... and people will become impatient, confused and distracted. (*Ibid*.: 212)

Similarly, if reengineering fails, then it is attributed to senior managers' inadequate understanding or leadership of the reengineering effort (*ibid*.: 213). Thus, despite a 'veneer of HRM-type ideas' (Willmott, 1995: 89; Grint and Case, 1998) the change process is reduced to a technical task which can only fail through lack of ability or persistence on the part of managers.

A precursor to BPR and often practised alongside it was the set of ideas associated with total quality management (TQM). Again emphasis was placed on the need to consider each step in the production process as a node of relationships between customers and suppliers. Suppliers (whether internal or external to the organization) had to 'get it right first time' with 'zero defects' so that their customers (either inside or outside) received a quality product. Although different elements were emphasized, TQM was partly about a series of 'technical' prescriptions concerned with the analysis and measurement of the production process and reducing errors (and costs) and partly about cultural change concerning the commitment of lower level employees to the idea of quality (Wilkinson *et al*., 1997; Edwards *et al*., 1998). Again, it is hard to see any theory of change that goes beyond an expectation and belief that this is the most efficient way to organize and should therefore be welcomed by all. If it fails, it cannot be the fault of the theory (see Knights and McCabe, 1997).

Change programmes which develop out of these approaches are ostensibly concerned to rebuild the firm, stripping out long hierarchies and creating an organization characterized by a flatter authority structure and multiple horizontal linkages between the inner core of the firm and its outside suppliers, contractors and customers. These changes have also given rise to the concepts of the 'federal organization' or the 'network firm', implying a central node of coordination, if not control (Handy, 1993), linked to smaller-scale enterprises and businesses where skilled labour and professional workers at least can exercise greater freedom and autonomy, albeit with increased accountability for performance. This blends together the level of vision and culture (close to the customer/the innovative organization) with a programme for organizational restructuring which minimizes expensive permanent labour and creates new market relations both within the organization and with those linked to it on the outside. The boundary of '*the organization*' becomes blurred. This approach to change is short on analysis of successful implementation where people have different interests and values. It assumes that organizational life is a non-zero sum game. In the end, everyone will win out. Presumably, those who are 'released' from permanent employment will find more rewarding forms of work in a self-employed capacity, and society as a whole will benefit from the extra productivity which these new-found efficiencies will generate. Those further down the hierarchy will have more freedom to innovate and initiate action in response to market changes.

Managerialist approaches to change such as those above have mushroomed over the last twenty years. New terminologies, concepts and gurus have emerged and declined as management has struggled to find a path through an apparently rapidly changing environment. 'Heathrow' organization theory has sold well (not just in airport lounges!) and made millions for its authors and publishers (Burrell, 1996; Collins, 1998). Three features, however, ought to be emphasized. First and perhaps most importantly, evidence of successfully achieving change through the self-conscious adoption and top-down implementation of such approaches is difficult to find. Instead their implementation tends to lead to partial success and partial failure where contradictory and unanticipated consequences emerge in the process of change (Burnes, 1996; Clark *et al.*, 1988). This reflects and repeats the longstanding dilemmas of management whereby control of a necessarily interdependent and unpredictable social world is sought but never quite achieved (see Barley and Kunda, 1992 for a discussion of this problem). Second and relatedly, such approaches offer a weak analytical framework for understanding how and why organizations change. They are concerned to offer reassurance through (re)packaged prescriptions that reduce complex reality to simple formulations (see Gill and Whittle, 1992; Huczynski, 1993). As Collins argues, they reflect either an under-socialized or over-socialized model of change – rationalist '*n*-step' guides are silent on problems such as conflicting values and interests, while culture-change prescriptions present them as manageable (1998: 127). Thirdly, however, no matter how analytically weak these theories may appear to be, they have been both informed by and become part of the language, consciousness and/or actions of many managers and consultants, albeit not always in a straightforward manner (see Watson, 1994; Keenoy, 1998). They have thus contributed to shaping the way these individuals talk, think and/or act and therefore at a secondary level to the way in which organizations are structured, reproduced and changed. Organizations do not change just because management gurus will it to be so, or top management introduce BPR or TQM. Nevertheless, these models of change become part of the way in which people understand and make sense of their world as well as becoming invested with power to change that world.

## Political approaches to change

In broad terms, we use this phrase to refer to all those approaches to change which reject the idea of a unitary frame of reference and conceptualize organizational change in terms of competing interest groups. In Fox's formulation of 'frames of reference' in industrial relations, the 'unitary' and 'pluralistic' (i.e., political) perspectives were both seen as managerialist (1974). Despite our different terminology a similar position is set out here. There are some exceptions. For example, the industrial democracy tradition in change literature (e.g. Elden, 1986) stresses 'democratization' rather than 'participation' which is characteristic of organizational development. It thereby posed a partial challenge to hierarchical relations even if it was assumed that conflicts were reconcilable within capitalism generally (see Dunphy and Stace, 1988). More recently, conflicting interests have been portrayed in terms of different 'stakeholders' and coalitions rather than focusing on capital–labour conflicts. Here, typically, the challenge presented to power relations is even more muted (e.g. Salancik and Pfeffer, 1978; Kanter *et al.*, 1992).

In such a perspective, the conflict between interest groups or, in more recent terminology, 'stakeholders', is understood by recognizing two other features of the change process. The first concerns the temporal dimension and the need to study change, not through snapshots, but over long periods of time in order to understand how groups and individuals interact and produce outcomes. The second concerns the need for the study of the *context* of the change process in terms of two or more levels – the *external* context (such as government, economy, competition, shareholders etc.) and the *internal* context (changing work processes, technologies, organization structures etc.).

These approaches focus on similar topics to those discussed above (e.g. culture, leadership, structure etc.), but seek to provide a framework for a better *understanding* of the change *process* rather than simply aim to present a list of prescriptions about how to achieve change. As we shall see, this does not mean that they shrink from prescription.

Rather, their prescriptions focus more on political and organizing skills than 'technical' procedures. The most prominent framework within this approach is that developed by Pettigrew in a series of studies of major organizational change conducted over the last decade, particularly that of ICI (1985, 1987, 1990; Pettigrew and Whipp, 1991; Pettigrew *et al.*, 1993). Pettigrew is critical of the acontextual, atheoretical and aprocessual nature of mainstream organizational change and development literature (see Pettigrew, 1985; Collins, 1998), and his work represented a significant analytical advance in the study of organizational change. In addition, although criticized for being impractical (e.g. Buchanan and Boddy, 1992; Dawson, 1994), it presents a distinctive approach to managing change. He argues that achieving major organizational change requires the successful management of three aspects.

First, all change programmes exist in the particular internal and external environment of the organization. The internal environment refers to all aspects of an organization's functioning but in particular to its culture, leadership, structure and human resources policy. The degree to which organizational cultures are homogeneous and the strength of such cultures will vary. Nevertheless, organizational change cannot be delivered unless it is either in line with the culture or the culture is somehow changed to 'fit'. The appropriate leaders with the skills for achieving change must be in place and able to shape culture, structure and human resource policy to fit the change programme. However, in any organization, there will be a number of groups and individuals competing for power and using internal structures and processes to their own advantage. The internal environment exists within a broader economic and political context. Leaders within organizations have to be able to utilize external changes to add weight to their own power and authority in the change process. Economic crises in the form of falling markets or new government regulation can become the opportunity, as well as stimulus, for managers to achieve change. The second aspect Pettigrew identifies is the management of the change process itself. Leaders have to ensure that there is a broad recognition of the need for change and then to ensure that the way in which change is introduced and managed is coherent and consistent with the organization's culture and goals. This in turn requires building success incrementally rather than going for 'quick fix' solutions. Thirdly, change management requires some content, a programme or vision towards which the change is directed. This needs to be sufficiently broad to be meaningful to everybody in the organization, but also to say something specific enough to provide a motivating force and be communicated accordingly.

Other political approaches to the change process share with Pettigrew a concern with certain central phenomena – political bargaining and negotiation within organizations and contextualizing and examining change over long time periods. They also share and even extend a prescriptive basis for management which focuses on the idea of political skills. Johnson and Scholes, for example, refer to Macchiavelli as a source for guidance on how to use language, symbols and rituals in order to promote change. They also identify how organizational resources may be used to 'build a power base ... encourage support or overcome resistance ... and achieve commitment' (1993: 407). Similarly, Buchanan and Boddy (1992) identify the need to synthesize the rational linear model of programmed change dominant among managers with the political processual model of emergent change. They argue that this can be achieved by identifying the key competencies of change agents which combine public performance skills (e.g. based on demonstrating expertise in rational planning) with backstage activity of persuasion and negotiation. Pettigrew *et al.* refer to this as the need to create receptive contexts for change (Pettigrew, Ferlie and McKee, 1993).

The political approach to change then promotes more sophisticated 'cultural engineering'. It recognizes the multiplicity of groups involved in the change *process* and the complexity and contextually bounded nature of change. It also recognizes the uncertainties and ambiguities of the change process which emerge from the interaction of the different elements. Mintzberg's work has particularly emphasized the point that the direction of organizational change is not always as top management might have expected or even wanted; he refers to the 'emergent process of strategic change' where outcomes are often the unanticipated results of the clash between a planned strategy set by senior management, and the responses and judgements of people at lower levels of the organization. Thus, strategic change is less a matter of planning and more a case of management skillfully 'crafting' outcomes through continued adaptations and iterations of formal planning procedures in the light of internal and external responses (Mintzberg, 1987, 1994; Mintzberg and Waters, 1985). However, partly as a consequence of the Business School/management/consultant audience to which such literature is often and increasingly directed, it still tends to be pulled towards a managerial frame of reference and reductionist prescriptions to achieve control (e.g. Kanter *et al.*, 1992; Dawson, 1994; c.f. Collins, 1998). In recognition of organizational pluralism and the necessarily interactive and informal nature of cultural (meaning) production and change generally, an, albeit limited, form of cultural democracy *may sometimes* be argued for. Nevertheless, management's role is largely unchallenged – 'managers may manage change but it is not they who exclusively decide on what that change should be' (Bate, 1994: 229).

## The social approach to change

As our review so far has demonstrated, the study of organizational change is populated by many researchers. Furthermore, in broad terms, there is, certainly among a growing number of academics, a degree of consensus in terms of the need to look at change from a longitudinal perspective taking account of context, content and process. However, in our view, the alternative approaches available to researchers are still too limited (see also Collins, 1998). Authors who reject the overtly managerialist approaches outlined earlier may be attracted to the political approach, but even here often find themselves drawn into an uncritical managerialist framework, whereby the politics of the change process is examined using essentially the same categories of understanding as the actors themselves (which are invariably managerial).

In this book, we argue that in order to understand change processes, it is necessary to examine the languages, concepts, categories and their associated practices which actors adopt to make sense of, construct and act in the world. These *discourses* are locally reproduced and transformed as social action, but also, and crucially, emerge from and produce distinctive social contexts. The term 'discourse' has come to be associated with postmodernist studies of organization such as those drawing on Foucault (1972). Although as a focus of analysis it also has a tradition in other theoretical approaches, for example symbolic interactionism and ethnomethodology (see du Gay, 1996; Reed, 1997), we share aspects of this more recent formulation of discourse as 'what *can* be said' (and done) (Jacques, 1996). Discourses become the way in which individuals explain themselves, their actions and organizations – both to themselves and to others; they also underlie the mechanisms of control and coordination, the framework for building and maintaining order, that managers construct within and across organizations. Bodies of knowledge are constructed which are often transmitted and translated by organizational participants into routines and procedures which, in turn, constitute or contribute towards the construction of new or adapted knowledges and practices. These bodies of knowledge become languages through which people speak about and understand organizational processes. From the point of view of organizational change, therefore, we need to understand what these bodies of knowledge and practice are which actors articulate as ways of understanding and achieving a sense of control over the world in which they are located. We also need to understand why these particular bodies of knowledge and practices have emerged as relatively enduring, and yet ultimately fragile, modes of understanding in particular contexts.

These themes echo concerns within critical social theory with underlying logics of change and with power and knowledge as well as those of a growing literature focusing on the proliferation of management ideas or knowledges (e.g. Gill and Whittle, 1992; Huczynski, 1993a; Grint, 1994; Abrahamson, 1996). One can identify five, sometimes complementary and sometimes conflicting, streams of relevant literature or perspectives which can contribute to understanding the way in which management knowledges and practices are generated, reproduced, transformed and resisted. All of these deal in varying ways with the issue of why and how managers take up certain modes of understanding of their own position and practices which then become ways of seeking to control themselves and their worlds.

*The Marxist approach*

The role and ideological function of management and social (and other) science ideas and applications in furthering and legitimating the managerial prerogative to organize, lead and control the labour process and reproduce power and inequality has been a central theme in Marxist writing (Baritz, 1960; Braverman, 1974; Anthony, 1977) and an important counter to managerialist and rationalist literature (Collins, 1998). A parallel and sometimes overlapping literature focuses on a similar relationship between management knowledge and patriarchal power and gender inequality. This is particularly evident in accounts of technological change (e.g. Cockburn, 1985; Sturdy *et al.*, 1992). More recently, attention has been given to the gendered (typically masculine) nature managerial knowledges and practices both generally (Morgan, 1986) and in specific cases such as strategy (e.g. Kerfoot and Knights, 1993; Jacques, 1996) and BPR (Grint and Case, 1998). However, overall and in common with the tradition in other areas of 'malestream' organizational theory (Wilson, 1996), organizational change literature has been gender-blind (Tienari, 1999; see also Chapter 7). The Marxist view contrasts with the political or pluralist approach to change, not by giving primacy to conflicting interests, but by presenting conflict as irreconcilable within existing social relations. In this sense, it would seem to point to continuity rather than change – organizational structures may be flatter and more global, but both hierarchy and the wage relation persist (Willmott, 1992). However, Marxist theory and, in particular, its use of the broader concept of dialectics – change as the product of internal tensions between opposites – can provide insightful accounts of change. For example, Marglin (1979) sees managerial problems (e.g. labour resistance or low commitment) as symptoms of inherent contradictions of capitalist social relations (e.g. between socialized production and privatized appropriation or the use and exchange value of labour to employers). Provided that these structural relations are preserved, attempts to solve problems, such as through the deployment of work humanization knowledges, will simply lead to new problems (see also Edwards, 1979). In spite of the intentions of management, control is followed by resistance or counter-control in a continuing cycle. In other words, the model of change allows for and predicts unintended or contradictory consequences and helps to account for the continued emergence of new management knowledges. Relatedly, the emergence and dominance of particular management ideas/functions can be explained in terms of conflicts *within* capital (c.f. capital–labour) as groups (e.g. accountants, consultants) compete for privileged positions and status within organizations and society by developing and offering profitable solutions (Armstrong, 1986, 1989, 1991; Sturdy, 1997b).

Such structural tensions need not necessarily be linked to Marxist theory. Abrahamson for instance, highlights 'technical contradictions' *within* organizations as shaping the flow of management ideas. For example, centralization (e.g. leadership) may stifle employee autonomy and thereby open up a market for decentralization-type solutions (e.g. 'empowerment') (1996; see also Child, 1984). He also points to macro-economic cycles of expansion and contraction as a key factor. Indeed, structural-economic forces are key in shaping the emergence, if not the form, of managerial problems and, therefore, ideas (e.g. Guillen, 1994). Moreover, within most Western organizations, it is the capitalistic form of economic exchange and its associated tensions which is central in framing change processes (Ramsay, 1976; Wilkinson, 1996; Smith and Meiksins, 1995; c.f. Whittington, 1992). Such a perspective on change is important in drawing attention to broad and contradictory structures of power which reproduce continuity as well as change. However, and as we shall see, it is insufficient to explain adequately the complex, varied and precise nature of change. Not only is the 'economic'/material often falsely separated from the 'social' (Sturdy, 1997a), but there is a danger of determinism and reductionism, treating discourses and practices as though they can be explained solely by reference to class interests. As a consequence, little attention is given to the subjective (mediating and interpretative) processes involved in change (cf Willmott, 1997; Casey, 1995).

*The psychodynamic approach*

By contrast, in the second stream of literature, accounts draw on the psychodynamics of management – the 'anxieties, fears and yearnings' (Fineman, 1993: 3) or ontological insecurity (Giddens, 1984) which underpin action and habitual behaviour. Here, the focus is typically on the proliferation and apparent transience of management ideas. For example, Abrahamson sees the demand for new management ideas as being shaped by a *competition* between 'techno-economic forces' such as those referred to above, and 'socio-psychological vulnerabilities' (1996: 274). Others give greater recognition to the complementarity of managerial anxiety and economic and organizational structures. For example, Gill and Whittle argue that 'new' ideas are simplistic and therefore flawed, but appeal to the unconscious anxieties and fantasies of managers which are reinforced by uncertain market environments (1993). Similarly, Huczynski (1993, 1993a) examines the historical emergence of different 'families' of ideas (e.g. human relations) in relation to a number of different context types. The 'motivational' context refers partly to persistent managerial and psychological 'needs' for predictability and control along with personal and social (e.g. occupational) esteem. These are appealed to and reinforced in the promotion of ideas by consultants and 'gurus' (see Chapter 5).

   In focusing on managers' adoption of new ideas in this way, there is a danger of presenting them as largely vulnerable or even gullible and of neglecting their instrumental or tactical use of ideas (Sturdy, 1997a). This is less evident in more ethnographic or case-study accounts of managers and the management process. For example, Jackall's account of executive anxieties associated with bureaucratic organizations in the USA refers to managers' use of new ideas to secure a sense of professional identity (1988). A similar theme is pursued by Watson in the UK (1994) echoing the work of Armstrong noted earlier, whereby ideas are related to the 'double control' aspect of managerial work – control of the organization and of personal identity and career. However, these concerns, combined with a confusing proliferation of ideas, are shown to result in rejection and cynicism as well as the adoption of particular 'flavours of the month' – managers are often equivocal or ambivalent (1994a; see also Scase and Goffee, 1989). Indeed, in contrast to Huczynski (1993), Watson examines how, and the extent to which, 'popular' ideas are actually taken on and applied by managers (see also Hollway, 1991).

*Organizational culture, meaning and identity*

Here, organizational culture(s) and, in particular, managerial attempts to shape and control it are examined, typically ethnographically (Kondo, 1990; Kunda, 1991; Frost *et al.*, 1991). The focus is not so much on knowledge and its diffusion, but organizational meanings and identities. Kunda (1991), in his study of managers in a 'strong culture' company, like Watson (1994), stresses their ambivalence. A tension is identified in managers which results from behaving in accordance with the rewards and security associated with adopting espoused values (and knowledges) and yet maintaining a sense of self as 'independent' (Kunda, 1991: 214, see also Hochschild, 1983; Scase and Goffee, 1989; Willmott, 1993). Other related tensions are revealed when attention is given to pre-existing and often competing cultures within/beyond the organization which may provide the basis of different and multiple social identities and of resistance and conflict (May, 1994; Ackroyd and Crowdy, 1991; Sturdy, 1998; Mabey and Mayon-White, 1993). This gives rise to a view of organizational and management culture that is distinct from the sense of normative consensus evident in managerial approaches and prescriptions. Rather, culture might be better portrayed as situationally-specific sets of factions and alliances (Parker, 1995), or as the outcome of a plurality of structural rules and enabling resources (Whittington, 1992). Such accounts provide a framework for the complex way in which managerial discourses are likely to be mediated and enacted by individuals and groups in particular settings. Indeed, although not always an explicit focus, language is analytically crucial in such studies. They typically draw on work from a symbolic interactionist perspective such as Cooley, Mead and Goffman where it is through communicative interaction that meanings are created and self (or selves) produced – as a *process* through the eyes of 'significant' or 'generalized' others. More recently, the traditional concept and focus of the individual as possessing one or more identities has been seen by some as problematic such that the self is viewed as a *relationship* over time based on narrative (e.g. Gergen, 1991). However, as Casey (1995) argues, in *both* formulations, the wider social context beyond interaction and the local is either ignored or inadequately addressed. By contrast, her study is concerned with the *relationship* between self-formation and historically-specific general changes – 'institutional processes of the new work in post-industrial (post-occupational) corporate culture' (*ibid.*: 5; see also Reed, 1997). We share a similar focus, albeit with greater emphasis on the more specific context of changes in financial services and less emphasis on the self as an overall theme.

*Institutional theory*

Broadly speaking, institutional theory demonstrates the variety of societal influences on organizational/management structures and practices – their institutional 'embeddedness' or, more actively, constitution. Institutions are conventionally seen as the state, church, professions, unions, family and so on, but in institutional theory they may be more diffuse and interacting social (sub-) systems, domains or fields which shape and are shaped by organizations (e.g. see Whitley, 1992a; Friedland and Alford, 1987). For example, Whittington (1992) charts political (state), communal (ethnicity; religion), domestic (household; gender), intellectual (professions; knowledge) and economic systems. These do not represent an external environment to organizations in the conventional sense (c.f. Pettigrew, 1985), but penetrate or constitute all aspects of organizational life. For example in relation to the 'intellectual' system, change and associated conflicts may involve an individual's identification with a management function or profession – it is part of them and their organization.

In relation to management practices and ideas, Greenwood and Hinings point to the 'importance of ideas and values within a sector that limit the range of likely organizational designs' (1993: 1057). Partly overlapping with studies of culture, the emphasis is on the symbolic aspects of organizations and environments and how ideas and practices are nurtured and developed within particular industrial and organizational settings. DiMaggio and Powell's original reformulation of the institutionalist approach to organizations (1983) identified three mechanisms towards what they termed institutional isomorphism – coercive isomorphism, arising from the need to secure resources by demonstrating conformity with the expectations of key power-holders; mimetic isomorphism deriving from organizations responding to uncertainties by copying what other, supposedly 'successful', organizations are doing; and normative isomorphism where the professionalization of management functions leads to the creation of standardized views which are transferred across different organizational contexts (see also Powell and DiMaggio, 1991; Zucker, 1987; Scott, 1995; Meyer and Rowan, 1977).

This approach points to the ways in which change processes are shaped by actors seeking support and legitimation from different institutional sources or belief systems. Institutionalist analysis emphasizes that these isomorphic processes 'proceed in the absence of evidence that they increase internal organizational efficiency' (DiMaggio and Powell, 1983: 153). This relates to the concerns of psychodynamic and ethnographic literatures with knowledge and managerial status as managers respond to uncertainty by seeking the security of copying others. This copying can be explicit through standardization procedures such as those which flow through benchmarking and badging, e.g. the achievement of BS5750 or ISO 9000 in relation to quality programmes. It can also be more implicit where various types of auditors (of accounts but also increasingly in the public sector of performance standards) expect the operation of certain forms of measurement, control and accountability (Morgan, 1990; Morgan and Willmott, 1993; Broadbent and Guthrie, 1992; Power, 1997; Clarke and Newman, 1997). Failure to meet these expectations can lead to both loss of business and income as well as public censure.

Changes like this concern the forced, voluntary and sometimes unintended transfer of practices and discourses between institutional and industrial sectors. However, a number of potential problems or questions remain as to their origin and process. A principal feature and contribution of institutional theory is in highlighting and explaining practices which appear to deviate from an economically rational logic of efficiency. So, for example, structures/practices may be adopted for symbolic reasons regardless of, or at the expense of, control or profitability issues. This allows for 'permanently failing organizations' (Meyer and Zucker, 1989; see also Meyer 1994) because 'legitimacy drawn from other social systems can buffer inefficiency in capitalist terms' (e.g. French CEOs sacrificing profit for social harmony: Whittington, 1992:

707). Certain authors have identified this as a fundamental conflict *within* various forms of institutionalism, distinguishing, for example, those arguments which emphasize that ultimately the process of institutional isomorphism is driven by (and conversely constrained by) rational-technological (competition) from those which take the view that all actions are socially embedded and cannot be reduced to (or confined by) economic necessity (Oliver, 1992; Granovetter, 1985; Tolbert and Zucker, 1996). Scott (1992) for example, argues that environments, and therefore sectors, vary in their level of institutionalization depending on how far removed they are from processes of economic competition. Indeed, early formulations of institutional theory were only applied to non-economic (e.g. public sector) organizations (Meyer and Rowan) because it was thought that the lack of market discipline meant that there were more options open to managers in this sector. However, more recently, economic efficiency itself is seen as socially variable or institutionally determined (Whitley, 1994; Di Maggio and Powell, 1991: Quack, Morgan and Whitley, 2000).

The tension between those for whom 'economic' factors operate, at least partially, outside of institutional contexts and can therefore be utilized as causes of institutional change, and those for whom the economic is also ultimately institutional and therefore cannot have either ontological or causal primacy, is endemic in institutionalist accounts of change. Oliver, for example, represents the first view when she states that 'institutionalized activities that begin to have significant [negative] implications for the economic success of the organization are likely to be re-evaluated' (Oliver, 1992: 572). Such problems or crises, along with a number of political and social pressures within and beyond organizations (e.g. regulation) are seen to account for change or 'de-institutionalization' (*ibid.*). Whittington, on the other hand, whilst he recognizes the 'centrality' of capitalist structures of resource allocation and conduct and the limited scope for managerial discretion (1992: 697, 706), states that managers are 'faced by a variety of conflicting rules of [and resources for] conduct' (*ibid.*: 705) and no one aspect (such as the economic) has priority. Guillen (1994), in his comparative and historical study of the adoption of dominant management ideas appears to give greater emphasis to technical-economic explanations and combines them with institutional considerations. He argues that organizational problems are experienced and perceived as a result of changes in organizational form (e.g. size), competition and structured (e.g. capital–labour) conflict. It is the final choice/adoption of 'solutions' (i.e. ideas) which is institutionally shaped through business elites, professions, the state, and the industrial relations systems. For example, he describes how Human Relations *ideas* in postwar Spain had considerable institutional support, but associated *techniques* were only adopted in those sectors where there was a structural 'need' (e.g. bureaucratic and large organizations) (1994; see also Reed, 1996; Grint, 1994; Bierstecker, 1995).

In theoretical terms, institutionalism does not resolve this problem. The focus on the social embeddedness of economic action creates a preference for understanding forms of organization, markets and competition in terms of the specific historical features of their construction and maintenance (e.g. Fligstein, 1996a, 1996b; Podolny, 1993; Whitley and Kristensen, 1997). However, such a focus often detracts from the shared structural characteristics of many work organizations across different sectors and contexts, notably the capitalist organization of the labour process. Associated economic values and interests (e.g. profit) both shape and draw upon other social institutions (e.g. professions, gender, community, 'lifestyle') – they are *interpenetrative*. From this point of view, there can be no pure economic nor institutional logics which acts as an exogenous force for change.

This point leads to another concern with institutional theory – over the meaning and importance of legitimacy and consensus. The approach has been criticized for its emphasis on consensus or 'shared definitions' and, therefore, stability or durability rather than change (Cohen, 1968; Oliver, 1992; Hatch, 1997). Although this is perhaps less relevant today where some accounts incorporate multiple institutional environments/competing belief systems (Friedland and Alford, 1987) or present institutions as the product of conflict (DiMaggio and Powell, 1991), some idea of a shared meaning remains central as providing the basis around which institutionalized practices accumulate. However, it is important that the notion of a shared meaning is treated not as the outcome of spontaneous shared interests but, as we have seen in discussing ethnographic literature, as a set of social relationships which are situationally produced and reproduced. As Oliver states, 'the cultural persistence of an institutionalized activity may be much more fragile and less inevitable than institutional theory suggests' (Oliver, 1992: 581). More generally, organizations and their practices can survive and even flourish without a common value-orientation particularly among labour – resigned acquiescence or the 'dull compulsion of economic [i.e. material] relations' may suffice (Wilkinson, 1996). Clearly, some shared understanding is required, but how much, for how long and by whom –

perhaps as Anthony (1990) suggests, it is only amongst senior management that shared meanings are important. Even where practices are (or come to be) seen as 'legitimate' and therefore to be copied more widely, attention needs to be paid to the political process through which this was achieved in order to avoid the impression that institutions or social identities are independent and pre-given, some sort of embodiment of what Durkheim referred to as the 'collective consciousness' (Durkheim, 1984). For example, Wilkinson highlights how, in the interwar period, business and state elites drew on the long-standing Japanese traditions in an appeal for industrial harmony to counter union power and support relations of domination (1996; see also Littler, 1982; Harris, 1982); it was not that these traditions in themselves ensured cooperation between managers and workers, rather they were selectively used as part of a variety of forms of management control aimed at subduing potential conflict. The claim to a continuous historical tradition of 'harmony' therefore needs to be considered critically as 'an institutionalized myth' (Meyer and Rowan, 1977).

This also implies the importance of not allowing institutionalist theory to become a form of sociocultural determinism (Wilkinson, 1996; Clark and Mueller, 1996; Oliver, 1992) where little scope is left for human (e.g. managerial) agency, organizational autonomy or selective borrowing and copying within a given institutional (e.g. national, sectoral) frame. Whittington (1992), for example, has sought to overcome this by integrating institutional theory with Giddens' concept of 'structuration' (1984) so that agency is derived from human reflexivity combined with conflicts, contradictions and complexity *within and between* a growing plurality of overlapping social structures/systems (see earlier; also Parker, 1995; Reed, 1997). Accordingly, individual actors' (e.g. managers') discretion and, therefore, organizational variation, is achieved through interpreting system rules and roles and from inter- (e.g. feminine versus professional versus managerial) and intra- (e.g. management of cost versus quality) system tensions and contradictions such as those associated with economic exchange (e.g. conflict and resistance in the work process). Combinations of complex social structures act as resources as well as rules and their multiplicity, interpenetration, situational specificity and tensions provide scope for agency. These characteristics are also important with regard to accounting for change processes. In particular, they allow for an element of chance, multi-directionality and unpredictability as well as order in the emergence and outcomes of change.

*Genealogy, discourse and change*

Following Foucault (1972, 1977), genealogical studies are historical projects concerned with discourse as productive of social life and subjectivity. They examine the conditions that make it possible for a discourse such as strategy to arise and 'assume pre-eminence . . . in order to capture both the discontinuity and uncertainty as well as the appearance of stability and coherence surrounding' that discourse (Knights and Morgan, 1995: 193). For example, Rose (1989) charts part of the social constitution (genealogy) of the individualized 'autonomous' or 'free' self in Western societies. In particular, he shows how the development of psychological theories and practices in the Second World War (notably the concepts of attitude, personality and the group) came to transform our very sense of ourselves through their application in public and private sector programmes to 'govern' populations. Of special relevance here is how the management of subjectivity became central to organizations in pursuing productivity and harmony from employees (and citizens) (see also Hollway, 1991). Similarly, Jacques (1996) examines the conditions of emergence and the form of management discourses in North America in the first decades of this century. He argues that knowledges which emerged subsequently as 'new' developments (e.g. contingency theory etc.) were nothing of the sort and still reflected the spirit of the earlier modernist age or were amended to do so. Consequently, Jacques argues that current dominant thinking is wholly out of step with contemporary conditions. By contrast, others with a less historical focus, intertwine management and organizational discourses with economy and culture (Casey, 1995). For example, du Gay and Salaman (1992) focus on the recent emergence and dominance of a discourse of 'enterprise' or 'cult(ure)' of the customer' enacted in business and public service organizations (see Chapter 6 and 7).

Such accounts strongly inform our own analysis of change by exploring knowledge, language and identity and their conditions and consequences. Indeed, the expressed aim of Jacques' study – 'to trace the construction of organizational knowledge in order to make connections between the form this knowledge took and the broader social currents within which it formed' – is very similar to our own concerns, albeit in a different context. These approaches differ from the largely ahistorical managerial and political approaches which present knowledges as rational techniques which may be constrained or mediated by immediate organizational politics, but must be learned in order to manage/adapt to the environment. As with some institutional theory, they are also distinct from Marxist and other economistic literature in not giving primacy to economic categories such as capital, labour, capitalism and so on. Instead, emphasis is placed on the detailed processes whereby forms of knowledge are constructed and become productive, as well as constraining, of forms of subjectivity and patterns of action. In Marxist accounts, management knowledge is treated as an ideology, a 'false view' which distorts reality and acts as a disciplinary mechanism, denying certain groups access to the 'truth' of their situation. Rose, however, argues that this implies a humanist notion of false consciousness and/or a pre-existing 'free' subject (Rose, 1989: 11).

Discourse approaches, on the other hand, see knowledge not as 'truth' but as power. Power stands behind knowledge, not as an 'invisible hand' which manipulates what is to count as truth but as the energy which runs through its veins, giving it 'effectivity', making it 'work' to change existing practices and expanding its reach into ever more areas of life. Out of power, comes knowledge and out of knowledge comes discipline. Self-discipline implies the project of producing a subjectivity (a sense of the self and its role/position in the world) out of knowledges. In this perspective, there is no knowledge separate from this 'will to power', nor can there be a 'subject' outside of these discourses, manipulating and shaping them (creating 'false consciousness'). Individual actors are in this sense constructed through discourse; even when they think that they are acting as free individuals, they are in effect just enacting a different discourse, one based on 'freedom' and 'resistance' rather than 'control' and 'discipline'. The logic of this approach is that the self-directing or mediating human subject is analytically insignificant or 'decentred' and no more than a 'convenient location for the throughput of discourses' (Hassard, 1994: 316). Thompson and Ackroyd are critical of this, stating that 'the shift towards the primacy of discourse and the text encourages the removal of workers from the academic gaze and the distinction between the intent and outcome of managerial strategies and practices is lost' (Thompson and Ackroyd, 1995: 629).

More generally, the issue of resistance has become focal in a debate between Foucauldians and their opponents. When acknowledged, resistance is seen by the former as a localized phenomenon which is integral to, rather than a reaction against, power. It provides the challenge to knowledge – to show how and why resistance has occurred and can therefore be overcome. Therefore, resistance can be 'insisted' upon rather than denied (Knights, 1997), but the meaning is fundamentally different than it is, for example, in Thompson and Ackroyd where resistance confronts power and changes its nature and effects. For the former approach, whilst employee reactions to being 'labelled from above' through new discourses are *necessarily* ambivalent (e.g. du Gay, 1996), the consequence is typically seen as the continued refinement of forms of knowledge, surveillance and control. In the latter approach, ambivalence is merely one of a range of possible responses from at the one end, commitment to and identification with the discourse to at the other end denial/rejection (Sturdy, 1998; Rosenthal *et al.*, 1997; Edwards *et al.*, 1998). This divide need not necessarily be so severe if a non-essentialist concept of the subject is adopted whereby a multiplicity of sometimes competing discourses exist (Boje, 1996) which may or may not have meaning for an individual actor. Individuals may privilege one or more particular identities as 'real', but self-identity 'is something that has to be routinely created and sustained in the reflective activities of the individual' such that its content varies socially and temporally (Giddens, 1991: 52). We return to these debates in the following section.

**Constructing a social approach to organizational change**

In this book, our study of organizational change draws from all these 'social' approaches in its concern to understand how and why knowledges, understandings and practices about organizations develop and change. In doing so, it steps beyond, and offers an alternative to, the dominant engineering models characterized by both managerialist and political approaches to change. From the foregoing discussion of the contributions and problems associated with the different 'social' approaches, we can bring together here some of the themes and assumptions which frame the analysis developed in subsequent chapters. Doing so heightens the risk of over-simplification and generalization, but is useful as a summary.

The dialectical/materialist approach characterized by Marxist analysis highlights the importance and interpenetration of structural and ideational tension in change processes, and the centrality and material and ideological basis of capitalist social relations. However, the complex and varied ways in which structures are subjectively mediated and interpreted tend to be neglected (c.f. Willmott, 1997). By contrast, by drawing on psychodynamic and cultural-identity perspectives, connections can be made between organizational and wider social structures and ontological insecurity and social identity. So, for example, new management ideas may be internalized, complied with and/or resisted and transformed on the basis of a preoccupation with maintaining a sense of control and identity in particular situations. Institutional theory can provide an understanding of the social and historical conditions and consequences for these processes and organizational change more generally. While typically underplaying the economic/capitalist and material basis of organizational life, its socially constituted, variable and changing nature is illuminated. This is understood through interactions, interpretations and tensions between and within a multiplicity of complex and dynamic social systems or their specific combination/ aggregation as organizational fields. In this way, crucially, a concept of human agency and a measure of unpredictability can also be incorporated into our analysis. In relation to management knowledges and practices, institutional theory focuses attention on the processes which create and constrain their adoption at the level of meaning. This may, however, exaggerate the importance, stability and extent of the legitimacy of a given practice. By contrast, the genealogical approach goes to the other extreme in exploring language and practice without reference to subjective meanings or social structures. Nevertheless, it draws attention to the vital link between organizational change and discourse in localized, cultural and historical forms.

Given that we share similar concerns with genealogical approaches, including the use of the term 'discourse', it is worth briefly setting out our differing position and understanding of discourse. Jacques provides a 'relatively usable lay understanding' of discourse as 'what *can* be said' rather than just what is said (1996: 19, original emphasis). But discourse is not merely concerned with the linguistic or textual. While it is not always explicitly linked with the term 'practice', discourse incorporates and connects material practices and the language through which they become recognizable or meaningful (*ibid.*). This corresponds to du Gay's understanding of discourse as ' ... the production of knowledge through language and representation and the way that knowledge is institutionalized, shaping social practices and setting new practices into play' (1996: 43). However, we depart from the associated ontological position whereby discourse is 'constitutive of social reality *in toto*' (*ibid.*: 38, original emphasis). From this point of view, as we have seen, there is 'nothing beyond discourse'. While the *existence* of material objects and events (practices) is acknowledged, they only achieve *being* through language. Thus, claiming to provide an account of (i.e. represent) an external reality (e.g. organizations, change) is seen as highly problematic, as privileging one discourse (reality) over others. Every discourse ultimately expresses a 'will to power' which produces 'truth' as its effect rather than being produced by it.

This argument now lies at the root of the emerging (and hardening) debate within organizational analysis between post-structuralism and critical realism (for the purposes of our argument, we leave aside those still working within some sort of positivist or neo-positivist framework, e.g. Donaldson 1996). The critical realist approach points to underlying and relatively stable, but fluid, logics and structures of action (for a major statement of this approach, see Archer, 1995). In the field of organizational analysis, Reed, in particular, has explicitly taken on poststructuralism using the tools of critical realism:

> the relationship between a discourse and that which it represents is not entirely arbitrary and independent of its anchoring in an extant set of material and social conditions: landlords and tenants, masters and servants, owners and workers can only be what they are as a result of the objectified material conditions and institutionalized social relations which inhere in respective systems of property distribution, social stratification and economic production. (1998: 211)

In the critical realist approach then, underlying structures can be identified. These empower actors in different ways and, in doing so, create the possibility to change the structures. Explanations for change, therefore, need to encompass both the original structure (and how it creates certain positions and powers) and the actions of social agents as they exercise powers in uncertain and conflicting contexts. For some, this position may seem untenable for it retains the distinction between structure and action, rather than conflating it to 'discursive practice' (see Reed, 1997: 30; Casey, 1995; c.f. Knights, 1997). It also locates itself at a remove from the argument that there are multiple discourses about reality which produce multiple 'truths'. It offers itself as a means of overcoming such fragmentation without the imposition of the rigid 'scientism' of positivism and neo-positivism. Critical realism may also be differentiated from Giddens' 'structuration theory' which, according to Archer (1995: ch. 4), elides the distinction between structure and agency. He is thus unable to account for differential powers of actors which are pre-given by structures, not constructed in social practice. He cannot, therefore, provide a coherent theory of how social orders change from one set of structures to another. For the critical realist, the underlying structure which determines the relative power of actors must be revealed in order to understand how these actors are then able to change structure itself, given certain other accompanying conditions. Clearly, these theoretical choices are not without political, practical and moral consequences. Fragmentation and multiplicity can be seen as opening up space for alternative views or abnegating moral and intellectual responsibilities depending on one's perspective. Similarly, the development of critical realist accounts of social order can be seen as either an imposition of a single view, or getting social theory closer to an understanding of reality (see the discussions in Parker, 1998, for the link between ontology, epistemology and ethics; also Bauman, 1989, 1993).

In what follows, our approach seeks to uncover underlying structures but we do also perceive that languages and discourses are central elements in any understanding of social stability and change. Accordingly, our position is that languages and associated practices – discourses – are socially structured and structuring as well as intersubjectively mediated. What *can* be said (and done) is then, for us, the basis of 'social action' rather than 'discourse'. In turn, what can be said can only be understood by examining the underlying structure and how this constrains and empowers actors in differential ways. Through the development of particular discourses, actors are able to reflect on and modify their practices. The modification of practices can reinforce or undermine the structures out of which they emerged. This modification may eventually entail a more widespread reflection on the existing underlying structures. These processes are played out to a peculiarly visible degree within organizations because of the simultaneity of formal rules and informal resistance, both of which express underlying structural arrangements and the powers given to actors by those arrangements. Furthermore, organizations regularly and invariantly absorb, adapt and produce knowledge and discourses about the process of 'organizing'. Therefore, structural arrangements and discourses coexist and need to be analyzed together in order to make sense of processes of change.

It might be argued that by drawing from what are sometimes theoretically incompatible streams of literature, we are guilty of some kind of theoretical pluralism or, even, piracy. However, to a certain extent, all theoretical frameworks are composites and derivative. Nevertheless and as we have indicated in our distancing from postmodern (discursive) ontology and the determinism of some institutional and Marxist theory, we seek to work within a coherent framework. While we do not set out and then apply a single theory or logic of organizational change, our aim is to develop a theoretically informed analysis which illuminates its complexity and multifaceted nature. The above literatures are drawn on to different degrees as appropriate to the particular chapter topics and 'layers of social reality'. This does not mean that we simply draw on the different streams, depending on levels of analysis, for example. Rather, we seek to address their weaknesses and develop their application, sometimes through combination and integration. In doing so, we hope to offer new insights into organizational change generally, as well as the chosen areas of focus (see below). We also believe that by going *beyond organizational change* this study can feed into broader concerns with how society is changing and what new forms of organizations and identities are being constructed and contested. In the remaining chapters of this book, we explore this process by concentrating on one particular industry, that of financial services.

## WHY STUDY FINANCIAL SERVICES?

Most studies of organizational change are, perhaps unsurprisingly, focused at the level of the *organization*. Clearly, this can reap rich insights, such as in the longitudinal studies referred to earlier. However, not only has the conventional concept of an organization as explicitly bounded become increasingly problematic in the current era, but the view of context as an externality is reinforced by such an approach. By focusing more broadly, on a 'sector', the problem is not necessarily diminished. For example, in our chosen area, financial services, new entrants (e.g. Marks & Spencers, Virgin, Tesco, Sainsburys) and forms of relationships are developing. Nevertheless, by exploring the constitution and transformation of a 'sector' and problematizing its meaning, a softer, more subtle and interpenetrative organization-context relationship is possible. This issue is introduced in the following chapter. Here, we outline the reasons why financial services (conventionally defined) is especially appropriate for a study of organizational change.

For fifteen years, we have been involved in research in the personal (c.f. commercial) financial services sectors – individually, jointly and collaborating with other colleagues such as those at the Financial Services Research Centre in UMIST, Manchester. We have explored a range of issues and deployed different methodological approaches although the case study and interviews have been most frequently adopted. Our research (see references) has included organizations in the following product areas: life and general insurance; investments and pensions, and; (other) banking services. As well as studies in banks, building societies and insurance companies and intermediaries (e.g. brokers), research has been conducted on regulators, industry bodies, management consultants and IT suppliers. Most work has been with large organizations established in their sector, but the emergence and impact of 'new players' and forms of distribution (e.g. telephone sales) has also been a focus. This volume presents and integrates some of our findings from the UK. In the course of the research, the frame-work for the social perspective on organizational change has gradually emerged. In retrospect we came to see that our study of this industry could reveal the limitations of existing approaches to change and therefore necessitated moves towards a new model. Four particular aspects of the change process in the industry were of significance to that awareness.

First, any discussion of the industry highlights the perceived rapidity of change and the associated rhetoric which occurred during the 1980s and early 1990s. In broad economic terms, the industry boomed during the height of the Thatcher years on the back of increased wealth and income, greater willingness to take on consumer credit in the form of loans and plastic cards, the housing market 'bonanza', personal pensions legislation and the privatization of the major public utilities. Since the late 1980s, conditions changed as house prices stabilized; consumers sought to reduce debt levels; stock market conditions became more uncertain; and scandals engulfed the pensions and invest-ment industry. This transition is typically seen to have arisen because the government 'deregulated' substantial parts of the market which had previously been sheltered from competition by government and industry action. On the other hand, the government also introduced new forms of regulation of the selling and marketing of investment products, as well as other areas of legislation on issues such as data protection which affected the industry. In the mid-1990s to date, the experience of change continued with, most visibly, mergers and indus-try and organizational restructuring.

Studies of organizational change in the industry (e.g. Pettigrew and Whipp 1991) typically see this context as the challenge/opportunity faced by senior managers in achieving successful adaptation. What they fail to consider, however, is the central significance of the way in which senior managers reached out for (and were sold) new ways of understanding their organization, its context and role. The industry had central elements in its self-image(s) which had been established for many decades and were part of the taken-for-granted routines of management, if not always other employees. During the 1980s and 1990s these have been gradually challenged, reshaped or replaced by new discourses, particularly those concerned with 'strategy', 'marketing', 'quality service and customer care'. Our encounters in the industry led us to see the central importance of the interaction and clashes between and within preexisting and new discourses. The latter were, for the most part, being carried into the industry from outside through, for example, the agency of management consultancies; government ideology and legislation; consumer groups; new types of managers recruited from outside the industry or trained in business schools; and 'stakeholder' expectations. We were struck by managers' concerns to learn, practice and develop what was meant by 'strategy', 'marketing' and so on, and the pressures on them to do so Their examination of existing practices in the light of these new knowledges led to conflicts at many levels. Individuals struggled to come to terms with the new language; departments struggled against each other to demonstrate their centrality to the new vision(s); senior managers struggled to make sense of it all and convince outside stakeholders that they had created a coherent and effective organization. It was impossible to understand the 'turmoil' within organizations without understanding the way in which many of the previous ways of working were being challenged and/or dismantled. Spaces opened up were being, and continue to be, colonized by the new, competing and sometimes fragile practices and ways of understanding being carried into, and generated by, organizations.

Secondly, whilst many of these discourses derived directly from management specialisms that were familiar in certain parts of British industry by the 1980s, and were to become more widespread, there was also a wider social and political climate that shaped the way they penetrated the industry. It is now commonplace to contextualize the changes of the 1980s by reference to Thatcherism, individualism and consumerism, but this had a particularly strong resonance within the financial services industry. The industry had been built around ideas of security and safety for families and their money. In the 1980s, the increased attention to consumerism, the opening up of credit opportunities, the lure of quick gains on privatization issues, the housing market and stock exchange transactions changed the climate for the industry pushing it away from the emphasis on security towards a wider variety of risk positions which could be 'chosen' by many individuals (Sturdy and Knights, 1996). This had complex effects in that some customers were looking for, and encouraged to seek, quicker and easier gains which could be achieved if companies took greater risks with their investments. Inside companies, there were struggles about how far to go with this. How could the public be made aware of the increased riskiness of their activity? Did it matter? Many managers felt that the public were basically ignorant and the choice was really about how far companies themselves should limit the risks by limiting their products. Others rejected this as an outdated paternalist view and wanted to offer customers a wider choice; whether this choice should be qualified by forcing consumers' attention to the risks involved was another question.

The point is, however, that these debates inside companies and the change processes that occurred cannot be understood outside the changes that were happening to consumers of the products of the industry. The two were integrally connected and as 'boom' turned into 'bust', people's attentions were dramatically turned to the risks which they had been often unknowingly running. A whole new perspective on issues of consumer protection and regulation emerged and threatened to fundamentally change the industry (Burton, 1994). Previous models of change were unhelpful in explaining this interrelationship between wider social changes and organizations in the industry.

Thirdly, the study of financial services highlighted the way in which ways of understanding and acting can become implicated into individual identities. The gradual dispersal or, possibly, pre-institutionalization of discourses around strategy, marketing and customer care also involved, sometimes intentionally, reconstituting the identities as well as the practices of the people who worked in the industry. They were expected to see themselves in new ways, to see their role in the organization from a new perspective, as an 'enterprising' actor in a much more commercially driven and uncertain entity, rather than a participant in an ostensibly genteel, respectable and stable institution. As has already been suggested, this process often involved resistance and/or painful personal adjustments for many people, including job losses for some. Also, to study the process of change without exploring the extent to which knowledges shaped and were (re)shaped by multiple social identities would be to miss a major element of what has occurred in this industry.

Fourthly, the changes in the UK financial services industry over this period also leads one to consider the national context of the process. As we shall see, in certain respects, financial services has a long tradition of international activity, even in personal products. Western banks, insurance companies and regulatory systems were set up in colonies and, for the most part, remained influential as empires declined and local companies and systems became established and dominant. More recently, within the EU, a single market in financial services may be accepted in principle, but it has only had a tangential effect in practice to date. Indeed, the challenge of thinking about financial services across borders, particularly with the existence of a single currency in at least part of the European Union, shows that categories which are taken for granted and used as though they are of universal relevance often reflect nationally specific ways of organizing social processes. The risk-averse nature of German financial institutions, the complex interrelationship between French financial institutions and the state, the overtly politicized nature of the Italian system, all of these offer simple but stark contrasts to the British financial services industry. Cross-national comparisons reinforce the central message of the social approach to organizational change. While this volume does not explicitly draw on our comparative research and studies of financial services in other countries (e.g. Morgan and Knights, 1997; Sturdy *et al.*, 1997; Sturdy and Morgan, 1993; Sturdy, 1997c; Morgan and Quack, 2000), it will hopefully serve to contribute to a growing literature from different nations which problematizes aspects of the organization and sector and seeks to understand how they have been socially constituted over time.

Our study of the financial services industry has forced us to confront a range of gaps in the existing literature; the failure to problematize central concepts such as strategy and marketing and therefore to understand how much of organizational conflict and change revolved around struggles between different discourses and tensions within them; the failure to see how wider social meanings and practices of the 1980s around themes such as the market, the consumer and the individual were both shaping and being shaped by organizational change and the sector's institutional domain; the failure to appreciate the central importance of the subjectivity of individuals as they struggled to attain symbolic and material security within competing and steadily emerging discourses; and, finally, the failure to appreciate the national business system context of organizational change and the need to reveal and problematize taken-for-granted elements of that context.

## THE STRUCTURE OF THE BOOK

In demonstrating the social approach to organizational change and the ways in which it can be utilized, our coverage of the changes in financial services is necessarily selective. Firstly, certain areas, such as information technology and, as noted earlier, cross-national issues have been explored from a similar perspective elsewhere (e.g. Knights and Murray, 1994; Sturdy, 1989). Secondly, and as already intimated, our concern is to examine change in depth which requires some degree of focus. Accordingly, we concentrate on four key and interrelated topics – *competition*, *regulation*, *strategy* and *marketing*. These areas, their dynamics, interconnections and contradictions, are explored progressively and in different ways. In doing so, a broad transformation is documented from a relatively persistent 'field' or set of institutional, regulatory and occupational relationships and tensions towards a situation whereby these relationships are challenged and upset and often self-defeating attempts are made to establish a new field or sense of order. New management knowledges as they relate to institutions and practices are shown to be central to this transformation to a state of flux.

In the next section of the book, contextual analysis of financial services as a sector is presented through developing the concept of an 'organizational field'. This is explored historically in terms of the form, control and distribution of money as it relates to changes in markets, regulation, competition and class structure. The period up to the 1960s is outlined (Chapter 2) and then set against what is seen as the beginning of a breakdown in the field of financial services from the 1950s–1980s (Chapter 3). This also provides a background to the subsequent section. This examines organizational change processes and outcomes in relation to developments in management discourses as modes of understanding and of control. Although interconnected and complementary, each chapter has a specific focus and may be read either independently or as part of the whole. The chapters explore the recent historical emergence and contemporary dissemination, contestation and contradictions of strategic and marketing discourses, both generally and in relation to specific organizational practices and subjective experiences. We examine the emergence and nature of the discourse of corporate strategy (Chapter 4) and develop this through a discussion of the role of management consultancy in IT strategy development (Chapter 5). The emergence of sales and then marketing practices in relation to changing patterns of consumption is then explored (Chapter 6) along with associated changes in career, work and gender patterns such as those inherent in 'customer care' culture initiatives – from 'black coats' to 'service smiles' (Chapter 7). The final section widens the discussion by returning to a principal focus on the organizational field. The development and consequences of strategic discourse are linked to currently emerging patterns of regulation, consumption and organizational structures and ownership. In particular, the nature and role of the different actors are shown to have been transformed through discourses of competition and individual responsibility for welfare (Chapter 8). We then summarize our analysis and discuss some of its implications for the study of discourses and organizational change (Chapter 9). Our approach to organizational change grew out specific research experiences within financial services, but we argue that it is applicable to change in other sectors and contexts. More generally, we hope to provide a response to recent calls for a 'more sociological and historically-grounded education about management' (Collins, 1998: 196).

# Part II
# The Organizational Field of UK Financial Services

# 2 Money, Financial Institutions and the Social Order

## INTRODUCTION

Financial services companies are in the business of making money from money: money lies at the heart of what they do and what they are. Yet, as Dodd notes, 'existing sociological analyses of money are relatively insubstantial' partly because of the 'failure to recognise its importance as a consequential social institution' (Dodd, 1994: vi). If, however, there is one thing which defines financial services companies it is their role in the management, control and distribution of money. In this chapter, we firstly examine in general terms the nature of money and its social construction. Through examining money we can identify the crucial underlying social structures within which financial institutions are embedded. Secondly, we elaborate the particular nature of that embeddedness in the British context. This involves understanding both the way in which the various institutions link together and the way in which the nature of these linkages are understood and articulated by social actors. This enables us to identify the key conditions for the reproduction of this embeddedness at both the level of the system as a whole and at the level of the social actors themselves. In the following chapter, we examine how these conditions for reproduction began to change from the 1960s onwards. As they changed, the interconnections between the elements of the system had to be renegotiated, a process which involved the reconstruction of the elements themselves into new entities. This also necessitated the development of new modes of *understanding* the system on the part of the actors. The interface between the changing interrelationships and entities and the changing understanding of the actors constitutes our focus of attention in the next part of the book.

MONEY AND FINANCIAL INSTITUTIONS

Although the paucity of sociological accounts of money is gradually being rectified (Dodd, 1994; Corbridge *et al.*, 1994: Leyshon and Thrift, 1997: Zelizer, 1994), the connection between these discussions and the organizational analysis of financial institutions is still limited; where it exists, it tends to focus on the role of the City of London. In this section, we argue that money needs to be conceived as part of a wider set of organizational and institutional relationships which have outcomes in terms of power and inequality.

Leyshon and Thrift's description of forms of money is a useful starting point. They argue that 'each form can be thought of as consisting of a particular set of formal *instruments* of money, a particular set of financial *institutions and practices* and a broadly conceived set of *interpretations* of what money is and what it does' (1997: 3; italics in original). The first key form of money in their discussion, for our purposes, is *money of account* which is where money is a measure of value. Here, money gradually loses its connection with precious metals; the power of money becomes embedded in 'claims' on others rather than in the materiality of gold and silver. Money can be stored as a credit or a debt through the accounts of banks or merchants and it can be transferred through paper bank notes. At first, this system was basically a private system. As Leyshon and Thrift note, 'responsibility for regulating the financial system fell to the growing band of private merchants and bankers who effectively oversaw and supervised the circulation of money and credit, often through informal but closely knit networks for the exchange of business and information' (1997: 18). The system which was established extended as the state became more involved. As European nation-states asserted their claim to control territories, they began to establish a single unified currency system, based on a national currency of account. As with the private banking system, paper money at first involved a claim to gold. However, the ability to 'create' paper money, once the state had the monopoly over coinage, led to the emergence of what Leyshon and Thrift refer to as '*state credit money*'. In other words, the state controlled the issue of credit through the issue of paper money. Where this led individual banks into difficulties, the state also acted as 'lender of last resort' to prop them up until they could reconstruct their accounts. It is with this last type of money form with which we are most concerned in the first part of this book. We therefore now explore it in more detail.

## Money, credit and the state

It is axiomatic in our discussions that however else money 'works', in a market society it works as a store of power. Possession of money involves power to spend; it gives the individual and/or organization power over their future in a way that those without money can never have. Yet as has already been implied, 'possession' of money is not entirely comparable to possession of other commodities such as cars or houses. There are a number of reasons for this which are highly relevant to understanding the role of financial services.

The first and probably most important of these reasons goes back to the idea that money is a 'claim' on something rather than the thing itself. In the past, money was a claim to a certain amount of gold or silver; thus currencies were fixed to the gold standard and, in theory, people could swop their notes for gold. With this they could buy commodities or services anywhere in the world. However, the claim which paper money makes is inherently unstable and therefore possession of money is always a risk. Why is the claim unstable? The answer is because, in the modern era, states control money supply (or at least have done so until recently). Through this control (and their willingness to print, borrow or lend money), states affect the 'value' of money, that is, the ability of any particular unit of account to purchase goods and services. Therefore, the metaphorical 'claim' which money made last year, which expressed in simple terms might have been to buy $x$ kilos of potatoes, is not the same this year when the same unit of account can only buy $x-1$ kilos of potatoes. In short, holding wealth as paper money is a risk as your possession is likely to decline in value. Other commodities decline in value but generally this is because of their use, not, as in the case of the person who hoards money in an inflationary era, because of its non-use! On the other hand, money which is used, that is lent on as credit, tends to increase in value. Both of these features mean that money is integrally related to time and risk. Holding, spending, accumulating, speculating – all of these are uses of money which actors may undertake, depending on the institutional infrastructure of the financial system. Money is also infinitely divisible and infinitely accumulable. This characteristic means that small amounts can be accumulated together and then divided up again *ad infinitum*. This process also means that, except in the sense of being valid only within the jurisdiction of the particular state which issued it, money is not fixed in spatial location by the position of its 'possessor'. Once it becomes a unit of account, particularly within a state credit monetary system, money becomes easily transferable within territorial boundaries provided there exists some type of organizational infra-structure for 'banking'.

This relates to a third characteristic of money. Unlike most other commodities, there is a sense in which the same 'money' is simultaneously possessed and used by a multitude of people. In the simplest case, money deposited by an individual in a bank is counted as part of the bank's assets for purposes of deciding how much the bank can lend; therefore the depositor, the bank and the borrower are all, in different ways, exercising rights of possession over the money.

Financial institutions are in effect the organizational means whereby these characteristics of money are given substance and reality. Financial institutions are concerned with the process of *intermediation*. They create channels through which money passes; these channels act as ways of funnelling funds, accumulating them, dividing them and passing them on to others. Individuals can place small or large amounts of money in accounts at banks located in their home towns; banks then become the means whereby these funds are accumulated and distributed. This process may be limited to the locality or the region, or alternatively the bank may be part of a national or international set of processes for the allocation of capital.

The financial institutions themselves are not, however, neutral containers of these funds. They are historically shaped by other forces, out of which emerges a particular institutional and organizational structure of financial services. The result is a particular confluence of structural and cultural features in the financial systems of different countries. Two of the predominant influences are the state and the existing distribution of power and inequality in society. As states shifted towards the state credit monetary form to which Leyshon and Thrift refer, they established the rules on which financial institutions could act. These rules could range from technical ones concerning the liquidity of the banks to more general ones, concerning, for example, the expectation that the banks should support industry by guaranteeing low levels of interest and long terms of repayment. These rules reflect the second aspect which concerns us – the relationship between the rich and powerful in society and the financial institutions. This is both an indirect relationship through the state and a direct one in terms of the control which this group exercises over the financial system. With regard to the former, the role which the rich and powerful play in setting the goals of the state clearly impacts on how the state structures financial institutions. In what follows, we aim to explore this inter-relationship. With regard to the latter, it is the rich and powerful who provide a significant proportion of the money for the financial institutions. Once again, this is an important aspect of our analysis.

From this perspective, financial institutions emerge in modern societies to control and manage the flow of money. The terms on which they do this emerge out of the broader social context within which nation-states are constructed. These processes of construction reflect and reproduce inequalities within society, in particular, the ways in which the rich and wealthy relate to the state and its forms and functions. Financial institutions provide the channels through which money flows to its various sites within society where it empowers certain actors and disempowers others. Financial institutions therefore are a reflection of the distribution of money and power in a particular society. However, because of their control of the system of intermediation (within the constraints set), they also contribute to and shape the distribution of power and money.

## ORGANIZATIONAL FIELDS, MONEY AND FINANCIAL INSTITUTIONS

In what follows we refer to this set of relationships, its institutional forms and its social and economic outcomes as the *'organizational field of financial services'*. The idea of an 'organizational field' is becoming increasingly common in the analysis of organizations stemming from institutional theory and the work of authors such as DiMaggio and Powell:

> By organizational field, we mean those organizations that, in the aggregate, constitute a recognized area of institutional life: key suppliers, resource and product consumers, regulatory agencies and other organizations that produce similar services or products. (1983: 148)

This concept of the field or societal sector goes beyond the notion of sector as used both by economists and sociologists by including organizations within the state as well as amongst consumers in its definition. It focuses attention on the gradual development of pressures towards homogeneity among the organizations operating in the field. These pressures arise not simply from a technical-economic imperative but from institutional environments which are 'characterized by the elaboration of rules and requirements to which individual organizations must conform if they are to receive support and legitimacy ... organizations are rewarded for conforming to these rules or beliefs' (Scott and Meyer, 1991: 125). The field defines a level of analysis embedded within a broader, *'business system'*. Developments within fields may shape and be shaped by the business system context. How fields are formed, how boundaries are sustained, how new actors enter, how rules and resources are reproduced, developed and transformed are empirical questions. The concept of the organizational field is inherently social; it refers to social actors and the relationships between them. It cannot be considered except through a relational type of analysis where events or episodes in one part of the field have effects for other parts.

However, the model of the organizational field needs to be elaborated further than is the case in the work of institutionalists such as DiMaggio and Powell and W. R. Scott. In particular, it is necessary to examine the underlying social mechanisms which construct the field. Organizational fields are also fields of power. At a simplistic level, an examination of an organizational field will reveal elements of hierarchy, with some organizations dependent on others for resources. Moreover, organizational fields clearly exist within, and serve to reproduce and/or undermine, other wider systems such as capitalism and patriarchy. Thus power relations within the field and between the field and other fields and structures are of central empirical interest.

On the other hand, the 'field' metaphor allows a deeper and more sociological understanding of notions of the market and competition. In a neo-liberal economist's model, the market represents the nodal point where buyers and sellers meet, prices are determined and messages signalled to producers about the quantity and quality of products required by consumers. A 'free' market exists where this process operates without interference and maximises utility for all the participants in the market. The concept of the organizational field develops a very different view of market exchange. Organizations construct norms and expectations about the sort of products which are to be sold, the sort of consumers who exist, the way in which the products are to be sold, the sort of competition processes which can or cannot be entered into. Markets are constructed within an organizational field; they do not exist separately from them, but are mutually constitutive. The organizational field can empirically consist of trans-national, national and local state and self-regulatory organizations (which set rules and regulations about types of products etc.), commercial organizations (which sell or distribute products), consumer organizations (which articulate and construct the 'needs of the consumer' or 'society' or 'future generations' etc.) and a range of other organizations which have interests in the field that may or may not be significant in particular change processes (for example, the mass media, trade unions).

From the point of view of financial services, the organizational field can be understood through an analysis of money, how it is socially constructed, maintained, circulated and distributed. As discussed, financial services organizations are located within a field which also contains the state and the existing structure of social order and inequality. This field in turn is located within an international context which influences forms of structure and action in the national setting (see Morgan, 1997). The structure of financial services differs between countries because of these differences in the nature of the state and the social order which influence when and how these organizations are founded and how they operate and develop (see chapters in Morgan and Knights, 1997: also Morgan and Quack, 2000). In the rest of this chapter, we explain how a particular structure emerged in the British context. We emphasize that this structure reflected the power of key actors to control money, how it was organized, where it went and who benefited. This structure linked the rich and the poor in British society through an intricate web of organizations, rules and routines. It created a field of inequality dominated by a particular set of relationships between actors and a particular structure of expectations about the rights and responsibilities of these various actors. Out of this, financial services organizations emerged which operated in distinctive ways to reproduce and shape these processes.

We firstly examine the role of the City and the Bank of England and its particular linkages to the state and the wealthy in British society. Within this context, a certain set of financial services organizations emerged with specific characteristics. However, unlike many authors who assume that they have understood the UK system once they have understood the City, we then go on to show that what was crucial to the evolution of the field of financial services was that as new organizations developed beyond the City to serve the emerging middle and working classes in the nineteenth and early-twentieth century, they became subordinated to and constrained by the existing City institutions. We emphasize that this subordination was not a 'natural', 'economic' necessity but rather the result of the actions of key actors with powers to shape the direction of the system. By constructing the system in this way, multiple mechanisms were brought into existence which linked different types of financial institutions into a web of cross-cutting networks of influence, power and regulation, centred on the City of London. It was this ability to control and dominate organizations and networks *beyond the City* which enabled the individuals and organizations located there to retain, reproduce and extend their wealth, power and influence over British society for so long. We show how the gradual extension of wealth and economic activity amongst industrialists and the emerging professional classes who lived beyond the metropolis potentially undermined the power of the City. However as a result of a series of social and economic pressures, this was avoided and instead the wealth of these groups was directed through the City, thus reinforcing the power of those institutions and the people who controlled them. In the final part of the chapter, we show how this power and influence was also exercized to ensure that the financial institutions established by and for the 'respectable' working class were constructed and regulated in such a way as to reinforce the dominance of the City. The result of these processes was the construction of a financial system which was organized and coordinated through certain central points in a complex network of relationships; at these points, the power to influence and shape the structure as a whole was located and it was used to reinforce a certain pattern of wealth and inequality.

Overall, we argue that what was created was a particular organizational field of financial services, where different types of institutions related to each other in particular ways. This field was hierarchically organized in terms of both its organizations and other actors. Some organizations and other social actors had more power than others to set the rules and therefore had greater access to money and capital. This hierarchical organization of the field was reflected in the expectations that the various groups of actors (within the state, the Bank of England, the various types of financial institutions and within the various social positions in society) held about their rights and responsibilities. These expectations added up to a coherent picture, not in the sense of a consensual view of the world and all its parts but in the sense of a *negotiated order* where the powerful and the less powerful tested out modes of surviving and living together. The limits of these modes of survival could be modified through conflict and compromise but as long as the basic distribution of power remained stable, these modifications would tend to remain minor. It was money that was at the centre of this process; it was money that did most to give the powerful their power. Not surprisingly, therefore, it was within the institutions which managed money (i.e. the organizational field of financial services) that the most effort was exerted to prevent change.

## THE CITY OF LONDON

There are now multiple accounts of the emergence of the City of London as a financial centre (e.g. Ingham, 1984; Michie, 1992; Kynaston, 1994, 1995; Cassis, 1994; Scott, 1982, 1997; Roberts, 1995). As Michie in particular emphasizes, the City developed out of the creation of a series of activities that became partially interlinked over time even though they remained organizationally separate. These links occurred through the creation of economic and social networks (based on family, educational and friendship ties) and through the role which the Bank of England took in coordinating and overseeing many of these activities.

Many of these activities emerged in the seventeenth and eighteenth centuries as the British state established its naval power over and beyond those of other European states, and thereby its centrality to the growing trade between Europe and other parts of the world. The process of trading across long distances and long time-spans was not unusual to this period or place, but its extent and importance was growing rapidly (see also Canny, 1998; Colley, 1992; Marshall, 1998). As well as its importance as the centre of the most powerful sea-faring state, London became central to this process because of the development of various facilities that enabled the trade to occur. One essential element of this was the creation of credit facilities for merchants involved in the uncertain business of buying and selling over long distances. These could be partially insured against by the establishment of various 'prepayment' facilities. Merchants could borrow 'on account' from other merchants who, as they became more specialized in this process, formed themselves into 'merchant banks'. In other words, they would borrow money on the promise that they would be receiving money for something which they had sold. Similarly, the merchant at the next stage could also borrow. The resulting system of borrowings evolved into a system of specialist institutions – increasingly known because of their role in this system as merchant banks – which would carry a merchant's debts in the expectation that eventually they would be paid.

Banks would only accept debts from those they believed would eventually repay.

However, to have one's debt accepted (by what was known as an 'accepting house') was equivalent to receiving money since the bank would not renege on their promises. As a result of this process, London developed a range of banking houses which swopped the debts and credits of merchants between themselves whilst taking a proportion of the value of the account each time it was traded. The same linkages to overseas trade also led to the development of insurance facilities for ships and goods through Lloyds (originally a City coffee shop, which became a place where insurance business could be done and which eventually outgrew its original setting to become a market for insurance in its own right). Finally, the position of London as an entrepot for various goods and services was reinforced by the creation of specialist intermediary brokers for commodities such as sugar, coffee, tea as well as metals of various sorts. Commodity brokers were closely linked to insurance and banking institutions as their business depended on the timely provision of credit and debt repayments. These were the institutions of the 'trading city' established during the late seventeenth and eighteenth centuries.

They were reinforced by the extension of credit beyond merchants themselves to the state and later foreign governments. The development of this function became crucial to linking the City to the government and thereby creating an alliance of powers which was to be mutually reinforcing for many decades. The central symbol of this integration has been the Bank of England. The basic reason for the formation of the Bank was the state's need to borrow money in order to wage war and maintain the fleet and the colonies; in other words to protect the trading wealth that Britain was building. Unlike its main European rivals such as France and Spain, where eighteenth-century monarchies were trying to reform and sustain absolutism, in Britain the Civil War had led to a system in which monarchs required the consent and cooperation of Parliament in raising funds through taxation. The opportunity to borrow funds through the emerging merchant banking system therefore offered a possible way of extending military power without directly confronting the rich and powerful in Parliament with the request for higher taxes. The Bank of England was therefore formed in 1694 in order to provide a loan of £1.2 million to the King. In return for the loan (which was charged at 8 per cent p.a. interest), the Bank was made the government's banker. It was used to manage the debts of the government through organizing its borrowing requirements and repayment facilities. Central to this was, firstly, the Bank of England's role in setting interest rates and therefore influencing people's propensity to lend or borrow, and, secondly, its close connection to the various parts of the banking system which were the source of funds for the government's borrowing needs. Through its knowledge, understanding and influence over the other merchants and banks in the City, it was able to ensure that the government's needs for funds were met, at the same time negotiating interest rates with the government that were favourable to its lenders. The Bank therefore developed close relationships with the merchant banks in the City to provide funds to the government as and when necessary at the interest rates negotiated by the Bank. As loans to the government were highly secure, this business was greatly prized by potential participants. The Bank wielded its power to decide who was and was not worthy to be a party to these transactions. This in turn became a mechanism whereby insiders (and those who supported the Bank in difficult times) could be rewarded, whilst outsiders could be kept out of this lucrative business. These processes reinforced the social construction of an inner core to the City.

The implication of these processes was not just the growing power and patronage of the Bank of England. Firstly, private investors found a strong outlet for their money in the national debt 'upon which capitalist fortunes were made' (Weiss and Hobson, 1995: 117). What was created was a close set of interconnections between the institutions of the City (which made money through acting as intermediaries), the wealthy (both in the City and outside, who made money safely and securely through funding government debt), the government itself (which was able to fund its various activities in the European and colonial wars of the eighteenth century) and the traders (who wanted a navy and a military presence to secure their rights to exploit new found resources and trade them across land and sea). Weiss and Hobson assert that 'overall, the state intentionally formed a strong "organic" or "reciprocal" relationship with the financial capitalists where both parties co-operated and gained power in a positive-sum game' (1995: 119).

These authors also note a second aspect of the process. The interest on the loan had to be paid in some way other than further borrowing or printing more money – both of which would have had the potential effect of increasing interest rates whilst 'devaluing' money itself. They argue that in order to achieve this, the state raised customs and excise taxes. During the eighteenth century (and for much of the nineteenth), the British state raised between two-thirds and three-quarters of its entire revenue from indirect taxation (Mann, 1993: 382). Referring to the main European states as a whole, Mann observes that:

> At least half of indirect taxes came from a handful of goods, usually, salt, sugar, tobacco and alcohol...Such taxes were usually supplemented by more general customs revenues, especially on imported foodstuffs. Indirect taxes thus fell disproportionately on subsistence items and on fairly universal drugs like alcohol and tobacco. They were regressive, especially hard on the urban poor. Eighteenth century states were fiscal reactionaries, especially commercially buoyant states like the Netherlands and Britain, deriving 70 per cent of revenue from indirect taxes. (1993: 387)

Weiss and Hobson refer to this as a policy of 'forced savings' and link it directly to class relations within Britain when they argue that as a result of the way in which these taxes were used to pay interest on the National debt, '...the state effectively redistributed money from the poor consumer classes to the rich investor classes' (1995: 120–1). Thus, the key institutions in the City (i.e. the Bank of England and the merchant banks) acted from their origins to shape and reinforce inequalities of wealth within the British system.

In the course of the nineteenth century, a range of further institutions was established within the City of London which reinforced these processes. In particular as the number of types of government stocks expanded, there emerged an institutional form (the Stock Exchange) for the launch of such issues and subsequently a secondary market in their sale and purchase. By the mid-nineteenth century, the Exchange was serving this function not just for the British government but also for foreign governments, and, gradually but slowly, companies. During the first half of the nineteenth century in particular, overseas companies, usually with a British merchant bank sponsor (known as the issuing houses), required large sums of capital in order to develop railway infrastructures or to exploit the mineral and agricultural wealth of areas beyond Europe.

The establishment of the Stock Exchange reinforced the power of the City and its banking communities. Stocks were brought to the Exchange by issuing banks. In order to improve the chances of an issue being fully subscribed at the interest rates proposed, the seekers of funds would have to buy themselves the support and advice of one of the existing merchant banks; the more prestigious and well-connected the bank, the more costly the advice. The bank would then use its connections into the Exchange (particularly with the major broking houses) and the surrounding financial institutions to ensure that there was interest in the issue. In the Exchange itself, there was, in theory, a strict demarcation between the jobbers (who held stock on their own account) and the brokers (who purchased on behalf of clients). Prices were supposed to be negotiated on the floor of the Exchange by the jobbers and brokers according to levels of supply and demand. Brokers worked on a commission basis for their clients, advising them on appropriate stocks to purchase. The rules of the Exchange were managed by its members who traditionally were small scale partnership firms.

As the Exchange expanded to include company stocks, its role within the City became both more central and more controversial. The Royal Commission of 1877–78 revealed some of the intrigues that surrounded the Exchange. For example, Kynaston quotes the evidence of one outside speculator who claimed that 'a conspiracy between his broker and other members had taken place to his severe detriment . . . secrecy permeates every branch, pervades all the acts . . . unbounded facilities for collusion between the broker and the jobber' (Kynaston 1994: 283). The Stock Exchange provided countless opportunities for forms of what later became known as 'insider trading'. Bankers, jobbers and brokers were members of the City elite; they attended the same public schools, the same events of the London season and the same country house parties. They married into each others' families and shared many of each others' secrets. They were able to brush off any demands for outside scrutiny, claiming that they were capable of self-regulation. In this atmosphere, information was freely shared amongst the inner circle who were able to use their forward knowledge to sell or buy shares in particular issues. Occasional scandals and complaints surfaced during the nineteenth century, but they had little impact on the system as a whole. On the contrary, the City grew stronger as it adapted itself to industrialization, the internationalization of capital and the new financial opportunities that were opening up through these processes.

It is hard to overestimate the importance of the early phases of development within the City for the subsequent development of the whole financial system in the UK. Before the industrial revolution had begun, key institutions such as the Bank of England, the Lloyds insurance market, the early City merchant houses, brokers and jobbers were all in existence and closely integrated in a locational and social sense with each other and the government. As the industrial revolution developed, its proponents found that a financial system was already well-established in the City. Furthermore, it was a system which had grown independently of industrialism and it saw no reason to change its structures rapidly to meet the new requirements. No other country in Europe industrialized in such a context. In most countries, the financial system and the industrial system developed hand-in-hand. In Britain however, the financial system already existed, but had little relation to manufacturing industry. In the short-term, the result was that new financial institutions outside London also developed in order to meet the banking needs of these new sources of wealth. Over the longer term however, these regional institutions were absorbed into the City.

## THE EMERGENCE OF THE MIDDLE CLASS: RETAIL BANKING AND LIFE INSURANCE BEYOND THE CITY OF LONDON

In this section, we examine how new sets of financial institutions evolved in Britain under the impact of industrialization. We focus in particular on two aspects of this process: firstly, we consider the institutions themselves and how a process of amalgamation and centralization occurred which brought them and their funds into the ambit of the City of London; secondly, we consider the nature of those funds, particularly from the point of view of the increasingly important middle class depositor of the funds.

Most of the financial institutions which were founded as industrialization began had developed as mechanisms to serve the needs of particular towns and cities. Those commerical banks, savings banks, friendly societies, building societies, provident societies and life insurance companies founded in the early-nineteenth century tended to be highly regional and local. They collected funds from the local urban and rural populations and lent them to local industry. In 1825, according to Sykes (1926), there were 554 private banks in England and Wales, most of which only had one branch, that is in their home town. Private banks were dependent on the capital of their partners and therefore limited in size and the ability to adapt in times of recession. The joint stock legal form, where capital was raised from multiple investors whose liability was limited, was only available as a special concession by the government until the 1840s. For that reason, banks with large amounts of capital were few and far between. As the government made the joint stock legal form more available, some banks began to adopt it. Although these banks generally had more capital available, their branch network remained small. In 1844, there were 106 joint stock banks with 604 branches – only around five branches per bank. However, Sykes (1926) calculates that the number of joint-stock bank branches increased rapidly from 1195 in 1858 to 8081 branches in 1923. At the same time, joint stock banks began to take over the private ones and to amalgamate or merge with each other. In 1885, there were 110 joint stock banks in England and Wales, each bank with an average of 10 branches; by 1920, there were only 20 banks with an average of around 350 branches each.

By the interwar period, the retail banking system basically consisted of the 'Big Five' (Barclays, Lloyds, Midland, National Provincial and the Westminster Banks) and six more regionally-based banks, known as the 'Little Six'. They comprised three independent banks – Martins, District and National – and three subsidiaries of the 'Big Five' that retained an independent existence mainly based on a regional identity – Glyn Mills, Coutts and Williams Deacon's. The disappearance of locally-owned banks was reinforced by the relocation of the remaining large banks (e.g. Lloyds and Midland) into the City of London. Unlike countries such as Germany and the USA, therefore, Britain rapidly developed a retail banking system which was centralized into one part of the country by the start of the First World War.

What occurred in the amalgamation movement was the transformation of a regional and local banking system into something completely different. It was not just that the institutions became centralized, but that the consequence of this was a fundamental 'lock-in' to the City of London and its practices. In the nineteenth century, there is little doubt that a close relationship existed between banks and businesses in the same locality. Once the national banks were created and headquartered in London, this relationship began to break down. What had previously been a direct relationship between local banks and local businesses was now mediated by rules and decisions of the London-based head office. Many economists and economic historians have seen this as a process of spreading risk. Local banks are dependent on funds from local savers and lending to local businesses. Where the local economy is in turn dependent on a particular sector, firm or industry, economic downturns can lead to bankruptcy. Therefore, banks look to spread their risks by amalgamating and thereby avoiding excessive dependence on a single locality. In the British case, the banking crisis of 1878 can be interpreted in this way as a number of provincial banks were bankrupted partly because, as Collins states, their 'businesses had become closely inter-twined with the commercial fortunes of a small number of industrial customers' (1990: 206). Amalgamations and a shift away from long-term lending can be seen as emerging from this crisis in the banking system.

However, this argument under-estimates the already established importance of the City of London and the way it shaped the development of the provincial banks. Local banks were already strongly linked to City institutions, developing 'correspondence' banking relationships in London which enabled them to deposit and invest funds on the London markets. The markets for stocks, shares and lending and borrowing facilities were already developed and offered high levels of rewards to those participating. The local banks therefore established linkages to ensure that this could be done well before they were actually amalgam-ated into the large national banks. Amalgamation on the other hand centralized power and decision-making in the headquarters of the banks which were invariably located in the City. The large national banks which emerged were thereby in direct contact with the other City institutions. Cassis argues that:

> The prime function of the London joint stock banks was to make pos-sible the financial and commercial activities of the private firms and the overseas activities of their partners by providing the required cash credit. This was a major factor in the confinement of the English joint stock banks to traditional banking activities and also explains why the professionals were subordinated to the amateurs in the joint stock banks. (1985: 311)

The funds which the retail banks generated from their national branch networks became the source for the loans and investments which the merchant banks and Stock Exchange members controlled. Thus, in spite of the vast resources at their disposal from local branch deposits, the joint stock banks were usually very willing to fall in behind decisions and practices developed in the City of London and by the Bank of England. Cassis states that:

> ...the big and lucrative international financial operations were under-taken by the private firms, the partners of which were directors of the major joint stock banks or by groups of private firms or individual

capitalists. The role of the joint stock banks was seen as providing the required cash credit rather than to undertake these operations on their own account or to head a banking group. (1985: 313)

By the end of the nineteenth century, then, the retail banking sector had been absorbed into the City institutions. It had lost its previously distinctive features and was now a mechanism whereby funds were generated that could be recirculated through the City. In fact, it had two sides to its operations. On the one side, the banks still dealt with customers on a local basis through their branch network, earning money on fees and interest rate margins. Here, they increasingly operated as a cartel fixing interest rates and charges between themselves to support vast infrastructures. So long as they acted in concert, customers had little choice but to continue to pay even though the systems were clearly expensive and bureaucratic. On the other side, the banks developed surpluses which they invested through the City institutions. Here, flexibility and informality ruled, decisions being based on individual status and position within the social networks. These networks provided many opportunities for banks to make profits on their deposits without substantial risk, or at least without a risk that was shared amongst the City institutions as a whole. Informality meant that wrong decisions could easily be taken but the institutions usually did their best to support each other lest the failure of one be seen as a more general culpability. Compared to the uncertainties of investment in manufacturing industry, the use of bank funds in the short-term money markets and in the underwriting and purchase of government gilts seemed relatively risk-free.

The social networks which developed to support this process of financial integration also had a broader purpose. Retail bankers met regularly with the Governor of the Bank of England and were entitled to seek support at moments of crisis. Reciprocal invitations on to company boards or public institutions cemented the links between the retail bankers and the other members of the all male City community and all of this was underpinned by growing social homogeneity organized through the public school and Oxbridge system (see Cassis, 1995; Kynaston, 1995 for detailed analyses of how this process of social and economic integration in the City occurred during the 'Golden Years' leading up to 1914).

These processes were reinforced by the growing importance of other institutions, particularly those of life insurance. Over the course of the nineteenth century, the growth of the life assurance societies provided large amounts of savings and deposits. Once the initial technical problems with mortality tables and the actuarial basis of the industry were overcome, the industry grew rapidly. In the period 1830–69, 321 life offices were formed, and although 262 of these discontinued business there was still a net increase of 59 to a total of 110 offices open at the beginning of 1870. During the same period, the total of life assurance funds increased threefold. From 1870 onwards, the industry grew even more rapidly with new entrants and old established companies gaining more business. In this period, many life assurance offices were established as mutual societies providing benefits for their members. Often the title of these mutual societies reflected their perception of their membership, their local origins and moral goals – the Clerical and Medical, Scottish Widows, Scottish Temperance, Equitable Life, Norwich Union and so on. Even those companies which were established as joint stock proprietary organizations emphasized a social role – the Prudential, the Guardian, the Refuge. Unlike the retail banks, there was no rapid amalgamation process in the life insurance sector. Strong local identities plus the problems of taking over a mutual society prevented the wholesale amalgamation process from occurring even though there was a high turnover in companies as they went into liquidation or voluntary merger.

Nevertheless, the industry did become increasingly concentrated with a small number of large institutions taking the bulk of the business. Moreover, from the late-nineteenth century onwards, these companies began to diversify their portfolio of investment out of government stock. As their own funds grew through individual and collective savings schemes, they became more active participants in the Stock Exchange and the money markets. This process in turn led to a closer integration between the head offices and the City and the companies with which they invested. Investment management departments grew and were increasingly located in, and staffed from, the City of London even if the headquarters remained 'out of town'. These departments led to strong links being created with brokers in the Stock Exchange and also with the merchant banks concerned with stock and share issues. Senior directors of the life companies could expect invitations to sit on the boards of City institutions, including the Bank of England. Once again, then, at this level informality and networks became vitally important as ways of finding investment opportunities. It is important to note that the life insurance sector was never as homogeneous in its practices or structures as the retail banking sector had become by the 1900s. There were too many companies which retained strong local and regional roots for them to act as closely in concert as did the banks. Nevertheless, the overwhelming impression is that they too became increasingly drawn into the system based around the City of London earning profits and social prestige from their involvement in these informal networks. Also, as with the retail banks, the insurance companies developed extensive branch networks across Britain to extract as much savings as possible from the population. As these extended, more of the growing wealth of the nation was being channelled through the City. It was invested in accordance with the dominant logic of the City insiders, many of whom were able to take commission and fees from the process.

**Class, status and money**

The processes which have been described depended on the existence of a growing middle class. In this section, we discuss briefly the nature of that class and how it relates to the organizational field of financial services. The term 'middle class' covers a multitude of occupational categories, and over the last two hundred years some categories have declined (shop-keeping) whilst others (particularly managerial and professional roles in the public and private sector) have increased. Perkins provides various estimates of its size in the nineteenth century, suggesting that it increased gradually through this period up to around 30 per cent of the employed population by 1913 (Perkins, 1989: 79). In general, the members of this class could be said to be distinguished from the working class (and to share amongst themselves) one main characteristic – their access to income was generally stable and the level of that income was usually sufficient to enable them to save. The latter point was particularly crucial because unlike the upper class whose inheritable wealth was so large as to make work irrelevant to their survival, the middle class could only survive by working. So long as they kept working, their ability to maintain a house, a family, servants and a 'middle-class' style of life was generally secure. Unlike the working class, where insecurity of employment was endemic except in a few limited trades, middle-class professionals such as bankers, lawyers, doctors and teachers expected to have security of employment. On the other hand, there remained something precarious about this position for a number of reasons. What if the professional fell ill or died young? How could the family be supported? How could the professional ensure that the family would remain middle-class? Furthermore, what about those struggling to enter the middle class – H. G. Wells' *Mr. Kipps* and his like? How could they get there and make sure that they and their family stayed?

Many of these issues revolved around the sense of responsibility which was held by this group. Central in turn to this was the vision of the bourgeois family with the wife's place in the home, looking after the children (and the servants). In return for submitting to the patriarchal family structure, the woman could expect the financial support of the man (see Davidoff and Hall, 1987, for an analysis of this in the period 1780–1850). Children also were to be obedient to the father. As both the woman and the children depended on the man's earning potential, they were threatened by the loss of that potential. Visions of genteel widows thrust into poverty by the loss of their husband haunted the respectable middle class of Victorian England; so too did the idea of orphan children sent out to stay with distant relatives after the death of their parents. As the century wore on, the middle class learned to understand their family responsibilities not just in terms of providing for today, but also insuring against the potential ill-fortunes of tomorrow. This meant building up savings in banks and insurance societies, rights to pension entitlements (particularly popular in state occupations), and finally investing in the family's future by ensuring a 'good education' (usually at private school but possibly at the local grammar school) could be bought for the sons of the house. What they were doing was building up the family's monetary and cultural capital in order to ensure the continuance of the middle-class style of life within and across generations.

These goals were articulated in the literature, culture and ideology of nineteenth-century Britain. The successful middle-class family was held up as the ideal. In the sphere of financial services, this ideal shaped government policies. This is graphically seen in the provision of income tax relief on life insurance policies which began in Gladstone's budget of 1853 'as a minor element in a minor part of the tax structure with, it was anticipated, minor impact. Until 1984, when it suddenly fell victim to monetarism, it was a major part of the tax structure with major impact' (Zimmeck 1985: 167–8). In the debates at the time about tax relief, a number of issues emerged. One issue concerned Gladstone's wish to cut state expenditure and therefore hold down taxes. As Mann notes, the balance between expenditure and revenue in Britain changed dramatically during the nineteenth century (1993: ch. 11). The primary reason for reduced state expenditure (in relative rather than absolute terms) was the lack of any major wars after 1815. However, this came about in a context where free traders were also seeking to reduce customs and excise taxes which would have meant that revenues would fall even faster than expenditures. Some of the reformers argued that a form of differentiated tax system (i.e. the rich paying the most) could fill the gap. Gladstone, on the other hand, preferred to cut state expenditure. Mixed in with these arguments were issues concerned with encouraging people to save and the role which the tax system should play in that. Zimmeck quotes the 1852 Select Committee comparing the professional man and the 'annuitant'; that is, in the terms used here, the person who has inherited wealth and receives an annuity from this wealth:

> The professional man... may be said in some measure to be an annuitant as regards his earnings; but the annuitant would draw his annuity whether he were in good health or a sick bed; but the professional man can only draw his earnings during the time of health, and a serious bodily illness or mental imbecility would annihilate his income altogether. (Zimmeck, 1985: 173)

The issue which concerned the reformers at the time was how to encourage the savings of the professional middle class whilst ensuring that any benefits were not also felt by the 'undeserving wealthy' living off their annuities and inherited wealth. In typical liberal fashion, Gladstone noted that the premium relief,

> is open to all those who choose to avail themselves of it; but while it is open to them all, we know that practically the classes who are in the habit of insuring their lives are just those very classes... of professional men and of persons who are dependent on their own exertions. (Quoted in Zimmeck, 1985: 180)

The government adapted to the self-help and thrift ideas which were dominant in the Victorian era whilst resisting any moves towards a differentiated tax structure. They laid the basis of a system which would encourage middle-class professionals to place their savings in life-insurance-associated policies. The result was a boom in the number of life insurance companies, up from just six in 1800 to 150–180 in 1850 by which time funds were worth £50 million (Zimmeck, 1985: 176).

Ideas of thrift, self-help and saving stimulated both banks and insurance companies. The funds which were saved flowed through the channels of the bank branches and insurance networks towards the City of London where they were invested in the markets. Thus, the middle class became partially incorporated into the existing system. The banks and the insurance companies offered them the means to save and ensure the survival, growth and reproduction of their families and their social position. Long-term savings, in particular, were generally safe and secure investments for the future. The middle-class savers were not active investors; they gave up their money to 'respectable institutions' which made a virtue of stability, security and moderation – the Equitable Life as one of the oldest companies had called itself. Within the City, the processes of investment might be risky and uncertain in some areas but, generally, operating through the right banks and brokers could guarantee conservative actuaries investment returns which would be sufficient to meet their liabilities. Similarly, deposit accounts in banks could be considered safe, 'as safe as the Bank of England' which stood behind them as lender of last resort in the event of potential crises. The government, the financial institutions and now the middle class were linked together in an alliance based on the ability of the City to continue to make returns on its investments. As many authors have noted, this alliance had little to do with home-based manufacturing industry and everything to do with the international orientation of the City and its ability to extract surpluses from trading and lending activities in the Empire and elsewhere.

## THE WORKING CLASS AND SAVINGS INSTITUTIONS

The structure which was emerging had then been extended to incorporate middle-class professionals, even if their role was subordinate and limited. What about the working class of Victorian Britain? How were they to fit into this structure?

The ideology of thrift and self-help was not confined to the middle class. It exerted a powerful hold over groups within the working class, though here the problems of survival *per se* were usually more important than those of long-term savings. Nevertheless, throughout the nineteenth century, institutions were formed which sought to encourage members of the working class to save. These institutions took many forms; some concentrated on insuring people for the costs of burial (known confusingly as 'life insurance'); some acted as collective savings mechanisms to enable the purchase of homes (the building societies). Others were based simply on encouraging people to save small amounts in order to tide them over unemployment and illness (the 'friendly societies', the trustee savings banks and later the Post Office savings banks). Finally, there was the Cooperative movement which sought to combine all these aspects with the establishment of shops and political activity. All of these institutions sought to fill the gap (which the nineteenth century state refused to acknowledge as its responsibility) between the precarious nature of working-class employment and daily life, and the means of ensuring the reproduction of the labour force (families and children) by providing sufficient food, shelter and education to survive. Seccombe (1993) labelled this process 'weathering the storm', referring to the difficulties of sustaining any form of stable working-class family life or system of biological or cultural reproduction consequent on the impact of industrialism and urbanism.

Each of these institutions had local origins based on the efforts of working-class people to pull themselves out of their precarious dependence on employment. Through regular and small-scale savings which were pooled and then redistributed according to certain agreed principles, there was an attempt to create institutions which could provide financial help and support to members when required. Up until the Royal Commission of 1874 and the legislation enacted in the following year, these societies could be set up with relatively little formality. Nevertheless, the numbers of people involved in some of the institutions were huge. In 1870, the Manchester Unity of Oddfellows (the largest) had 434 100 members and the Ancient Order of Foresters 361 735 (Hopkins, 1995: 31). The Oddfellows had 354 lodges scattered throughout the country in 1865–75 (Gosden, 1973: 72). Referring to friendly societies as a whole, Gosden states that their 'known membership . . . in 1872 was 1 857 896 but . . . the [1874 Royal] Commission concluded that there were probably 4 000 000 members of friendly societies and about 8 000 000 persons interested in them as beneficiaries. These members were distributed over 32 000 societies, registered and unregistered, possessing funds of about £11 000 000' (1973: 74). There were also around 4000 building societies in England and Wales in 1870 with a membership estimated at anything between 212 000 and 800 000 (Hopkins, 1995: 42). In the period up to the Royal Commission, there was concern about the precariousness of these societies. This was based on a combination of the fact that they were dependent on their members maintaining their savings rather than withdrawing them. Therefore in periods of economic downturn, particularly where membership was local and likely to be hit by the same conditions, there was always the risk of collapse. There was also fear of incompetent and/or fraudulent committees losing or stealing the money.

In the early part of the century, the construction of this network of financial institutions was central to the attempt to stabilize the conditions of reproduction (both moral and material) of working-class families. The state stayed away from any direct involvement. However, by the last third of the century, the 'condition of England' question was increasingly leading reformers and others to consider how to maintain social order in the face of the continued growth of the working class in cities and the gradual establishment of trade unions. Over on the continent, Napoleon III and later Bismarck were beginning to construct paternalist state welfare systems which explicitly sought to reduce class conflict by providing various unemployment and other benefits (Esping-Andersen, 1990: ch. 1). In Britain, these issues gradually came to a head at the turn of the century with the reforming Liberal administration of 1906 and the emergence of the Labour Party. For most of the Victorian era, the emphasis was on self-help. By the time of the Royal Commission, however, it was recognized that the state needed to do more than simply encourage self-help. It had to provide the conditions to ensure that fraud and incompetence did not undermine either the achievement of self-help or faith in it as a possible strategy. The 1875 Act 'was to make these societies more reliable as insurers and to achieve this by getting them to manage their financial affairs more efficiently' (Gosden, 1973: 74–5). The Act increased the powers of the Registrar of Friendly Societies and required more regular auditing of the accounts of the societies; failure to comply would lead to suspension of a society. Gosden reports that between 1875 and 1890, this power was used 785 times (1973: 86). Building societies were also brought into this system of regulation.

The friendly societies and the building societies were generally founded and organized by the working class. The trustee savings bank movement on the other hand was 'set up by the middle class to encourage working-class saving and keep them off the poor rates' (Hopkins, 1995: 48). Hopkins notes that the depositors had no right to participate in the management of the banks. The Trustee Savings Banks were organized under various Acts of Parliament, one of which from 1817 required the trustees to place their balances at the Bank of England to a special account with the National Debt Commissioners in return for a fixed rate of interest. This link to the state encouraged the formation of more savings banks. On the other hand, the deposits of the working-class customers of the savings banks were being used to pay off the national debt. In the first half of the century, there was discussion and debate about the significance of this. Although the prevailing interest rate on savings bank funds often drifted above market rates in this period, Gosden states that:

> ... it could be – and was – argued by supporters of the banks that the free use of their deposited funds by the Chancellor of the Exchequer had saved the Treasury far more than the subsidy had appeared to cost it. When Goulburn was Chancellor, he used the money of the savings banks as a reserve from which to pay off dissatisfied fund-holders when he succeeded in reducing the rate of interest on government paper from 4 to 3.5 %, then to 3.25 % and finally to 3 %. The saving to the state from these manoeuvres amounted to £750 000 annually. Again, the savings banks' funds were also useful as a way of avoiding the costs of loan raising in the Crimean War. (1973: 221)

Gosden also shows that the savings banks were still subject to potential fraud and incompetence and, in the 1850s, a Select Committee was appointed to look into their operation (1973: 222–4). The debate centred on the state providing a guarantee for the funds of depositors, and this in turn led to the argument that the state should not only guarantee savings and use them but also collect them. The idea which emerged was that there should be a bank based in the Post Office – and what became known as the Post Office Savings Bank was set in 1861. Later in the century, the Post Office claimed that its 'Savings Bank rapidly became an important factor in the general development of thrift in the country, not only by the assistance which it rendered to thrifty individuals, but also as an ally of the associations for self-help' (quoted in Gosden, 1973: 238). By 1895, there were 5 776 000 accounts in 10 887 offices with an average annual total of £83 million on deposit. The Post Office was generally considered to pay a low rate of interest, around 2.5 per cent, which was lower than that of the savings banks. Thus, the savings banks were not put out of business by the Post Office savings banks. Indeed, from 1861 savings banks were allowed to invest a proportion of their funds beyond the national debt, enabling them to improve interest rates further.

It is interesting to note that these financial institutions served a dual purpose. Firstly, they were integrally tied into the ways in which the state conceived of its roles and responsibilities. Unlike most continental

European countries, where paternalism and forms of cooperation between rich and poor (albeit on highly unequal terms) were becoming established as the basis of the modern state, the predominant ethos in Britain was one of self-help (see Crouch, 1993). Class conflict was not to be controlled by state paternalism, but by individualizing the working class and reducing forms of collective identity. The ideology of self-help was central to that as was the establishment of financial institutions which could offer the chimera, if not the reality, of financial autonomy to the working-class male and his family. Eventually, even the liberal Victorian state came to recognize that this could not be achieved without some sort of state regulation.

Secondly, the funds which were collected were used to reduce the national debt and thereby reduce pressure for increased taxation. In many ways, this reproduced what we described earlier in Weiss and Hobson's account of the late-eighteenth century where, in effect, there was a redistribution from the poor to the rich. In this case, the savings of the poor were used to reduce the need to tax the rich. Ironically, in seeking to help itself, the working class also helped the rich.

This set of linkages between the state, the working class and the financial institutions articulated through an ideology of self-help and thrift remained unstable. In particular, as the poverty researchers of the late-nineteenth and early-twentieth centuries showed, there were many people who just had no residual income at all to invest in these institutions. Hopkins quotes the 1892 Royal Commission on Labour as stating that:

> there is still a deplorably large residuum of the population, chiefly to be found in our large cities, who lead wretchedly poor lives, and are seldom far removed from the level of starvation. (1995: 54)

He goes on to argue that 'the plain fact is that although self-help had provided a powerful means of self-protection for the majority of the working classes in the nineteenth century, for an important minority, it provided no safeguards at all. This was particularly so in old age' (Hopkins 1995: 54). Even for the majority, employment conditions led to uncertainty and insecurity which could not be overcome purely by individual savings. As membership in trade unions increased and working-class political activity inside the Liberal Party as well as outside (e.g. in the Independent Labour Party) grew, the debates about the role of the state increased. Harris states that the 1890s and 1900s...saw the emergence of a new form of contingent property rights in the form of social welfare entitlements created by the state...The introduction of workmen's compensation in 1897, old age pensions in 1908 and national insurance in 1911...in form and substance they were just as much genuine property rights as the voluntary savings institutions. (1993: 112)

Similarly, Runciman argues that the changes which occurred in these spheres and others in the period from 1915–22 were in fact sufficient to identify an 'evolution from one to another sub-type of the capitalist mode of production' (1993: 53). He noted that, firstly, the taxation system was fundamentally altered: 'the rate of income tax remained [after the war] some four times higher than it had been in 1914. Death duties [on estates of £1 million or more] were raised from 15 per cent in 1914 to 40 per cent in 1919; by 1930...they were 50 per cent and by the outbreak of the Second World War they had been raised again to 60 per cent' (*ibid*.: 57). These taxes were a fundamental blow to the rentier system of the Victorian era, and shifted the balance of state expenditure and revenue dramatically. 'Before the First World War, the working classes had been paying out more in taxes than they received in social services; but thereafter they received more than they paid' (*ibid*.: 57).

Secondly, this development went alongside a major expansion of social welfare expenditure. By 1918, Britain was almost a democracy, with young women the major group still disenfranchized. Politics was undoubtedly changing and whilst it can be debated how significant the shift from the Liberal Party to Labour as the main alternative to the Conservatives was for the events which followed, 'it is hard to doubt that wages would otherwise have been lower and welfare benefits less generous' (*ibid*.: 60). 'Between the wars, the proportion of national income spent on the social services roughly doubled...by the 1920s, the state was irretrievably involved in the provision of welfare in a manner and to a degree that would have been unthinkable before 1914' (*ibid*.: 57). Interestingly, the moves in Britain towards extending welfare benefits actually ended up excluding most of the friendly societies and contributing to their decline, a trend which was reinforced by the manner in which the National Health Service was created after the Second World War (on pensions, see Macnicol, 1998; on the NHS, Webster, 1998). On the other hand, building societies and the trustee savings bank movement continued to thrive.

The financial institutions of the working class were then integrally related to the struggle of this class to carve out conditions of survival in the type of capitalist economy which emerged in Britain during the nineteenth century. These institutions were reflections of that struggle and of the role of the state in a context where the ideology of self-help and thrift was powerful. Nevertheless, by the end of the century a form of collectivism had become established which changed some of these parameters by involving the state more closely in the provision of security. However, state involvement was still limited and the power of the idea of self-help remained strong even in the interwar years when economic depression made it even more difficult. Self-help was carried through into the post-1945 period and into the heyday of the welfare state by the continued existence of these working-class financial institutions.

## CONCLUSIONS: MONEY, POWER AND CLASS

In this chapter, we have outlined how the organizational field of financial services emerged. We have shown that there were strong elements of historical continuity even in periods of change. The direction of development was set by the establishment of the institutions of the City which built and reinforced a system for dealing with money between the government and the rich and wealthy long before the industrial revolution. As other sources of wealth were created outside the landed aristocracy and the merchant class of London and the major seaports, new financial institutions emerged. Over time, however, they became integrated into the circuit of monetary and social capital which centred on the City and reinforced the power of the insiders. Thus the City was eventually strengthened and revivified by the supply of new capital from the industrial areas of Britain. At the same time, whilst dividends and interest payments might flow back to these areas, large sums of capital did not. Instead, they were directed overseas to the formal and informal empire over which Britain ruled and to Europe and the USA. Thus, though the institutional structure of financial services became more complex and the range of funds which were being intermediated, accumulated, distributed and managed increased hugely from the nineteenth century, the City retained its power. The middle classes in particular were incorporated into this process through the new banks and insurance companies which promised them safe havens for their funds and the prospect of sustaining their class position and that of their families in times of illness and old age.

On the other hand, the British working class stood predominantly outside of this system. The City was willing enough to see its funds used through the Savings Banks and the Post Office to reduce the national debt and the pressure for higher taxes. It also recognized the working-class institutions as ways of reinforcing the ideology of self-help and thrift which could in turn ensure that the British worker remained more individualistic than some of his/her continental counterparts. It was therefore willing to support increased regulation of the sector to reduce problems of fraud and incompetence. However, as the ultimate weakness of this became clear, the City and the rentier class generally fought against Lloyd George's budget of 1909 which tried to introduce a super-tax on incomes over £5000 and a new succession duty on estates passing on death. Such was the opposition to this that a constitutional crisis was created which eventually led to the reduction in the power of the House of Lords through the 1911 Parliament Act.

In conclusion, we have sought to demonstrate that the financial institutions in Britain were structured through distinctive processes associated with the class nature of British society. Oberbeck and D'Alessio (1997) refer to the 'bon mot' of the German economist Adolf Weber:

> Summing up the findings of his comparative research on the British and German banking industries at the beginning of the twentieth century, Weber used to say that the British banks were developed for people who had money, whereas the German banks were developed for people who had none. (*ibid*.: 102)

In contrast to this, we have argued that while the system was certainly designed by, and even more importantly for, the rich, what was crucial was that the middle and working classes were granted their places within this system. From this point of view, we cannot conceive of change in financial services without recognizing that this is simultaneously implicated in a reconstruction of class relations. This illustrates in part what we mean by the *social theory of organizational change*. In the next chapter, we begin to explore these simultaneous and interconnected processes of social and organizational change.

# 3 National and International Money: Restructuring British Financial Institutions

## INTRODUCTION

In this chapter, we examine how a range of social, political and economic changes in Britain associated with its location in the wider international political economy impacted on the structure and organization of financial institutions. These changes made it increasingly difficult to sustain the structure of the system which was described in the previous chapter. They began to undermine the network of social and economic linkages which held each type of financial institution in its place within the hierarchy of functions managed and ordered primarily through the Bank of England. The ability of the Bank to maintain the structure of incentives and controls which had ensured the reproduction of this hierarchy declined as new actors and dynamics emerged.

Central to this process was the changing nature and distribution of money within both the national and the international context. In the postwar period, the nature of money began to change from what Leyshon and Thrift describe as 'state credit money' to 'virtual money'. They state that:

> the history of money is . . . a history of what Marx and others called the *dematerialisation* of money. Money is no longer a commodity which is transported hither and thither. It no longer even consists of paper, in the main. Increasingly, money is a set of double entries etched in computer memories. (1997: 22; italics in the original)

They go on to argue that this process also concerns space 'because money is a means of linking what are often widely scattered interchanges, connecting credit and liability' (*ibid.*). In doing so, they draw on Giddens:

Money is a means of bracketing time and so of lifting transactions out of particular milieu of exchange. More accurately put … money is a means of time–space distanciation. Money provides for the enactment of transactions between agents widely separated in time and space. (1990: 24)

These changes in the nature of money profoundly affected the dynamics of the financial institutions within the UK. As money became more international, it became more difficult not just for national governments to control, but also for nationally based financial institutions to sustain their traditional ways of working. Some financial service firms began to seek advantages and profits beyond those which could be guaranteed and managed within the UK context. This destabilized existing power relations and led to growing differentiation within the system which in turn created further demands for changes in the formal and informal regulatory processes. The internationalization of money was also part of a process whereby nation-states were having to adapt to new challenges arising from the more open world economy. As well as searching for ways to manage the macro-economic context in the light of these changes, governments in the West faced particular problems in terms of managing their systems of welfare in ways which controlled taxation and expenditure. The money that was international was also national, and national state coordination of the two became increasingly complex and secondhand not least because it involved influencing companies with their own sets of largely profit-oriented objectives which were no longer confined within the national context. Finally, money was also personal – it belonged to people. In the postwar economic boom more money and wealth was being created in the UK. This was changing the nature of British society through creating a larger and more affluent group of consumers for whom money was no longer a scarce item but rather something which was more central to constructing their own identities and lifestyles. Money now had multiple and, for some, more realizable meanings and uses (Bauman, 1998b). To a greater degree than ever before, money was not just associated with the battle for survival. More and more, individuals and families sought, as best they could in conditions of uncertainty, to plan their approach to money as part of an evolving lifestyle and lifetime approach to identity. Financial institutions acted as both contributors and mediators in this transformation of money (Sturdy and Knights, 1996).

In this chapter, we firstly examine the internationalization of money in the period up to the 1980s, and how this impacted on the UK financial sector undermining the previous order and increasing uncertainty and instability. In the second section, we reveal how this process placed increasing pressure on the state as it attempted to manage the consequences of these changes. Finally, we consider how all of these related to the changes in the nature of consumers and their expectations of financial services, focusing particularly on the transformation and growth of the middle class. In conclusion, we argue that as money changed, so the organizational field of UK financial services changed – the financial companies themselves, the forms of regulating and managing their behaviour, the way in which the state related to the financial sector and finally the nature of the consumers of financial services. By the mid-1980s, these were all in a state of fundamental transformation. How key actors sought to make sense of that transformation and restore order is the subject of the next section.

## THE INTERNATIONALIZATION OF MONEY

In the aftermath of the Second World War, the system established at Bretton Woods was aimed at encouraging international trade whilst reducing some of the tensions which were thought to have led to the instabilities of the 1930s. There was a presumption that the major industrial states would open their borders to competition in manufactured goods, and also that competition would be based on various national monies which had exchange rates fixed against each other. This competition would lead to countries building up surpluses and deficits which would have to be rectified through some sort of internal macroeconomic management. On occasions, it might be necessary for countries to call for support from the International Monetary Fund in order to reduce their deficits, or, even more unusually, there might be the possibility of a devaluation of the currency to restore its international competitiveness. In the main, however, the expectation and hope was that the system could combine increasing international trade in manufactured goods with what Block (1977) referred to as 'National Keynesianism', that is national systems which were managed (at the governmental, sectoral and firm level) according to their own historical and political logics. Across Western Europe, therefore, national systems would differ. The relative power of trade unions and workers, the different structures of the welfare state and production systems could all be sustained and managed through national macroeconomic management of supply and demand as developed in Keynesian economics (see for example Crouch, 1993). Money was still predominantly national and so were the financial institutions which controlled it. Central to this was the right of nation states to control capital flows; major sources of funds could not be transferred from one country to another. This was supposed to ensure that governments were able to maintain control of money and credit within their boundaries (Block, 1977: Ruggie, 1982: Morgan, 1997).

National Keynesianism was, however, based on an implicit internationalization of a specific type of money. In the period up to 1914, international trading between countries had been based on the gold standard and the fact that national money had a fixed rate of exchange against gold. In so far as international transactions were conducted in paper money, they tended to be conducted in pounds sterling since, as the dominant economic power, it was believed that the British pound was 'as good as gold' and highly unlikely to be devalued. Following the disruptions of the interwar years and the decline of the British pound, it was the US dollar which took on the role of providing liquidity for the international system, and it became the unit of account for many international trading transactions. In this sense it stood outside and above the other 'National Keynesianisms' of Western Europe because, unlike them, it was highly international – possessed and used by a wide range of states and organizations to settle their accounts.

This was possible for two main reasons. Firstly, US companies were the most international in this period and were therefore building up and developing businesses in various countries with the use of the dollar. Secondly, the US government with its global military and diplomatic commitments was using the dollar to pay for them. As a result, during the 1950s, the US dollar became a global currency in a context where its value was expected to be sustained and fixed relative to all the other currencies in the world. Dollar surpluses were built up in various parts of the world, but particularly in Europe where they were known as *eurodollars*. US banking regulation, which had been considerably tightened in the 1930s and 1940s in the aftermath of the Wall Street Crash to reduce speculation, discouraged dollar holders from depositing their funds in the USA. 'Regulation Q' limited the rate of interest that US banks could pay on deposits, and as a result, many of these eurodollars were deposited in the financial institutions of the

City of London. In 1957, foreign currency deposits in the UK banks had been $196 million; by 1964 the figure was $3600 million, the bulk of it held in dollars.

The existence of the eurodollars threatened national Keynesianism in Europe in a number of ways. Their availability as a form of credit reduced the control which national governments had on the tools of macroeconomic management since eurodollars could be accessed as forms of credit with no central bank control. They also provided a 'safe haven' into which funds could be switched out of currencies that were perceived to be potentially weak and therefore open to devaluation pressures. Finally, their existence made the US increasingly vulnerable to outside pressures. Unlike other countries, there was no obvious pressure on the US to reduce its balance of payments deficit; on the contrary, other countries were for a time happy to see it grow as they accumulated dollars. However, as European and Japanese industries rebuilt, they became increasingly competitive against the USA, thus increasing the US balance of payments deficit. These events gave rise to the feeling that the US would have to make some adjustment in the value of its currency, that is by devaluing it against the strong deutschmark and yen. This began to increase uncertainty in the international system, particularly after Britain devalued in 1967. By the mid-1960s, there was sufficient weight of trading in currencies to make some, such as the British pound, vulnerable to speculation and enforced devaluation. As currency trading began to be loosened from the control of central banks by virtue of increased international trade and the holding of 'offshore' monies such as eurodollars, the pressures for a major realignment of currencies began to build up. The US dollar was seen as overvalued as opposed to the rising currencies of Germany and Japan.

From the late 1960s through to the early 1970s, there was conflict among policy-makers at national and international level about how to resolve these difficulties. Some countries such as Germany and Japan had benefited from the system. Their fixed exchange rates against the dollar had become more competitive as their productivity levels had increased, thus building up their dollar surpluses. The USA sought to reduce this competitive advantage by forcing a realignment of the international monetary system. The Germans and Japanese recognized the need for readjustment, but hoped it could be achieved within a system that retained fixed exchange rates and discouraged speculative capital flows (thereby reinforcing national Keynesianism). US policy-makers, however, were moving towards a more radical solution involving floating exchange rates and a reduction in capital controls. Helleiner describes this shift as follows:

> the failure of the European and Japanese initiative to introduce co-operative controls marked the collapse of the Bretton Woods principle that liberalism in financial affairs should be sacrificed to preserve exchange rates. As the introduction of a floating exchange rate system after 1973 encouraged further speculative financial movements, states were then forced to consider giving up the second Bretton Woods principle: that of defending the policy autonomy of the Keynesian welfare state. (1994: 167)

By the mid-1970s, the trend towards internationalizing money and loosening its embeddedness in national regulatory systems was firmly under way. Currencies were now being traded continuously in markets and their values were rising and falling on the basis of these trades. Although most countries retained some control over capital until the 1980s, the network of relationships linking different national monies (particularly in the industrialized West and Japan) to each other through market trading was increasingly dense as trading currencies either directly or through swaps and futures became common. This meant that national money was inevitably embedded in an uncertain and unstable international context. As a result, interest rates and inflation were influenced not just by factors internal to the national system but also, increasingly by the location of the national system in an international context of trading of commodities, currencies and capital.

One result of this process was the opening up of many new areas of business for financial institutions. In the sphere of foreign exchange itself, instead of simply providing foreign exchange for their clients as required by business and personal circumstance, financial institutions were now able to deal on these markets on their own account, effectively to bet on movements between currencies. Goodman and Pauley state that 'in the midst of the currency crisis in March 1973, $3 billion were converted into European currencies in one day. In the late 1970s, the daily turnover around the world was estimated at $100 billion; a decade later, that figure had reached $650 billion' (1993: 57). By 1995, the figure was up to $1000 billion (Roberts, 1995). Crucial to this further expansion has been the process occurring since the 1970s of the gradual abandonment of capital controls. In 1974, the USA removed such controls, and the UK was the first European economy to do so soon after the election of the Thatcher government in 1979. Germany followed in 1981 and France a few years later in the wake of the Socialist government's U-turn in economic policy after 1983 (Schmidt, 1996: chs 4, 5). Through the 1980s, other European economies and Japan gradually removed their controls over capital (Helleiner, 1994), a process which spread into the emerging economies of East Asia during the 1990s, partly under the sponsorship of international agencies such as the IMF and the World Bank, but also as a means of accessing capital for the industrialization drives of these countries (on the politics and economics of these debates, see Wade, 1990, 1996; Wade and Veneroso, 1998). The ability of capital to move in and out of countries reduced the ability of governments to manage the macroeconomic framework. The decisions of financial and industrial companies to invest was increasingly shaped by global comparisons in terms of present and perceived future economic performance, which governments could affect but not determine. The removal of capital controls also reinforced the tendency to trade on the values of currencies. If currency values were likely to change, it became necessary to hedge against this risk by securing futures contracts. Creating various ways of hedging against currency risk not only produced new and more complex financial products, it also created new ways of betting on currency movements. The result was an increasing array of financial products which linked bonds in particular currencies with mechanisms for hedging and protecting as well as gaining from changes in currencies.

These processes also affected the functions of corporate finance. Funds for investment could be more easily transferred from one area to another. It did not matter what currency they were denominated in so long as any risks arising from switching to a new currency had been laid off. Thus the market for international lending expanded and with it the role of corporate finance departments within banking institutions. This in turn related to the expansion of investment and dealing in stocks and shares. Financial institutions, either on their own or through their clients' accounts could purchase stocks and shares on foreign stock exchanges. Coleman and Porter (1994), for example, show the growing degree of internationalization in financial services from a number of perspectives. With reference to bank assets, they state that in 1970, 46.1 per cent of the assets of British banks were foreign-owned, a figure which increased to 48.4 per cent in 1989–90. In France for the same period, this figure increased from 15.9 per cent to 36.9 per cent, in Germany from 8.8 per cent to 16.2 per cent, in Japan from 3.7 per cent to 16.1 per cent and in the USA from 2.6 per cent to 9.4 per cent. They also state that eurobond issues (i.e. bonds issued in a currency other than the domestic currency of the borrower – see below) accounted for 25 per cent of all bond issues in the UK by 1990. In terms of equities, by 1990, 25 per cent of trade in the UK was conducted by foreigners (*ibid.*: 192–6).

In the course of the period from the 1950s to the 1980s, therefore, a fundamental change occurred in the nature of money. It increasingly became an internationally traded phenomenon in its own right. National money was also international money in a new sense. In the past, its 'international' nature was expressed in the fact that it could be traded at a fixed rate with other currencies. In the new era, its value was variable, not fixed, determined by the operations of the financial markets within this emerging international trading system.

## Internationalization and its impact on UK financial institutions

The arrival of the eurodollar funds in the City of London was an opportunity which initially attracted only a small number of banks, but gradually, as the scale of fees and earnings was realized, more institutions entered the market. A key innovation here was the creation of the eurobond market. These were in effect the invention of one of the newer and more aggressive merchant banks in the City, S. G. Warburg, which developed the idea of offering for sale bonds in dollar denominations with fixed rates of interest. Acting for a fee on behalf of the client requiring the loan, they would estimate likely demand for the bonds and how this affected rates of return and periods of repayment. They would also underwrite the bond issue, guaranteeing its take-up by committing to purchase any bonds leftover. However, using its reputation, influence and network of contacts in the UK, Europe and beyond, the bank could generally find purchasers. As the eurobond market grew, syndicates of banks became involved as arrangers and underwriters. Like shares, bonds became tradeable, but unlike shares they provided a guaranteed rate of return as well as a higher priority in the queue of creditors if a company went bankrupt. Bonds therefore offered less risk and less variation in rewards and losses than did shares. Interest rates paid by bond issuers could also be set to reflect perceptions of the safety and security of the loan. In the initial launch of bonds, financial institutions made their money out of the fees which they earned for their advice, issuing, underwriting and trading. They were also able to use their knowledge to trade the bonds in the subsequent markets.

The eurodollars and later the other currencies which found an off-shore home in the City of London created a vast new source of business and profits for institutions based there. Foreign banking institutions soon saw that unless they too were present, they would lose the business of some of the largest of their own national firms. The result was that the number of foreign banks operating in London increased rapidly from around 70 in 1960 to 199 in 1975 and 312 by 1985, of which around 25 per cent were of US origin. Also, the scale of annual syndicated loan business in foreign currencies went up from $200 billion in the early 1970s to $1.3 billion in 1980 and over $6 billion in 1990 (Brearley and Kaplanis, 1994: 5). This market received a massive boost by the oil crises of the mid-1970s which suddenly redistributed large numbers of dollars and other currencies to economies in the Middle East that had little capacity for immediate investment. The funds were placed back in London where they fuelled a massive investment boom. During the 1970s, these funds were circulated in two directions – firstly into the UK economy where banks and other institutions borrowed in order to lend on to business and personal customers, particularly in the property market, and secondly into the provision of loans to governments in the 'less-developed' countries.

**Money, credit and crisis in UK banking**

This expansion of lending which became possible during the 1970s created serious difficulties for the way in which the Treasury, the Bank of England and the financial institutions had sought to manage credit and monetary expansion in the heyday of national Keynesianism. During the 1950s, the Bank of England was still using its powers of influence and moral persuasion to manage credit. As we saw in the previous chapter, this was part of its traditional role exercised for two centuries in which it acted for the government in managing interest rates and the provision of credit. In the Keynesian period, this became even more important as the government sought to manage the macroeconomic context to achieve full employment. The Bank of England was closely tied into the Treasury and economic policy-making, acting in the financial markets themselves in order to ensure the government's goals were achieved. In the language of the period, the Bank would make 'requests' to potential lenders to restrain their activities. In the case of the Clearing

Banks, who dominated the credit markets in the 1950s and were closely connected to the Bank of England, restraint was maintained in a number of ways. Firstly, the banks were expected to keep up to 30 per cent of their deposits in liquid assets; within this total, 8 per cent had to be made up of cash. Secondly, the Bank of England operated a system of special deposits: when a call was made, each bank had to lodge a cash deposit of a specified percentage of its total deposits. In general, this meant that the banks had to call in some of their loans, in effect resulting in a credit squeeze and a rise in interest rates. Thirdly, the Bank also operated quantitative ceilings on the growth of lending to the private domestic market. In 1965, a limit of 5 per cent annual growth was placed on this lending; in 1967, there was to be zero growth, in 1968 4 per cent; in 1968, a reduction of 2 per cent over four months was proposed.

These measures, which were aimed at managing the provision of credit and liquidity in the system and therefore either stimulating or reducing demand according to the government's assessment of the broad macroeconomic environment, were particularly aimed at the clearing banks. In the earlier part of the century, as described earlier, these banks had been integrated into the City system and through their branch network were key to the provision of credit and, therefore, demand in Britain as a whole. However, during the 1950s new institutions were set up known as *finance houses*. Like the banks, these institutions also offered credit though it was increasingly based on their own ability to borrow from elsewhere and then to lend on to personal customers; they did not set up a branch network to collect funds. Up to 1200 finance houses came into existence in the period up to 1959. Unlike the banks, however, they did not have to make special deposits with the Bank of England. As the eurocurrency markets expanded, more funds became available for this 'fringe' or 'secondary' banking sector as it became known. As Moran states; 'The consequence was that big [financial services] companies who voluntarily exercised restraint found their business nibbled away' (1986: 21). While finance houses strengthened their position in the personal credit sector, the building societies took advantage of the constraints on the banks to become firmly established as the main source of saving and lending for home purchase. Indeed, clearing bank deposits fell from 43.4 per cent of sterling deposits in 1962 to 31.2 per cent in 1976; over the same period, finance house deposits increased from 3.8 per cent to 12.5 per cent, whilst those in building societies rose from 21.2 per cent to 37.7 per cent (London Clearing Banks 1977: 56).

The consequence for both the clearing banks and the Bank of England was serious. The former began to demand to be able to compete in these growing markets on equal terms. As the largest banking institutions in the country, they resented the way in which they were losing business to new entrants who were less constrained than they were by the rules of the Bank. Yet the Bank of England and the government were reluctant simply to do away with the controls over the banks without getting something in return. The clearing banks may have lost certain freedoms by cooperating with the Bank, but they gained others, such as the right to act as a cartel in price setting. It was therefore unrealistic to expect that they would be freed from their obligations to cooperate with the Bank whilst being left with the privileges which had originally come from that role.

The position of the clearing banks was also being undermined by growing criticism of their cartel-like practices. This debate was furthered when the Prices and Incomes Board reported in 1967 on their activities. The report was scathingly critical about the level of service provided by the banks and the charges which they made for these services. It also saw no reason why banks should be allowed to maintain hidden reserves and thus distort their profit figures. These criticisms were strengthened when a further wave of amalgamations began in 1968. First the National Westminster Bank was created from a merger of the National Provincial and the Westminster; a few days later, it was announced that Lloyds and Barclays were also to merge and then take over Martins Bank, one of the few remaining smaller banks. The government referred the Lloyds/Barclays/Martins merger plans to the Monopolies and Mergers Commission, the final report of which turned down the proposals on the grounds that they would be harmful to competition.

These arguments over merger and amalgamation did not resolve the problem of the relationships between the clearing banks, their new competitors and the management of the monetary and credit systems through the Bank of England. 'Existing credit controls were being avoided on a large scale, and . . . the diversion of credit outside officially controlled and monitored institutions made official indicators increasingly unreliable' (Moran, 1986: 49). The Conservative government which took office in 1970 responded to these difficulties with the introduction of a new system of Competition and Credit Control (CCC). This placed all banks (i.e. the secondary, fringe banks as well as the Clearing Banks) under the same obligation to maintain 12.5 per cent of eligible liabilities in specified reserve assets. For the clearing banks which had been previously subjected to a 28 per cent minimum liquidity ratio, this involved a considerable relaxation in how they were controlled. In return, the clearers had to abandon many of their long-standing cartel agreements. In September, 1971, their interest rate cartel was discontinued, and in the months which followed a series of other interbank agreements were wound up in areas such as charges for encashment of cheques by customers of non-clearing banks; commissions on traveller's cheques; charges for the management of employees' accounts for large firms (i.e. payment of salaries, pensions etc. by direct transfer); and minimum commissions on overseas business (London Clearing Banks 1977: 175). The result was a heightening of competition between the clearing banks themselves and between this group and the so-called fringe banking sector. In particular, the clearers were now freed to look more directly to the money markets both as a source of funds for new lending and as a destination for their funds. In terms of capitalization, Barclays, Midland and NatWest were amongst the 30 largest banks in the world during the 1960s and 1970s, but they had not yet become much involved in the growing international financial markets. From the early 1970s, however, they plunged into both international lending and property lending in the UK with gusto, to the extent that they were amongst the biggest losers in both areas when the UK property boom collapsed and the debt crisis of the 'less-developed' countries blew up in the late 1970s.

The impact of CCC was that credit as a whole became much easier to obtain as the relaxation of monetary constraints led to a rapid growth in monetary supply – 28 per cent growth in M3 annually in both 1972 and 1973, and a doubling between mid-1970 and early 1974 (Clarke, 1986: 27). This massive expansion of credit led to speculative bubbles, particularly in the UK property market. From 1971–73, house prices doubled (Saunders, 1990: 120), whilst rents for office properties particularly in London also increased rapidly. Property developers sought funds for speculative building, in the process reaching gearing levels on the basis of their loans of the region of 90 per cent (Clarke, 1986: 29). The result was that the clearing banks and the fringe banks all became enmeshed to varying degrees in a speculative boom. In 1973 and then more rapidly in 1974, (following the OPEC oil crisis and the Labour Party victories in the two general elections of that year when interest rates rose from 7% to 13%) property companies began to go bankrupt, drawing their bank creditors into danger as well. Whilst it was predominantly the fringe banks which were directly involved in lending to the property sector, the clearing banks were lending to the fringe banks and therefore the potential for contaminating the whole banking system existed. In 1974, according to Clarke, even 'the NatWest was forced to issue a statement denying that it was receiving Bank of England assistance' (1986: 40).

The Bank of England did try to stabilize the system in late 1973 by bringing the banks together to provide what was termed a 'lifeboat' for the ailing institutions. As in the past, the Bank wished to avoid a crash which might effect other banks. When it was informed that Cedar Holdings, a fringe bank, was on the point of closure, it summoned the chairmen of the clearing banks to help provide the £72 million necessary to save Cedar. The clearers put up 90 per cent of this sum and the Bank itself 10 per cent. These were lent at between 0.5 and 2 per cent above the prevailing money market rate, but it was not clear how long it would take the rescued firm to repay the loan. However, Cedar Holdings was only one of many that were getting into difficulties as property prices fell and loans became non-performing. The clearers and the Bank found the numbers seeking help increasing, so that by September 1974, £900 million had been lent. In March 1975, the sum had reached £1200 million which represented 40 per cent of the total capital and reserves of the clearers. At this point, the clearers refused to lend any more and the Bank had to assume sole responsibility for any further rescues. Fortunately, by this time, the crisis had almost run its course though the Bank was forced to rescue Slater Walker, one of the most famous of the fringe banks because of its connection to the flamboyant Jim Slater and the Conservative politician, Peter Walker. In terms of the clearers' refusal to put more money into the rescue, Moran states that:

> the Clearing Banks had divided interests; they had a collective interest in preventing the collapse of the banking system but individual interests in minimising their own contribution to the cost of rescue. (1986: 106)

In effect, this was the last time that the Bank was actually able to organize a 'lifeboat'. In 1984, Johnson Matthey Bank (JMB) (a small secondary bank which through its connection to the old established bullion merchants, Johnson Matthey was treated as part of the City insider group) got into trouble because of the failure of two of its largest loans. The Bank sought to organize another rescue, but the Clearers, in particular, were highly resistant and the Bank was forced to put up most of the money itself for what was effectively nationalization of JMB. Moran states that 'the clearers, having bitterly resented the scale of their involvement in the mid-1970s crisis, were determined not to become as deeply embroiled in another costly case' (1986: 169).

## Overseas lending

The same loosening of controls which prompted credit relaxation and property speculation in the UK encouraged the UK clearing banks into lending to 'less-developed' countries in the early 1970s. Kapstein argues that encouragement to lend was also provided by the support of government and intergovernmental agencies such as the IMF (Kapstein, 1994: 66) to such an extent that between 1974–76, non-OPEC 'developing' countries borrowed $25.5 billion within the euromarkets. Armstrong *et al.* argue that the 'banks faced with limited outlets for profitable lending in the advanced countries competed madly to attract OPEC deposits to lend to the South. It seemed safe enough. Many loans were at variable interest rates, guaranteeing a profit regardless of interest rate changes' (1984: 362). By 1983, LDC ('less-developed' countries) debt had reached $400 billion and, within that, the proportion of debt held by private banks had risen to nine times its level of 1973 whereas that to governments and international agencies such as the World Bank had grown to only three times its 1973 level. The UK banks were major participants in this debt and therefore highly dependent on the debtors' ability to pay back the loans at the agreed rates. George states that by 1984 Lloyds Bank had lent 165 per cent of its capital value (measured in terms of shareholders' equity) in loans to Mexico, Brazil, Argentina and Venezuela alone; the Midland had lent even more (205%) to the same group of debtors (1988: 33). She also notes that at the end of 1984, the British big four banks (Lloyds, Midlands, Barclays, National Westminster) had loaned about £16 billion to Latin America which she describes as 'vastly more money than they actually had' (*ibid.*: 35).

According to Spero and Hart (1997), the debt problem emerged on three fronts. Firstly, rising interest rates increased the costs of servicing the debt. Secondly, there was a switch in the length of lending from three to five years, which had characterized the pre-1979 period, to a more short-term orientation allowing lenders to leave more quickly in the event of possible crises. Finally, they note that the new lending was increasingly used for consumption purposes rather than investment in productive capacity. The result was that, by 1982, it was becoming increasingly difficult for the major Latin American borrowers to pay back their debts at the agreed rates. The crisis initially hit in Mexico where the external debt totalled $85 billion. On 12 August 1982 the Mexican finance minister announced that his country would not be able to meet its interest repayments to foreign banks. It was clear that other Latin American countries would face similar problems. All lending to these countries abruptly ceased whilst negotiations began involving the IMF, the debtor states and the banks. These negotiations went through a series of stages in the 1980s and early 1990s and led to a process of rescheduling the debts.

The negotiations around the debt crisis were clearly most significant for the populations and governments of the debtor states and for global structures of inequality (see the discussions in Kapstein, 1994: ch. 4; Strange, 1998: ch. 6; Shepherd, 1994). However, they were also import-ant to the British banks which had invested such large sums during the 1970s. They were placed under pressure to restructure the loans and allow countries longer to repay them. This in turn meant that they had to revalue the loans as assets on their balance sheets as well as re-calculate payback contributions to their revenues. Over the course of the 1980s, they had, in effect, to write off much of the interest repayment and prin-cipal sums in order to get them off their balance sheets. The process through which they did this varied across the main banks. For example, Lloyds took it as a message to get out of international banking entirely and over the 1980s reduced their exposure to overseas risk. The Midland Bank on the other hand, acted slowly to restructure its balance sheet, in fact compounding its mistakes by purchasing a US bank, Crocker Bank, which also turned out to be highly exposed in Latin America. It there-fore found itself carrying a high level of non-performing debt which weakened its performance on the stock market to such an extent that it became a takeover target, eventually succumbing to the Hong Kong and Shanghai Bank.

**From debt crisis to competition: the breaking of boundaries in UK financial services**

The loosening of credit controls and the access to international money led British banks into overexposure when the markets in which they had invested declined. In order to deal with the problems that this was caus-ing them, the banks focused more strongly on their home markets. This focus pushed them into markets that had previously been the province of other institutions, particularly building societies and insurance companies. Traditionally, the building societies had dominated mortgage lending for house purchase (in 1977, the banks had only 3% of this market). They were also the favoured destination for personal savings since they generally paid better rates of interest than banks, which at this stage continued to charge customers to hold their money in current accounts. Not until the early 1980s did the banks begin to tackle this competition directly. Using money raised on wholesale markets (which were by then open to them but not to building societies), they launched an attack on the societies' position in the mortgage market, pushing their proportion of lending up to 38 per cent in 1982 (Bank of England Quarterly Bulletin, 1983: 371). They also overhauled their current account system and launched 'free banking' for accounts in credit. In turn, the building societies argued that it was necessary to loosen the controls to which they were subject. In the 1986 Building Societies Act, they were given some limited freedoms to borrow on the wholesale markets as well as to offer unsecured lending. They were also given the opportunity to loosen themselves entirely from the constraints of building society legislation by becoming public limited companies with the consent of their members. In the 1980s, only the Abbey National took this conversion route though all the large societies began to exercise their rights to borrow money in new ways.

These changes meant that the banks and building societies began to compete more strongly against each other for savings and mortgage business. The building societies had the advantage of their long-standing historical role in the provision of housing finance. Banks were also generally perceived to be less friendly to deal with for this purpose. As mutual institutions, the building societies did not have to worry about paying dividends to shareholders. On the other hand, the banks could access more funds from the wholesale markets and their own shareholders to launch aggressive marketing campaigns to win customers.

Even more important than winning mortgage business however, was the battle for personal savings and investments which extended the competition further, this time into the life insurance sector. Traditionally, these activities had been dominated by the life insurance companies with their large salesforces and the local brokers who advised customers on products and companies. As the banks developed their own investment management and later market-making capacity, they began to move into the sphere of selling investments. Whilst margins from money transmission and lending were tight due to increased levels of competition, the returns from the fees which the client paid for insurance and investment were higher and further strengthened firms' investment management and market-making capacities. During the 1980s, therefore, banks moved into what they termed '*bancassurance*', that is the provision through the bank branch network of insurance-based savings and investment products. The development of bancassurance occurred at varying rates in the different institutions and soon extended both to the building societies (which also began to offer a wider range of savings products) and eventually to the insurance companies themselves (which started to look at ways of providing a banking service) (see Morgan, 1994 for a discussion of the different routes to bancassurance). In its early stages, bancassurance was often characterized by ties between a bank and an insurer, with the bank selling the insurer's products through its branch network and receiving commission for this. However, banks and building societies soon began to argue that they were losing all the income from managing the policies and investments which came when savings products were sold. They therefore began to set up or purchase their own insurance companies, further extending their interests and enhancing the conglomeration effects arising from elsewhere in the system.

**The City institutions and money**

The changes which have been described were reinforced by changes occurring in the City institutions. In the 1960s and early 1970s, for example, the traditional City merchant banks played a central role in extending the international lending, equity and foreign exchange markets. However, as the bond issues and the foreign exchange markets grew, these institutions (generally based on a partnership structure with limited capital) found themselves being out-competed by the large foreign banks entering London. Although some of them began to seek outside capital, Hamilton states that the 'average UK merchant bank was still capitalised at only around $200 million by the early 1980s' (1986: 89). By contrast, Merrill Lynch had shareholder equity of $2 billion and Shearson Lehman and Salomons were both capitalized at over $1 billion (*ibid.*). Size of the capital base together with access to potential investors was increasingly crucial to this market. After their initial dominance, the British merchant banks had to battle against more powerful US, European and later Japanese financial institutions for a role. By the 1980s, it was increasingly clear that the battle was lost and, one after the other, the merchant banks disappeared into the welcoming embrace of larger financial institutions. The clearing banks and other retail banks were particularly tempted to extend their operations in the UK by purchasing a merchant bank. For example, TSB which had shifted from a loose agglomeration of savings banks to a single ownership and management structure over the course of ten years, purchased Hill Samuel in 1987 in order to diversify from its retail banking base. Thus, at the same time that they were developing bancassurance in the retail market, banks were extending into other markets and creating themselves as conglomerates stretching across the full range of financial intermediation.

This process was pressed forward in the name of competition and the idea that personal and business customers wished to be able to access a range of services through a single provider rather than having to shift between specialist organizations. From the point of view of the company, this meant looking at how these relationships could be developed in order to maximize profitability. The logic of this drove the companies towards further extensions in their range of services. In particular, the sphere of investment management offered a tempting target. Companies generating huge sums in retail savings looked for ways to invest the capital and to benefit not just from investment returns but from the process of investing and managing the investment itself. The merchant banks had traditionally developed major capabilities in this area offering expertise in fund management to insurers and pension scheme managers. Through this connection, these funds joined the circuit of capital that was operating through the City. Unlike other European countries, which tended to operate severe restrictions on how these types of funds were invested (often limiting them to low risk assets or in the case of pensions allowing investment in the companies for which the beneficiaries were working), there was considerable freedom for the investment managers in the UK. The result was that fund managers developed a portfolio approach to their investment, placing money across a range of bonds, shares, futures, gilts and other financial instruments. Once capital controls were removed in the UK in 1979, these funds were available for investment in other countries as well as Britain, causing a significant shift into overseas investment.

The growing importance of institutional investors also impacted on the field of governance and the market for corporate control. Competition in the field of fund management was intense. Selling out in contested corporate takeovers for the highest return was part of the game which was being played, and the institutional investors were key to such battles and bidders constructed their terms to win this support. The advisers in this process were often the same merchant banks which were in charge of the funds that would be crucial to the success of the bid. In theory, 'Chinese walls' kept the two parts of the bank separate and prevented 'insider trading' on private and confidential information. The difficulties of maintaining this separation increased in the 1970s and early 1980s as there was inadequate supervision of the markets. The City's own Takeover Panel and its Code of Conduct was meant to act as a disciplinary force but its success was problematic. For fund managers, success depended on showing the ability to manage the growth of these funds in ways which encouraged further investment. A major impact could be made on this by selling out to bids which offered a quick and instant return through inflating the price of the stock in a bidding war. There was little to hold the fund managers back from this approach to developments in the market, particularly as deals grew larger and new forms of financing were constructed by the merchant bank advisers. Thus the market for corporate control extended throughout the 1970s and early 1980s, fuelled by the increase in savings from pension and life assurance and the necessity for the fund managers to retain business by showing high returns.

One of the main barriers to this process remained the Stock Exchange which through the 1970s was still observing its traditional demarcation between brokers and jobbers with their minimum fixed commissions. As we saw in the previous chapter, members of the exchange were small, privately-owned firms divided into the two categories of brokers and jobbers, who, between them set fixed commission rates on all deals. Investors, such as pension funds, insurance companies or banks, who wished to purchase large amounts of stock found themselves with very little room to bargain or negotiate rates. They also found it impossible to purchase large lots from a single jobber as jobbers lacked sufficient capital to hold on to stocks and shares in the numbers often required by large investors. Thus, the investment managers and corporate financiers were increasingly frustrated by the Stock Exchange. The result was that some firms sought other ways to raise finance in the international money markets and dealing off the Exchange was beginning to increase as was the threat to deal in other centres such as New York. In general, however, there was increased pressure to reform the Exchange which was seen as an anti-competitive cartel. The clash between the Exchange and its critics led the Office of Fair Trading to refer the Stock Exchange rule book to the Restrictive Practices Court. In the next few years, the Stock Exchange worked frantically behind the scenes to ensure that the new terms on which it was to exist were advantageous to the old members. The result was a series of compromises which opened up the Exchange by enabling its members to sell out to other firms. The new membership system allowed firms to buy and sell shares on their own account and on behalf of clients, thus abolishing the jobber and broker distinction. Market-makers were supposed to offer best advice to their clients and not sell them shares at an inflated price in order to relieve themselves of a loss. Commissions were to be negotiated between the parties to the contract and the old fixed minimums were abolished. All of these changes took place in the midst of technological changes which were undermining the old trading floor of the Exchange and leading to electronic screen-based trades from the dealing rooms of the new institutions.

It was long anticipated that these changes would radically alter the nature of the City. One after the other, the City's financial markets had gone through a period of explosive growth fuelled by new funds from outside and inside the UK. The old City institutions had similarly enjoyed a period of sustained growth. However, each time a limit was reached beyond which the old structures could no longer be sustained. It was not just the specialist knowledge and skills and social relationships which the City networks had incubated and sustained over centuries that were required. Capital in large amounts was necessary to provide the funds both to manage increasingly complex businesses spread across the world and to take calculated risks in the markets where huge profits beckoned for the successful. In order to get to this capital, the old institutions had to sink their identity into larger banking conglomerates from the USA, Europe, Japan and the UK itself. What was known as 'Big Bang' was seen as the final piece of the jigsaw because now the banking conglomerates could stretch over every area of the wholesale markets from investment management to market-making, foreign exchange dealing and corporate finance. For a brief period of time after 1986, some of the main UK merchants banks sought to establish themselves in this vein by buying broking and jobbing houses. Warburgs, for example, bought the brokers Rowe and Pitman together with the jobbers Akroyd and Smithers. Kleinwort Benson bought Grieveson Grant (brokers) and Charlesworth (jobbers), and Morgan Grenfell bought Pember and Boyle (brokers) and Pinchin Denny (jobbers). However even these, the strongest and largest of the merchant banks, had disappeared within ten years into foreign ownership. Only the clearing banks were able to really sustain the objective of creating a universal banking conglomerate. Barclays bought De Zoete and Bevan (brokers) and Wedd Durlacher (jobbers); Nat West bought Fielding Newson-Smith (brokers) and Bisgood, Bishop and Co. (jobbers); and Midland through its merchant bank subsidiary, Samuel Montague, bought W. Greenwell (brokers). This trend was also followed by the large European and US banks; for example UBS bought Phillips and Drew, Credit Suisse bought Buckmaster and Moore, Merrill Lynch bought the jobbers Giles and Cresswell.

By the end of the 1980s, then, the structure of the UK financial institutions had substantially changed. The old City institutions of merchant banks and stockbrokers were now mainly integrated into large financial conglomerates which had interests in both retail markets and the more complex wholesale markets. This disconnected them from their previously close integration with the Bank of England. Many of these conglomerates were from outside the UK, operating their businesses in the City and elsewhere as part of a broader portfolio of national and international financial interests. Some of the different segments of the system which had existed in the nineteenth century were increasingly being tied together in shared competitive markets. Banks, building societies and insurance companies competed against each other in most of the areas of the personal market and even in some of the more specialized sectors of market-making and investment management. The old system of the City had been run on the basis of close relationships between the merchant banks, the clearers and the Bank of England. By the mid-1980s, however, the City was a different place. Many of the merchant banks, discount houses and stockbrokers were integrated into UK or foreign financial conglomerates. They were no longer independent and able to deal with the Bank of England on the basis of long-term social networking. Furthermore, all the agreements over which the Bank had presided, such as interest rate cartels and commission agreements, had been dismantled. The institutions were now more and more vulnerable to the demands of their own shareholders, making cooperation in the interests of the City or the country as a whole extremely difficult to achieve. Competition and the deregulation of barriers to entry had created financial conglomerates which had interests at home and abroad in a wide range of financial markets. The former bases for cooperation had gone and what emerged was increased emphasis on differentiation, not between sectors (which had character-ized the old system) but between organizations (see Morgan and Quack, 2000, for a more detailed discussion of this process in the UK, comparing it to the German context).

## THE STATE, REGULATION AND FINANCIAL SERVICES

In the previous chapter, we argued that the relationship between the British state and financial institutions during the eighteenth and nine-teenth centuries had been primarily constructed to ensure that the financial needs of the government could be met through borrowings in the City of London. The Bank of England acted as the crucial mediator between the state and the financial institutions, granting rights and privileges to the institutions in return for their cooperation in managing the state's finances. For most of the eighteenth century this related to funding military spending; during the nineteenth century the balance shifted towards expenditure on forms of infrastructure and social welfare. Crucial to this was the integration between the financial insti-tutions and the different groups within society. The City-based institu-tions and the large banks and insurance companies served the wealthy and the growing middle class, whilst the working class developed its own institutions which were linked in a specific way to the state. Self-regulation was managed within a rhetorical context of thrift, self-help and minimal state intervention.

In the first half of the twentieth century, however, spending on edu-cation, health and welfare services began to grow. Expenditure on all social services increased from 4.2 per cent of GNP (at factor cost) in 1910 to 16.1 per cent in 1951, rising gradually in the 1950s and then more dramatically to 28.8 per cent by 1975. Relatedly, between 1923 and 1975 the number of state employees rose ten-fold from 637 000 to 7 242 000 (all figures from Coates, 1994: 173). Many of these changes were driven by the increased role of Labour in the government and politics of the twentieth century. In this period, collectivism and social democracy were established and, in certain respects, triumphed in the postwar period. The sociologist, Marshall (1948), looked at this in terms of the gradual extension of citizenship rights, from political citizenship (equality before the law and the right to vote) to social citizenship (the rights to education, health and social welfare) into the sphere of economic citizenship (rights at work). Particularly in the

1940s and early 1950s, debates on these citizenship rights became a way of mediating between individualism and collectivism. The rights of the individual were defined by their position within a collectivity. In this context, ideas of self-help were subsumed within a collectivist morality of the individual's contribution to the whole, and the rights and responsibilities of the individual to pay taxes in return for the right to be provided with welfare.

Many of these ideas were articulated in a form which became known as Keynesian welfarism because of the way in which the rights and responsibilities of the state and the individual in the political, social and economic spheres were articulated. Keynes argued that the state could manage the economy and sustain full employment through a combination of measures designed to increase or reduce demand. These measures could involve direct state expenditure on infrastructure and welfare spending, or loosening the constraints on credit granted to individuals and businesses, thus generating more demand from them for goods and services. So long as the demand generated from this was primarily met from within the national system, the result would be managed economic growth. As described earlier in relation to Bretton Woods, orderly international economic relations could be maintained by all governments following similar policies with the possibility of periodic adjustments of exchange rates managed through institutions such as the IMF in order to reduce heavy balance of payments surpluses or deficits.

Macroeconomic policy was to be supported by a taxation system which balanced social objectives (for spending on infrastructure and welfare) with the more strictly economic concerns of managing demand. Borrowing by the state was the means whereby the gap between expenditures and revenues could be covered. So long as this gap could be kept relatively narrow, the system could be managed. If expenditure increases could not be matched by revenue increases, for example due to resistance to increased taxation, then government borrowing would also have to increase. This would be difficult to manage without causing increases in interest rates, leading to rising inflation. This in turn would impact on international competitiveness leading to a potential spiral of decline in that firms would go out of business, leading to reduced tax revenues and increased welfare expenditure on larger numbers of unemployed. In the Keynesian system, therefore, it was necessary that national firms were competitive enough to minimize the impact of foreign imports whilst maximizing their own export earnings. Success in this arena would produce the tax revenues necessary to support infrastructure and welfare spending. However, it was also necessary that demands for state expenditure were limited as taxation could not be raised indefinitely. This required constraints on citizens and politicians in order to reduce a potentially inflationary bidding up of expectations about what the state could and should deliver.

In this context, financial institutions were seen as playing an essential role with respect to the finances of the government, business and the personal customer. In broad terms, that role can be described as providing efficient markets for saving and borrowing. Failure to provide capital and liquidity at internationally competitive rates would undermine the efficiency of British industry; failure to provide borrowing facilities for the government at the most efficient rate would potentially push up interest rates; and failure to provide efficient services to personal customers would inhibit savings and could cause demands for further state spending on welfare services. This combination of circumstances led to two effects on financial institutions. The first was that they were increasingly scrutinized in ways which had not occurred previously when their activities were managed and controlled within segmented areas of the market according to criteria agreed amongst relatively small groups of key decision-makers. For example, the retail banks suffered muted criticisms for maintaining interest rate cartels and rationing access to credit. The second effect, however, was that the ideology of citizenship, home-ownership and the consumer society neatly dove-tailed with a growing sense of economic prosperity and a willingness of the financial institutions to support that through lending and savings schemes.

These effects became more important as the system of Keynesian welfare went into crisis in the 1970s. Out of this crisis arose Thatcherism which gave an even more central role to the financial institutions. The crisis began to emerge during the 1960s when the relative failure of British industry to compete in both the home and overseas markets started to have an impact on the whole process of economic management. Lack of economic success failed to constrain workers' expectations both of wage increases and improvements in social welfare. The result was escalating wage bills and increased public expenditure, neither of which could be managed without increased levels of borrowing (for a comprehensive review of the debates on UK decline, see Coates, 1994). The oil price rises of the mid-1970s further increased the problems for the government as the resulting pressure from the workforce for inflation-protected wage rises meant that

British wages and prices moved even further out of line with most of their competitors.

The inflationary spiral of the mid-1970s had a number of effects on the state, financial institutions and their customers. With regard to the British state, this period saw the dramatic emergence of what O'Connor called the 'fiscal crisis of the state' (O'Connor, 1973). State expenditure was rising inexorably in an attempt to mitigate the problems of increasing unemployment and industrial decline. However, there was not the willingness to increase taxes to fund this expenditure. Bridging the gap through deficit financing only served to exacerbate the problems by further fuelling inflation and undermining international competitiveness. Inflation reached the mid-20 per cent per annum range by the mid to late 1970s and had become a focus in industrial conflicts and wage demands. Although there were various attempts by both Conservative and Labour governments to reduce wage inflation by a combination of coercive incomes policies and negotiated corporatist solutions (based on agreeing wage increase targets with trade union and employer associations), the result was to exacerbate conflict. Hay, for example, argues that 'in the construction of the Winter of Discontent [1978–9] as a crisis of an "overloaded" state "held to ransom" by the unions, the post-war settlement was symbolically shattered. The assumptions, compromises and practices which had sustained it were torn apart. In this strangely liminal moment of transition, Thatcherism as a state project secured state power.' (1996: 120)

**Rolling back the state: Thatcherism and 'self-help'**

The Thatcherite discourse which was constructed during the 1980s was crucially related to the role of the financial services as a set of competitive institutions, but also to their role as key intermediaries in the construction of the conditions for the integration of individuals, groups and families within the existing social order. The Thatcher government promised to 'roll back the frontiers of the state' and give more responsibility back to the individuals; the 'nanny state' was to be replaced by measures aimed at encouraging self-help. In this way, it was hoped that state expenditure could be fundamentally reduced and inflation squeezed out of the economy, allowing a reduction in both taxation and borrowing which would in turn help British industry to become more competitive in world markets. In the long term, there would be a 'trickle-down' effect whereby those who suffered in the early stages from the reduction in welfare benefits would eventually find there were new job opportunities arising for them in the newly-competitive atmosphere generated by the Conservative government. In order to achieve this transition, the government was going to have to rely greatly on the financial services institutions as a key part of its strategy was to encourage individuals to save for their own education, health and old age. With judicious legislation and tax incentives, the financial institutions were expected to create the products to serve this purpose and then market and sell them to the mass of the population. This would allow state expenditure on these items to be reduced. It would also encourage and reward individuals who were 'strategic' in their purchases. Hay states that:

> consecutive Thatcher governments not only sought to secure the active consent of their many beneficiaries, but also engaged in strategic attempts to reconstruct the interests of large sections of the population. The (scarcely veiled) aim was to recast the material circumstances and conditions of targeted constituencies (principally potential home- and share-owners) such that their new interests coincided with those of the free market and a 'streamlined' state (rather than those of the public sector and the welfare state). (1996: 149)

What this meant was that the basic social democratic model of the welfare state, which had operated with varying effectiveness in the period since the Labour government of 1945, was placed in question. In the new evolving Conservative philosophy, individuals were to be given the 'choice' as to how to spend their money. This involved reducing direct taxation, providing more 'choice' in various state services (including through privatization) and encouraging self-provision and self-help – a return to the themes of the nineteenth century. Clarke and Newman argue that the New Right were able to tell

> a particular – and particularly effective – story about the conditions of crisis and to lay the ground for the reconstruction of the relationship between the state and social welfare. This story was constructed around three central themes: the costs of social welfare, the effects of state welfare and the problems of the welfare state itself . . . they targeted the welfare state as an active agency in the process of national decline, rather than simply an economic drain on the country's resources. (1997: 14–15)

The Conservative government proceeded to try and reduce public expenditure in a myriad of ways, most of which necessitated help from the financial services institutions. In the core social welfare services such as education and health, the government proceeded carefully for fear of electoral unpopularity. Nevertheless, it made clear its predilection for private forms of provision over public. In education, its assisted places scheme opened up public schools to children from less-well-off families, whilst its establishment of grant-maintained status as an option for erstwhile state schools created a new type of independent school. Coupled with the boom of the Lawson years, this atmosphere led to increasing numbers of children attending independent schools, often financed through savings with financial institutions. Although the government briefly toyed with the idea of providing specific tax incentives for this sort of saving, in the end it backed down, though the message was obvious – the best education comes from the private sector. Similar developments began to occur in the National Health Service, though here the combination of technological advance and an increasingly ageing population meant that costs were escalating year on year just to provide the same level of service. The government thought about providing tax incentives to take out private medical insurance, but once again backed down in the face of political opposition and uncertainties over whether the private sector could actually take on the business.

One area above all others – the provision of pensions – became the symbolic and practical core of these issues as far as the financial services sector was concerned. The issue of the state pension system had arisen again in the 1970s as the Labour government sought to close the gap between those in occupational pension schemes and the rest of the population, by creating the State Earnings Related Pension Scheme (SERPS). This was designed to provide an earnings-related top-up for those not in occupational pension schemes since it was generally agreed that the flat-rate state pension entitlement was not sufficient to provide for the needs of people. Although the scheme was designed to be self-financing and had originally been supported by both Labour and the Conservative opposition, it soon became a test-bed of the Thatcher government's approach to welfare. The New Right argued that the changing demography of the population meant that maintaining the basic pension in line with growth in earnings and funding SERPS would force state spending upwards until well into the next century (Waine, 1992). It also argued that the occupational pension schemes which had become popular since the 1960s (see Hannah, 1986), were no longer relevant in an era of flexible labour markets. The more people moved between jobs, the more difficult, time-consuming and expensive it was to keep track of their entitlements in particular company pension schemes. Instead, it was argued that individuals should make their own 'choices' about how and when they wanted to save for their retirement. The pensions debate brought together a whole range of themes about the 'failure of the welfare state' such as: increasing state expenditure leading to higher taxes; reducing motivation to work and to save; and creating dependency on the state. After various consultations, the Thatcher government implemented what was presented as a compromise solution in that it added a third tier of pensions to the state and the occupational systems rather than dismantling them entirely. Whilst the basic state pension was to remain in place (though pegged to prices not earnings – which effectively meant its long-term devaluation), a system of personal pensions was to be brought in to replace SERPS. Personal pensions were to be based on a contract between the individual and a pension provider (i.e. a private sector company, likely to be a bank or an insurer), the individual contracting to place a certain amount a year into a pension fund. In the early years, the state was going to grant tax concessions as well as SERPS rebates to encourage individuals to take them up. The savings would be invested by the provider in a personal pension fund, and when the purchaser retired the value of the fund would be realized and used to buy a retirement annuity. The value of the fund was dependent upon a number of factors. Firstly, it was dependent upon how much the person invested each year and over the course of a lifetime. In this sense, the changes chimed in exactly with the Thatcherite message of individual responsibility and self-help. However, the value of the fund was also affected by the nature of the contract purchased (i.e. the charges which the pension provider made for expenses in the sale of the contract and the management of the funds) and by the investment gain (or loss) achieved by the investment managers over the duration of the contract. The degree to which the personal pension system worked was therefore not just dependent on the ideological appeals of Thatcherism, but also on the reality of what happened to people when they bought these contracts. Here, Thatcherism was actually partially placing its fate in the hands of the financial institutions and markets.

This was not the only sphere where the fate of the two was being intertwined. Once the government had decided that privatization was going to be a major and permanent part of its programme, it had the job of managing the sales process. Here, it combined with the banks and insurance companies as underwriters and potential purchasers of the shares to create the image of an emerging 'people's capitalism'. Massive advertising and marketing campaigns were launched to convince individuals to purchase shares in the various privatization issues. As well as the financial impact on government finances that came from periodic sell-offs, it was important to present them as exemplars of 'people's capitalism' in action. The process thus fitted in with the broader philosophy of individualism and self-help which the government espoused. In order to be effective at this, the old institutions of the Stock Exchange had to be much more flexible in terms of dealing charges. The privatization issues therefore reinforced the government's determination to open up the Exchange and create the 'Big Bang' described earlier.

Another area which benefited from the government's ideology was home ownership. The Labour Party continued to espouse public housing as part of the welfare state, but Thatcherism targeted this from early on as part of the 'nanny state', reducing financial allocations to councils for house building and repairs as well as establishing the rights of council tenants to purchase their own homes. The government made clear its preference for home ownership in its pronouncements and actions. Some in the government recognized that this was creating distortions in the economy by taking money and savings away from more direct forms of collective investment in stocks and shares, as well as creating an inflationary boom which impacted widely but selectively on other areas of the economy. There was much talk of creating a 'level playing field' which reduced the advantages accruing to certain sorts of savings and investments, particularly mortgages and life insurance products. As Chancellor, Nigel Lawson was able to abolish tax relief on life assurance premiums thus reducing the tax efficiency of endowment mortgages (though by this time, the speculative fever of the mid-1980s and the advantages for the companies were so strong that it had little actual impact on the numbers buying this product). He was also able to abolish the dual tax relief which some couples were getting on their mortgages. He was not, however, able to persuade the Prime Minister to abolish tax relief on mortgage interest payments. Pressed by the financial institutions who were benefiting from the housing boom to continue it, the Prime Minister refused to go so far as Lawson wanted in creating the 'level playing field' with other forms of investment. Tax relief on mortgage interest payments was retained in spite of a considerable lobby of all political complexions calling for its abolition as a socially divisive and economically harmful policy.

### Thatcherism and regulation

The rhetoric of individual choice depended on the existence of a market in which people could choose. For this market, the government had to rely on the financial institutions; it would be the products which they designed and marketed which would provide the choices for the newly 'liberated' consumers. The government definitely did not want the public to be inhibited from buying these products because of a fear of being cheated, defrauded or simply being given poor value services. This was the danger that was lurking in the background of the strong domestic business growth achieved by companies in the 1970s, and the Thatcher government soon realized that it would not go away in the 1980s. Throughout the 1970s, the large banks had been repeatedly criticized for their failure to be responsive to customers; their opening hours (often restricted to 9.30–3.30 with no opening on Saturdays) and their charges were frequently criticized in the emerging consumer press. In the City itself, as discussed previously, there were a number of scandals which indicated the problems with self-regulation (Clarke, 1986).

The result was that the government initially set up a small-scale review of the operation of the system of investor protection led by an academic lawyer, Professor Jim Gower. In 1982, Gower issued an interim report on his work followed by the final report in 1984. At first it had been assumed that Gower would concentrate on the most obvious problem areas identified in the late 1970s, particularly the problems at Lloyds and in some of the fringe investment houses in the City. However, it soon became clear that he was in fact probing far more deeply into the nature of the financial services industry and how it worked. His broad conclusion was that there was a high level of potential for abuse and fraud in the industry, particularly as far as personal customers were concerned. This came from his concern that consumers had too little understanding and knowledge of what they were buying. This meant that plausible tricksters could persuade them to buy products that were not suitable for them personally, or poor value compared to other products on the market. At their worst, these tricksters could actually take clients' money and use it for their own purposes, perhaps in the hope that in an era of inflation it is best to get the money up front and worry about how to pay it back later. More dangerously for the industry as a whole, Gower felt that many of the firms operating in the industry were also relying on clients' ignorance and the pressure of commission selling to gain business. He felt there were no real controls over how firms recruited, managed and controlled their sales forces. The advice which was being given could not be trusted in Gower's view because the client could not tell whether it was based on a genuine evaluation of the client's circumstances and a recommendation based on an adequate market search, or alternatively whether the recommendation was based purely on what would earn the most commission for the seller. Gower's criticisms took in all investment products though he recognized that when it came to inter-business dealings there was less inequality of information and therefore the dangers would be less.

Gower's evaluation applied in particular to the areas which were essential to the Thatcherite programme of establishing a 'people's capitalism' – ownership of homes, savings towards old age, health and education and ownership of shares, either directly through involvement in the privatization issues or indirectly through life insurance policies and unit trusts. The implication of his report was the necessity to establish a new regulatory system which would enforce certain standards of conduct on the financial institutions. So broad and sweeping were his condemnations and subsequent recommendations that they were greeted with incredulity or denial by many in the industry. Yet it is equally clear that the Thatcher government realized the importance of taking at least some of its findings seriously if it was going to proceed with its overall programme. Thus, a government which espoused *deregulation* and the free market, was ironically driven to initiate a whole new system of *regulation*.

The result was that between 1984 and 1988 a new regulatory structure was set up for the financial services industry. Following discussions on Gower's report, legislation was introduced which reached the statute book in 1986 as the Financial Services Act (FSA), with an implementation date of 1 April 1988. The structure that arose from these debates was a mix of self-regulation and statutory duties. The essential element of the FSA was that it would be illegal to offer investment advice without being 'authorized'. In order to be authorized, a firm would have to apply to join one of the regulatory bodies set up under the Act. The only regulator specified was the Securities and Investment Board (SIB). This had overall responsibility under the Department of Trade to ensure that all firms were operating under the terms of the Act.

However, SIB could delegate some of the more detailed supervision to other bodies if they met certain criteria. These other bodies were known as the Self-Regulatory Organizations (SROs) and the Recognized Professional Bodies (RPBs). The RPBs tended to be the traditional professional associations in law and accounting whose members offered investment advice in the course of their other business. The SROs, on the other hand, were formed as firms operating in a similar part of the industry joined together to create a regulatory body. In the early stages before implementation, a number of SROs were established and applied to the SIB for recognition. For the selling and marketing of life insurance and unit trusts, LAUTRO (the Life Assurance and Unit Trust Regulatory Organization) was formed. Other SROs at this time were The Securities Association (TSA – mainly based on stock exchange dealing), the Investment Management Regulatory Organization (IMRO), and the Financial Intermediaries and Brokers Regulatory Association (FIMBRA). In order to gain SIB recognition, the SROs had to demonstrate that they had embodied the key rules and principles recommended in the FSA and that they had procedures to ensure that only firms which complied with these rules both at the moment of entry and subsequently would be permitted membership. Once SROs were recognized, a similar process occurred with the firms themselves. Each of them had to make an initial application to the SRO indicating how they matched up their practice with the principles of the Act and how they intended to make sure that this continued over time.

Following Gower, the Act laid particular emphasis on clarifying the status of the adviser. There was a fundamental distinction drawn between an *independent adviser* (who advised clients on products from the whole market) and a *company adviser* (who advised the client on the products of just one company). Individuals and companies were supposed to disclose their status and, in either case, fulfil two core duties. The first was to offer '*best advice*' from the products for which they were authorized (which obviously differed dramatically between the independent and the company adviser). The second was to '*know your customer*', that is show that sufficient information about the client's financial circumstances had been collected to ensure that a good match was made between these circumstances and the product which was eventually sold. At this stage, there was not yet any firm decision about the issue of commissions and how to deal with them. The companies in particular resisted detailed disclosure of commissions whilst others, including Gower and the Consumers Association, insisted that without knowing about commission customers would not be able to trust the advisers. Such debates over consumer protection not only highlighted some of the contradictions of Thatherism, but continue to the present day.

Thus, to summarize our account so far, dismantling the welfare state required the cooperation of the financial institutions. However, as we described earlier, they were increasingly locked into a complex international environment where the drive for profitability and extensive competition created huge uncertainties. When these institutions looked to their home markets they were less willing to voluntarily submit to the constraints and controls of the Bank of England. Nevertheless, the shift which the government was seeking to make towards a society based on individual 'choice' and self-help opened up large new markets for the financial sector which they were determined to maximize. Moreover, the government was made increasingly aware that its political project depended on the way in which the financial institutions cooperated. If they failed to be innovative enough, consumer interest in shifting from state provision to private provision might decline. If, on the other hand, the companies failed to offer good value or were perceived to be 'cheating' the public in some way, this would also pose a threat to the political project of Thatcherism. Regulation of the industry was therefore perceived as essential in an attempt to ensure that scandals were reduced and public confidence increased, though few people predicted how far this would evolve and with what effects.

## THE DECLINE OF THE WELFARE STATE AND THE RISE OF THE MIDDLE CLASS

Although the Thatcherite discourse was constructed as a unifying rhetoric in which 'individuals' made choices and there was 'no such thing as society', it was addressed predominantly to those middle-class groups who were perceived as embodying the virtues of self-help, thrift and morality. 'The enemy within', for Thatcherism, was first of all the trade unions, and secondly the 'welfare scroungers'. The constituency to which it appealed, on the other hand, were those who were providing for themselves or those aspiring to do so. As with so much of Thatcherism, this appeal built on very real changes in British society, but attempted to construct their meaning in a distinctive way in order to link it to the broader political agenda which was being pursued. However, these changes were actually more complex in their impact and fed into the restructuring of the financial services in unexpected ways. In this section we examine the changing patterns of income and wealth that drew more of the population into direct and indirect relationships with the financial institutions. We then relate this to broader accounts of the changing class composition of British society. This leads into a brief discussion of the relationship between consumerism, social identities and financial institutions. Our main point is to emphasize that as much of British society became more 'middle-class', its demands on the financial sector increased not just in terms of provision of new products but also in terms of expectations of the nature of the services and their value.

**Wealth, income and inequality in British society: home ownership and occupational pensions**

In the postwar period, Western Europe experienced 25 years of economic growth. In the UK, GDP had grown from a base of 100 in 1913 to only 133 by 1938. By 1950 it was still only 161, but by 1965 it had risen to 247 and in 1990 to 431 (Therborn, 1995: 134). Compared to many other countries this postwar growth was slow, but in terms of its broader affect on British society it was crucially important. One study showed that mean weekly household incomes (before housing costs and at January 1994 prices) rose from £140 in 1961 to £165 in 1971, £186 in 1981 up to £258 in 1991 (Goodman and Webb, 1994: 19). Between the same dates, home ownership rose from 40 to 68 per cent, whilst car ownership rose from 46 (per thousand population) in 1950 to 366 in 1989 (Therborn, 1995: 142). In these and absolute terms, then, there was a rise in average living standards over this period.

Within this absolute increase, there have also been some changes in relative positions. In the early part of the period into the 1960s, there appears to have been a move towards slightly less inequality as the poorest sections of the population were incorporated into the welfare state's system of benefits, whilst higher rates of marginal taxation at the top end of the income distribution dampened down growing income disparity. Later, and particularly from the mid-1980s, there has been a growth in inequality with the rich getting richer (thanks to changes in the tax system and the emergence of new ways of getting rich) and the poor becoming poorer (as a result of changes in the system of welfare benefits as well as high rates of unemployment). For the bulk of the population, the distribution of inequality is also affected by the number of earners in the household, the nature of their employment (whether it is full-time or part-time, permanent or short-term, skilled/professional or unskilled) and the number of dependents. Increased levels of divorce contributing to an expansion of single-parent families has led to a growing number of households trapped in unemployment or low-paid jobs, particularly amongst women. The changing demography of the population has also led to an increasing number of elderly people for whom inequalities established during the working life are often magnified (e.g. the distinction between those reliant on state benefits and those who have access to an occupational pension referred to earlier).

The expansion of the GDP and overall living standards has therefore had a complex effect on income and inequality and its relationship to financial institutions. At a very simple level, increased earnings contributed to more people opening up bank accounts and savings policies. This was partly induced by employers who sought the ease and convenience of paying wages and salaries directly into bank accounts rather than dealing with large amounts of cash, but it also reflected a more general change whereby a larger group of the population than previously could actually begin to plan their finances beyond the immediate necessities of the future because they were in stable, relatively well-paid employment. This linked to the growing expansion of credit facilities which occurred through this period, particularly as the use of credit cards became more popular. Thus it was not simply increased income, but also new ways of becoming indebted which were evolving since debt also requires some sort of future planning (Ford, 1992).

On the asset side, however, there were two important aspects to this process which have become increasingly significant. The first was the use of savings to establish home ownership. Unlike other societies where large amounts of private property were available for rent, Britain in the postwar period became rapidly divided into a nation of home-owners and council tenants. For many in the growing middle class and the affluent working class, as it was termed at the end of the 1950s, home ownership was a central objective, acting as a material and symbolic representation of 'going up in the world'. For the Conservative politicians, in particular, it represented a political goal – the home-owning democracy in which people had a 'stake in society'. Access to home ownership was dependent on saving with a building society and thereby gaining the chance of getting a mortgage. Although the idea of savings was closely linked to ideas of home ownership, it also became part of a more general emphasis on 'home and family'. This goal was supported by generous tax relief on the interest paid on mortgages. It was also fuelled by the way in which the housing market worked to create periodically spiralling house price increases which distributed windfall gains across the population of home owners. Although the distribution of these gains was uneven amongst home owners depending on where one lived and how one moved in the market, those left out of the market (i.e. in the rented sector) were completely left behind. For most of the period up to the 1980s, this group was disadvantaged by the accrual of wealth and speculative gains which occurred in the housing market. In the 1980s, however, the Thatcher government's policy of giving council tenants the right to buy their houses at substantially discounted rates provided a means whereby the better-off section of this group could join the ranks of the home owners.

Buying a home had meant queuing for a mortgage as the numbers of mortgages granted was controlled by the amount of deposit funds available to the building society. As we have seen, during the 1970s this began to change due to the removal of restrictions on lending, but up until then it had led to a growing mountain of savings in the building society sector. Indeed, more generally, financing home ownership was a crucial step in bringing many more people into a direct relationship with financial institutions. Furthermore, this relationship was not a simple, single tie between a lender and a borrower. Repaying 25-year mortgages inevitably involved elements of risk for the lender. Certain of these risks such as the death of the borrower could be insured against, and mortgages were therefore granted on condition that there was adequate life insurance. Gradually, this led to the development of endowment-linked mortgages. Life insurance policy-holders had enjoyed tax relief on their premiums since the late nineteenth century. A savings scheme linked to a life insurance policy was therefore a tax efficient way of saving. This tended to distort the savings market as other forms of collective investment such as unit trusts could not offer the same advantages. It also meant that individual share ownership, which anyway carried much higher risks, remained confined to a very rich minority.

Over the previous century, the life insurance companies had developed savings plans which were effectively forms of *collective* investment. Policy-holders paid a premium which gave them a certain level of life cover. The rest was invested by the company according to its own view of the markets and the necessity to cover potential liabilities. Life insurance companies began to develop large funds which were buying and selling stocks and shares on the markets. When policies were purchased on a 'with-profits' basis, each year the life company decided how much of its investment profits it could afford to distribute to policy-holders while still maintaining adequate coverage of its liabilities. At the end of a policy, the customer received back a sum based on these bonus payments, which were in turn affected by rates of return in the markets. 'With-profits' policies enabled the life company a high level of discretion about how it distributed investment returns. Traditionally, they were highly cautious, preferring to build up large reserves and only paying bonuses when they were certain they could afford them.

During the 1960s, the idea of paying back mortgages through investing in a with-profits endowment policy gradually began to develop. Instead of a straight repayment mortgage, where the purchaser paid back a mixture of capital and interest over the length of the contract, the home buyer would pay back the interest (on which there was tax relief) and pay towards a life insurance savings policy (gaining tax relief on those payments as well). At the end of the period, it was expected that there would be sufficient in the funds which the policy had built up to pay back the principal of the loan as well as provide a capital sum to the saver. This idea was also gradually extended to linking savings in unit trusts to mortgage funding. Unit-linked savings policies differed in that, instead of earning a bonus at the discretion of the insurer, the funds were invested directly for the saver in units which could either go up or down. The saver could see directly what was happening to the value of the units and, in effect, took all the risk. By the early 1980s, the number of straight repayment mortgages was declining – with-profits endowments were the most popular, with many of the banks entering the market offering unit-linked mortgages.

This change, like many others in the sector, cannot be accounted for simply by the preference of customers (see the discussion in Chapter 6). Banks and building societies pressed them hard to purchase these types of mortgages because the way they were structured guaranteed the lenders a higher rate of return than an ordinary repayment mortgage. On the other hand, these changes also brought customers into a more complex set of relationships with the financial institutions; whilst many did not fully realise what had happened, the way in which they owned their own home and were paying back the loan on it was now integrally and more explicitly tied with wider processes of investment in the capital markets.

The same process was occurring in a more indirect way as expectations about pension entitlements grew. Britain had seen the development of a framework for a state pensions system in the first half of the twentieth century (Macnicol, 1998). This framework developed in the context of a society where there were already a number of established schemes within particular sectors, and firms which aimed to provide pension benefits to employees. The private schemes evolved and developed as the specifics of the state scheme were constituted. In particular, it became clear that the state scheme for old age pensions was never going to provide more than a minimal level of support. As a result, it encouraged those who were able to continue to make their own provision for savings in old age. For a large proportion of, particularly male, employees this meant saving in an occupational pension scheme.

The term 'occupational pension scheme' is in some ways a misnomer. It refers to all those schemes which provide a pension to the employee according to a combination of that person's level of contribution, years of service and final salary. The scheme may be based on all or some members of a particular firm or public sector institution (such as the Post Office, the railways etc.) contributing together. Pension schemes may be administered in-house by a specific department though this is only likely in the case of extremely large and complex pension funds in the public and private sector. It is more likely, particularly for the private sector, that the management of the scheme is contracted out to a specialist pension management team, usually part of a larger banking or insurance institution. Many employers as well as employees eventually became willing to establish occupational pension schemes because they acted as a way of maintaining loyalty amongst the workforce as well as a means whereby benefits could be increased without infringing the sorts of incomes policies which became common in the 1960s and 1970s. For employees, occupational pension schemes served as a means of spreading the cost of supporting themselves in their old age across a wider population pool. In 1936 there were 1.6 million members of private sector schemes, and 1.0 million in public sector schemes; by 1956 these had grown to 4.3 million and 3.7 million respectively, making 33 per cent of the workforce covered by occupational pension schemes at this time (13 per cent in 1936) (Hannah, 1986: 41). By 1967, the numbers in occupational pension schemes reached its highest point of 12.2 million, almost half the working population (*ibid.*: 66). Following this, growth of occupational pension schemes began to decline from 53 per cent in 1967 to 49 per cent in 1987 (Johnson and Falkingham, 1992: 115).

The expansion of occupational pensions schemes once again saw more people becoming tied into the capital markets through the investment of their savings. The sums at the disposal of the financial institutions (banks and insurance companies, as well as specialist investment managers) managing these funds grew immensely and contributed to the massive expansion of institutional investment in the British capital markets. For individual savers, the process was more complex, as Johnson and Falkingham indicate:

> it seems simply implausible to believe that more than a handful of pension scheme members posses the knowledge of pension scheme rules and the actuarial abilities required to calculate their optimal date of retirement, and even if they manage this they need remarkable prescience and good fortune for their projections about interest, inflation and growth rates during their years of retirement to be a close approximation to reality... Yet it is clear that most people do make some financial plans for their old age, that many do have some degree of choice over when to retire and these saving and retirement plans are viewed as important issues rather than trivial decisions. (1992: 115–6)

Between 1950 and the 1980s, then, the growth of wealth and income in Britain drew people more tightly into relationships with financial institutions. In the past, many people had no relationship at all with any sort of bank or building society. Now, through savings, home ownership and pensions, they were connected not just to a single institution but to the capital markets themselves. Traditional building societies, savings banks and industrial life insurers no longer insulated their savers and borrowers from the risks of these markets. Instead, everybody was being plunged into them, albeit within the relative security of collective investment schemes where portfolio management could generally reduce the worst of the risks. On top of this, personal expenditure was increasingly funded through loans and credit cards where changes in interest rate levels could have a dramatic impact on individual's spending capacities.

This development created a fundamental change in the field within which financial institutions were working. We have seen how it previously operated with a small group of rich benefiting from direct involvement in the City, a small middle class with limited savings in stocks, shares and life insurance, and finally the large mass of the population who either had no direct connection to the financial institutions or were connected with a limited group of institutions, insulated and isolated from the capital markets. By the 1960s and 1970s, this was changing.

### The rise of the middle class

A crucial part of this change which deserves separate and further consideration is the continued expansion of the middle class or, in sociological discourse, the 'service class'. In the class schema developed by Goldthorpe, this category refers to people engaged in professional, managerial and administrative occupations. It is distinguished from routine non-manual employees, technicians and small proprietors. Goldthorpe argued that the 'service class' had grown from around 5 per cent of the population in the early decades of the century to in excess of 25 per cent by the early 1980s (Goldthorpe, 1982: 172). It is this group which has become most directly involved with financial institutions. Hamnett (1995), for example, shows that by 1990, in households headed by those in professional/managerial occupations, 90 per cent owned their own homes (up from 67% in 1961), compared to 78 per cent of intermediate/junior non-manual occupations, 73 per cent of skilled manual, 49 per cent of semi-skilled manual and 38 per cent of unskilled manual. The mean value of houses owned by the professional and managerial groups was around £103 000 in 1991 whereas amongst other non-manual workers, it was £74 000. Furthermore, the mean equity value of housing (i.e. the estimated sale value less the outstanding mortgage debt) was £63 000 amongst the professional and managerial groups and £34 700 amongst the partly skilled manual workers. This division has been furthered by the growing impact of inheritance. Hamnett notes that 'the chance of inheriting [housing property] is five times as great' for the professional/managerial group as it is for the unskilled manual worker (1995: 271). As the first generation to benefit from the expansion of the economy and service class jobs began to die out in the 1970s and early 1980s, its sons and daughters inherited large amounts of property and capital which they looked to invest for themselves and their own families. Thus, not only were they looking after their own housing, they were now liquidating the housing investments of their parents and turning them into new forms of saving.

This group has also been most affected by the expansion of occupational pensions. Those who benefited most from these schemes were the people who spent much of their lives in the same occupation. For many male professionals in public service or the nationalized industries, such as local and national civil servants, teachers and university lecturers, it was natural to stay in the same occupation throughout their lifetime, thus accruing the maximum pension rates to which they were entitled. Managers and administrators in the private sector were also fairly secure in their jobs until the 1980s (Scarbrough and Burrell, 1996). By contrast, manual workers (other than those in the nationalized industries) and the majority of women were less likely to be included in the schemes *per se*, and even if they were tended to have lower wages and more insecure conditions of employment which led to any entitlements often being lost entirely (as they shifted jobs or moved in and out of paid employment) or being very small. Johnson and Falkingham (1992) calculated that, whereas the top quintile of pensioners had a total gross income of £254.80 per week in 1987 (made up of 64.50 in social security payments, £78.40 from occupational pensions, £78.60 from other savings and investments and £33.30 from employment), the bottom quintile had a total income of £47.50, 90 per cent of which came from social security payments with occupational pensions worth only £1.66. Even amongst the fourth quintile, occupational pensions were only worth £21.70, whilst total income was £109.80, 65 per cent of it from social security payments.

The constitution of this privileged group as a social category is reinforced by recent research on social mobility which indicates that once an individual 'arrives' in the service class, a major concern is the strategic use of assets in order to ensure that there is no downward mobility either intra-generationally or inter-generationally. Savage *et al.* (1992) identify these assets as 'property, bureaucracy and culture'. In effect, the service class uses its advantage both to pass on wealth and position (e.g. through inheritance as mentioned earlier) and to inculcate 'cultural capital' into its children (through informal socialization and expenditure on education – most obviously in the case of public schools, but also less visibly by strategic location decisions to move within the catchment areas of certain schools and by financially supporting their children through higher education). Similarly, as Lockwood states: 'Personal initiative is the hallmark of the middle classes. They have always used their superior moral [sic] and material resources to full effect, above all by giving their children a competitive edge in the main site of social selection: the educational system.' (1995: 10). These processes increasingly require the strategic use of financial products – to set up savings plans for private education, to minimize taxation on income, savings and inheritance, as well as to maximize returns on investments. Furthermore, many of those in the service class are now directly engaged in occupations in the financial services or associated professions such as accountancy and law. Many others will have familiarity with financial issues through their role as managers. Others, who are independent professionals such as doctors and architects, may have responsibility for their own taxation arrangements as well as that of their employees.

The rise of this service class group is particularly important within the overall changing nature of wealth and income inequality in Britain. Unlike the old upper class which was part of, or connected to, the City of London elite and benefited from its practices, the service class is separate and distinct. It is geographically spread throughout the country, even though it is particularly concentrated in the south-east of England. It is crucially reliant on the strategic management of its financial assets in order to sustain itself inter-generationally. This has become an essential part of its cultural identity as can be revealed in any cursory glance at the broadsheet Sunday papers or magazine and book shelves of newsagents with their sections on Personal Finance. This is not an argument to state that all members of this group are active and knowledgeable at the same rates and at the same time. Rather, the point is that this group as a whole have increasingly come to recognize the importance of financial services to their social position. It is not too far from this recognition to develop some critical awareness of how financial services operate. The steps towards this awareness can be made through the critical intervention of the financial press and other media – the emergence of scandals about criminal fraud, bad advice/service or high charges; the impact of housing booms and slumps; and, increasingly, job insecurity. Or, it can arise from direct personal experience of such phenomena. As we shall see in later chapters, it is also, paradoxically, a consequence of the marketing activities of financial services themselves. Whichever of these is most relevant, it is clear that it involves a significant change for the financial services industry which was used to an almost completely ignorant and quiescent group of clients. These changes are still emerging and do not necessarily give rise to distinctive social movements though it is clear that the growth of more active consumerism has been significantly driven by a growing sense of the inadequacies of the financial services industry (c.f. Burton, 1994). For example, since the 1970s, the Consumers Association has produced a growing number of publications where it critically examines many of the products, services and practices of the industry. While actual individual membership of the Association may not be large or wholly representative, its publications and associated publicity help contribute to the overwhelmingly middle-class practice of looking to maximize their strategic financial advantages (see Aldridge, 1994, 1997).

In this section, we have looked at the field of financial services from the point of view of predominantly middle-class consumers. In the period between the 1950s and 1980s, many more consumers came into relationships with the industry through savings, investments, house purchase and pension schemes. One result of this was that much more money was passing through the industry creating employment and opportunities for people in the financial sector. Another result, however, was that the industry found itself faced with, and even actively contributed to, the increasingly difficult task of meeting the expectations of these consumers. Within the broad category of purchasers of these products, the rise of the service class created a group who were relatively well-educated and also increasingly motivated and encouraged to behave in a strategic manner towards their financial needs. It also follows that this group was likely to be adept at expressing its concerns and interests at a political level. As the industry grew and involved more people, these people (or at least a section of them) began to learn about how the industry was operating. They and their political and media representatives began to understand that competition was limited by interest rate cartels; that service levels were generally low; that there was a great deal of insider dealing (both on the Stock Exchange and in institutions such as Lloyds insurance); that supervision was imperfect leading in some instances to fraud and in others to reckless risk-taking at the expense of investors; and that information disclosure was generally low making it difficult even for the most discerning consumer to choose between products and firms. Realization of these problems did not occur instantaneously in individuals or groups, but over the period with which we are concerned awareness increased and continues to do so.

CONCLUSIONS

In the previous chapter, we showed how the structure of the financial services sector had been shaped by the interaction of the state, the different groups within society (and their relative wealth and power) and the institutions themselves. The resulting structure reinforced power and inequality in the system whilst managing it through the informal interaction of the Bank of England, the state and the City institutions. This system depended on sustaining a coherent view amongst this group of the role of the different institutions. In this chapter, we have shown how a range of pressures fractured that coherence:

Firstly, the increasing internationalization of money opened up new possibilities for the financial institutions. It became more and more difficult for the Bank of England to control and limit their activities. Instead, the financial institutions became increasingly driven by priorities of profit and extended their operations both nationally and internationally. This process increased the differentiation between the organizations, making it more difficult to sustain traditional modes of working. Competition at home and abroad became more intense as did the uncertainties with which the companies had to deal. These pressures made it increasingly necessary for particular businesses to be able to rely on support to weather downturns in their business. This contributed to reducing the number of privately-based institutions in the sector and favouring the emergence of larger financial services conglomerates with business interests across both corporate and personal business, national and international business, retail markets and wholesale markets. Thus the structure of the industry began to change as the international framework of money and its management changed.

Secondly, however, these changes were also linked to the changing role of the state. During the twentieth century, the role of the state in the provision of welfare had increased. The old nineteenth-century model of self-reliance had really only worked for a minority – the upper and middle classes. Although there were a range of financial institutions developed by and for the working class, the level of income and precariousness of employment for most of them meant that there was never really sufficient income to consider saving a substantial proportion of it for old age, employment or illness. One of the main aims of the Labour movement in the first half of the twentieth century was therefore to ensure that basic rights to welfare could be provided through the state (though this involved mainly a redistribution within the working class from the young and healthy to the old and infirm rather than a redistribution from the rich to the poor). In the heyday of Keynesianism and the welfare state, there was at least something of a fit between these social welfare goals and the macroeconomic context. However, the internationalization of money also undermined this system as it had undermined the way in which the Bank of England had managed the financial sector as a whole. In the conflicts of the 1970s and early 1980s, a discourse was (re-)constructed around self-help and self-reliance. This discourse explicitly referred to 'Victorian values', contrasting them with cultures of state dependency and high taxation. It opened up an increasingly wide range of opportunities for the financial institutions in providing various savings and credit products for consumers as part of the rhetoric of market choice and individual self-responsibility. Thus, the Thatcherite political project succeeded in redefining the relationship between the individual and the state, particularly in the sphere of money and savings. However, the project was dependent on the emergence of a new form of regulation, one which focused in particular on ensuring that the companies offered appropriate products to the customers. The Thatcher government feared that poor performance by the companies would turn people away from the rhetoric of self-help and back towards state provision. They therefore sought to inject competitive pressures into the industry and a regulatory structure which supported those pressures.

Thirdly, these trends were reinforced by the increasingly middle-class nature of much of British society. Increasing wealth and income, particularly amongst the growing service class of managers, professionals and state employees, extended the market for savings and lending products. The centrality of house purchase in the British context, reinforced during the 1980s by the Conservative government, led more people into the financial institutions and into new ways of saving in order to pay for their houses. Pensions also became a growing issue for many in this group as they sought to ensure (as their predecessors had in the nineteenth century) that their standard of living was sustained in retirement. These groups were not only increasingly enmeshed therefore into the financial system through their mortgages, pensions, credit cards and so on, but many among them were also becoming more knowledgeable and well-informed about the sector. From the late 1970s, personal finance became the subject of specialist magazines and subsequently began to appear more regularly in newspapers and on television. This was part of a broader process of emerging 'consumer consciousness' which was reinforced by the individualistic rhetoric of the 1980s. Consumerism started to become embedded in British society. It soon found one of its easiest targets in the financial services sector where a range of practices could be criticized as offering poor value for money.

By the 1980s, therefore, the financial services sector had begun to undergo fundamental transformation. The organizations themselves were no longer the same, the role which the state played was different and finally the consumers were also changing even if some sectors of society continued to be largely excluded. The old expectations about how the system should work, the roles which particular institutions and individuals should have in that system could no longer be sustained. This left the actors with high levels of uncertainty. Whilst there were various rhetorics which they could espouse linked to consumer sovereignty, market competition and value for money, these said little about how the firms should organize themselves internally. Whilst the old models (based on informal networks, self-regulation, cartel-like behaviour, bureaucratic administrations) were disappearing, new ones were only gradually emerging. In the following section of the book, we examine the emergence of new discourses and how they impacted on the financial institutions.

# Part III

# Changing Discourses: Process and Outcomes

# 4 Introducing Strategic Discourse

## INTRODUCTION

This chapter marks a shift in our analysis of change towards the dynamics of organizations operating within and simultaneously shaping the contexts which we have described earlier. At a broad level, our approach is to examine how organizations and fields link together through the development of particular discourses and practices. As we described in Chapter 1, discourses constitute ways of understanding situations and thereby relate to modes of acting upon and controlling contexts. As discourses emerge from a set of material and social conditions, they give the social world a new form and meaning and may become embedded in distinctive managerial practices. Thus, the discourse establishes the 'truth' of its presuppositions through constructing a world in its own image. This 'truth' defines and works upon the subjectivity of actors as well as the material practices in which the actors are embedded. Such a process does not necessarily imply acceptance and internalization on the part of the actors. These latter states are only one of a range of, often fragile, responses to managerial discourses – others may include rejection, resistance, adaptation or ambivalence. Furthermore, there are multiple, competing and sometimes contradictory discourses which exist in modern societies, and therefore it is crucial to identify which discourses become particularly dominant and influential in particular contexts, why and what their consequences are. This defines our interest in discourses within financial services. Our previous analysis of growing uncertainties within the sector has led us to the view that in response to these changes, discourses began to emerge to reestablish a sense of stability and control. These discourses were elaborated and carried into the financial services sector by many different actors. In what follows we seek to describe this process and how it impacted on the various actors analysed in the previous chapters.

Our key concept in this respect is what we term 'strategy discourse' (see Knights and Morgan, 1991, 1995 for earlier discussions of this issue). We argue that the way in which actors have sought to understand and control the changes in the field of financial services can be best understood through exploring 'strategy discourse'. Strategy has become the main language through which actors make sense of, respond to and thereby help realize these changes. It has become an over-arching framework for actors and organizations, providing a language of 'truth' to make sense of the world. As we seek to show, strategy discourse constructs this 'truth' at various levels – as a framework of knowledge about the world, as a set of managerial practices, controls and measurement systems in the world, and as a group of subjective identities for managers and employees. The discourse of strategy plays this key role because of its claims to be central to *integrating* the different functions and parts of the organization and its context. In this chapter, we seek to explain the distinctive characteristics of strategy discourse.

## STRATEGY DISCOURSE

Our general argument is that strategy discourse is a distinctive phenomenon that arises in a particular historical time-frame, which, in the UK, is the period from the 1960s onwards. 'Strategy' is not *natural* in the sense of something which all organizations at all times have had. To talk and act "strategically" has a specific set of meanings within the field of organizations. These meanings have to be constructed, enacted and then worked on continuously in order to be reproduced. They do not become dominant within particular organizations without conflict, nor are they unchallenged or unchanging. Our approach seeks to bridge those forms of discourse analysis which remain locked within a 'linguistic' framework with those types of institutionalist approach which seek to understand the social conditions which make certain forms of discourses and practices meaningful and *socially* effective at specific historical moments. In terms of its linguistic history, Whipp points out that 'the word "strategy" derives from the Greek *strategia*, meaning "generalship", and was first used in English in 1688' (1996: 263). However, as a term used to identify a specific function of management with a particular role within organizations as a whole, the term 'strategy' only developed from the 1960s in the USA. From the start however, 'strategy discourse' was characterized by two key features.

The first feature is represented in the work of Alfred Chandler, beginning with his book *Strategy and Structure* (1962). Chandler's work was based on a series of detailed historical studies of how US firms developed in the first part of the twentieth century. This was then extended historically into earlier periods as well as into the analysis of the evolution of industries and organizations in other countries. A central thrust of Chandler's argument was that *'structure followed strategy'*. In other words, management decisions on the nature of the markets and products in which they were to be involved necessarily led to certain structural requirements in the organization of the firm. In effect, growth and diversification required the shift from functional organization towards the multi-divisional structure.

Chandler naturalizes 'strategy' in the sense that he assumes that all firms 'have strategies' whether they know it or not. The outside observer can identify 'strategies' whether the insiders or contemporaries use that terminology or not. We would not wish to disagree with the argument that outsiders can sometimes see patterns which insiders cannot and therefore it is legitimate to import terminologies which were or are not accessible to participants to explain social phenomena. Nor do we disagree that it is possible to identify that firms (whatever their internal conflicts) may interact with environments in ways which can be characterized as consistent and patterned. What we do find problematic is importing the terminology of 'strategy' into that discussion. We wish to argue that the term 'strategy' is part of a specific way of looking at the organization and its environment which arises only at a specific time. To talk of strategy implies a certain way of characterizing the world and a certain set of practices to relate to the world. Thus, we do not find it surprising that Schendel and Cool (1988) comment on the Anglo-American management literature that there was little use of the word 'strategy' in a management context before 1979. Indeed, it is our view that the terminology, frameworks and practices of strategy had to be constructed by managers, academics and others in order to define it as something distinct from and superior to what went on before. It was not the case, as Chandler seems to imply, that managers had been doing it all along even if they had not named it as such. Once 'strategy' becomes named as a 'truth' to which organizations and managers should conform, a new context of knowledge, practices and subjectivities begins to be constructed. It is this new context in which we are interested.

The second theme of 'strategy' writing in the 1960s was exactly concerned to 'name' strategy, to tell managers what it was and get them to think in new ways about their role in leading the organization. Since the 1960s, there has been a massive outpouring of articles, journals, books and courses explaining the importance of strategy for management.

Most authors who have examined this phenomenon (e.g. Schendel and Cool, 1988; Whittington, 1993; Whipp, 1996; Knights and Morgan, 1991, 1995) are agreed that up until this period, there was very little explicit attention paid to what is now construed as central to organizations' functioning and success, that is strategy. However, it is characteristic of most discussions within the strategy literature that this is barely considered except as indicative of a failure on the part of previous generations to properly understand business (or, rather, and here there is the link to Chandler, to properly explicate the principles of business from which they were working). Henry Ford's comment 'History is bunk' would seem an apposite epithet; strategy discourse and its proponents are, generally speaking, unreflective about the historical conditions of the emergence of this way of thinking. So powerful has the 'naming' of strategy become that it is extremely difficult today for most actors to see it as anything other than a natural and unproblematic part of the organizational world. Accordingly, strategy has become intimately linked to power within organizations and as a result, its presuppositions are not to be questioned. As Whipp says:

> Clearly, the leading authorities in the subject have constructed a meaning for the word 'strategy' which both exploits its purposive military origins and invests heavily in the rational expectations of those wishing to direct and manage an organization. (1996: 263)

Central to this process of naming strategy was the way in which it became a means for differentiating those who engaged in strategy formation from the rest of the organization. Strategy-makers were thereby separated from mundane, operational and functional issues and elevated to the role of the key actors 'steering' the organization as a whole. Deciding strategy became the prime role of the leadership of firms and organizations. In terms of Marglin's (1976) classic question 'What do bosses do?', strategy is now the medium through which senior management both legitimate their existence and structure their actions. Such a role, initially at least, required distance from the operational details. The central importance of this theme is illustrated by the vehemence with which one of the doyens of 'strategy discourse', Michael Porter, returned to it recently as the core of his approach. His article, 'What is Strategy?', in the *Harvard Business Review* has as the heading of its first section 'Operational Effectiveness is not Strategy' (1996: 61). Porter is deliberately defending his concept of 'strategy' (which relies on this separation) in the face of the influence of Japanese companies and their focus on process and operations. Another sub-heading states that 'Japanese companies rarely have strategies' (*ibid*.: 63). Rather than treat Japanese companies as having a different framework for understanding the relationship between firms and their environments (e.g. see Whittington, 1993), Porter forces onto them his own framework and evaluates them, not surprisingly, as not living up to his expectations. 'If they are to escape the mutually destructive battles now ravaging their performance, Japanese companies will have to learn strategy' (Porter, 1996: 63).

The central importance of this distinction between strategy and operations is that it separates out a group of managers who act in the wider interests of the organization. In steering the organization as a whole, this group also exercises power and control over operational areas, seeking to enforce, in the name of strategy, a tighter process of integration and control over functions, activities and individuals than was previously the case. From this perspective, the construction, enactment and reproduction of strategy as a discourse is a problematic process within organizations, sectors and nations as it requires the exertion of power and the existence of resistance.

The 'truth' of strategy is established by reference to the idea of success in the marketplace; strategy is perceived to be the key to organizational success. The language of evaluation of firms by shareholders and analysts for example, is highly complex and contingent. Whilst the evaluation of a firm is fundamentally driven by financial performance within the Anglo-American context of capital markets, it also consists of a 'negotiated' reality which increasingly concerns the ability of senior managers to communicate their intentions and strategies. For instance, Holland (1999) in a study of large firms and their institutional shareholders in the UK has revealed the complex communication mechanisms which are constructed in order to enable the two sides to discuss strategy without contravening Stock Exchange rules against the selective disclosure of price sensitive information. These communication mechanisms are reinforced by more general comment in the business and financial press concerning the degree to which companies have or lack 'strategies'. The impact of these comments and constructions on firms' ability to raise funds in the capital markets or to stave off takeover/merger bids is part of constructing the 'truth' that strategy matters (c.f. the title of Whittington's book, 1993, *What is Strategy and Does it Matter?*). Constructing a successful strategy legitimates the power and prestige of top management. It separates them off from operational managers and enables them to define their 'singular' importance by reference to performance and outcomes in the capital markets. Similarly, it becomes the mechanism which justifies linking the rewards of top managers to stock options and other externally generated measures of performance (see Lazonick and O'Sullivan, 1995, on the significance and impact of the access of top managers to ownership income in the USA from the 1980s).

Those building the truth of 'strategic discourse' must create and/or have an audience for their ideas (through books, conferences and consultancies) who in turn become additional carriers of the language and its associated practices into organizations and new audiences. As we shall see, the process involved here is complex, linking academics, management consultants, civil servants, politicians, journalists and business people in an ongoing reflection and refinement of the meanings of strategy and its mechanisms of enactment and implementation. The implications of these constructions had to be dealt with in specific organizational settings with actors who at first were as likely to be indifferent or hostile to the discourse as to embrace it. However, as the 'truth' of strategy becomes dominant, it exercises power over the actors inside and outside the organization. They are constructed as different types of subject within the discourse with distinctive roles in the development and implementation of strategy. 'Strategy' becomes embedded in organizations and made into a 'natural' way of acting and thinking about how they work, survive and prosper.

This process of *naturalizing* strategy requires three main elements:

- Firstly, it requires the generation of a commitment to the general idea that there is only one legitimate or 'best' way to look at an organization's position, structure and role in the world. This must involve the acceptance of strategy simultaneously as the 'steering mechanism' and 'the steering principle' of the organization.
- Secondly, this general idea must be linked to a set of more specific frameworks concerned with how to position the organization to best effect. This implies the existence of a set of linking concepts which show how to decide and implement strategies. These links will, in principle, involve the *integration* of the various parts and practices of the organization and their subordination to the requirements of the overall strategy.
- Thirdly, strategy is embedded in the organization through the construction of a linked series of practices which articulate the 'truth' of

the organization through the language of strategy. Crucial to this is the measurement of performance and the creation of a series of techniques to track this against strategic goals and to create feedback loops into the behaviour of individuals and groups. Whilst these measurement and control techniques may be originally developed and maintained within particular functional areas (such as accounting or personnel) (e.g. Power, 1997; Hacking, 1991), within strategic discourse they become linked as part of the overall decision-making process.

In the following section, we examine each of these aspects in more detail.

### Strategy as 'a way of looking at the world'

Strategy discourse shares with managerialism more generally the assumption that there is an objective separation of the environment and the organization (see Alvesson and Willmott, 1992 and 1996). The environment exists 'out there', separate from the organization. In the spirit of modernity, it is there to be tamed and conquered, but only if the internal organization is properly 'machined'. Management becomes concerned with the development, elaboration and implementation of a series of techniques which are intended to predict and control the internal and external aspects of the organization. Out of these processes grow specific functional areas of management and professional groups, making claims to expertise, knowledge and power. As Alvesson and Willmott argue, 'when management is represented as a *technical activity*, a blind eye is turned to the *social relations* through which managerial work is accomplished and upon which it ultimately depends' (1996: 10). The development of these processes, the groups which claim knowledge and primacy, the techniques of control, surveillance and monitoring which are established have become central to critical studies of organizations (e.g. Armstrong, 1989). Alvesson and Willmott (1996) review some of these specialisms such as accounting, operations research, marketing, organization theory and information systems. They also examine the case of strategic management as one of this series of 'management specialisms'. In this respect our approach differs, because in our view strategy is not simply one of a number of specialisms within management. Rather, whilst it shares many characteristics with those other specialisms (e.g. the emphasis on techniques and objective knowledge which masks its own social process of construction within a specific context), it has come to stand above and beyond those specialisms in its claim to be *the* synthesizing and integrative moment in the management process.

Whilst all parts of management can and do make the claim to be essential to the overall success of the organization, strategy discourse, in effect, claims the right to adjudicate on those arguments and, in particular contexts, to set the 'operational' parameters for the rest of the organization. The point is that such claims from other groups can only be legitimated by reference to strategy discourse *per se*. As specialisms, these functions have had to show how they fit the broader strategic orientation of the organization – strategic human resource management, strategic accounting, strategic information systems and so on. The first prerequisite for 'strategy discourse' is for this argument to be accepted. In other words, for there to be no question whatever the context that it is crucial to 'have a strategy' and to be able to implement that strategy through a series of requirements that must be followed by the operational, functional parts of the organization. The 'truth' of this presupposition is embedded in the practices which mark out business success and failure. Although actors may recognize these practices as multifaceted, top management ultimately construct them in terms of successful or unsuccessful strategies and look for solutions to problems using this framework. This can promote conflict and dissent within top management and amongst shareholders as they seek to come to terms with the situation and out of these processes, winners and losers may emerge strongly, for example in cases where some of top management are replaced because of loss of faith by shareholders, non-executives or other top managers. The framework which links strategy, success and top management is reinforced through these conflicts, not undermined.

Strategy and those who control access to its making and implementation become divided from the rest of the organization. They are the 'steering mechanism'. They stand above the operational, setting the requirements for others who have little choice but to follow and accept the parameters of what is 'strategic' (and therefore of central importance, prestige and power) and what is merely 'operational'. Once this becomes accepted, functional areas have a number of choices. They can adapt to these demands or they can seek to reconstruct themselves in the image of strategy (e.g. by transmuting into a strategic version of their previous selves). Thus, as we shall see later, marketing becomes 'strategic marketing' and personnel increasingly became 'strategic human resources'. Moreover, as this process continues, all practices, however apparently mundane or 'operational' (e.g. customer service), take on an explicit strategic significance or connection in terms of organizational goals.

Establishing strategy as the terrain on which everything has to be exposed and judged by the strategists does not occur automatically. It has to be carried into the organization, accepted and learnt by certain key actors. It may be carried in through the action of certain key outside stakeholders, for example shareholders or public owners demanding that the organization 'has a strategy' (c.f. Clarke and Newman, 1997, on the importation of managerial discourses into the public sector) or, as we shall examine in detail, management consultants invited in to examine a specific issue, but eager to sell their wider expertise and/or legitimatory power in strategy. This process may be speeded up by the introduction of new managerial elites, schooled in strategy, either through previous experience, for example in more 'advanced' industries (where strategy has already become dominant) or in management consultancies or in management education (such as MBAs which have long placed the study of strategy in the centre of their programmes) (see e.g. Thrift, 1998). In particular, however, strategy has become a way of making sense of and seeking a form of control over contexts which have become increasingly complex and uncertain. Thus where existing organizational fields have begun to break down and with them traditional ways of managing have also become seen as less effective, then there is likely to be an attempt to develop new forms of meaning and new mechanisms of control. This is what strategy discourse has come to offer managers in UK financial services (and elsewhere) over the last thirty years.

It is in this context that one needs to evaluate the contribution of the processualist school of strategy associated with authors such as Mintzberg (1978, 1987, 1990, 1994) and Pettigrew (1985: Pettigrew and Whipp, 1991). In parallel with the distinction between managerialist and political approaches to organizational change discussed in Chapter 1, these authors differentiate themselves from the rationalist, prescriptive approach to strategy through their detailed studies of processes of implementation. Mintzberg offers a view of strategy as 'emergent' and a 'craft' process in which senior managers muddle through and adapt their strategies to the unintended consequences of actions undertaken by other groups in the organization. Pettigrew's longitudinal perspective emphasizes the complexity and uncertainty of strategy making and implementation and the role of power and culture in setting limits to a rationalist implementation model. These studies are valuable correctives to the more prescriptive views of strategy which are discussed in the following section. However, they remain embedded within the discourse of strategy, in effect creating an elaboration of the uncertainties which face managerial action. This in turn gives rise to its own style of prescription focusing on sensitivity to difference and the need to build coalitions of support. The 'truth' of the discourse of strategy *per se* is not denied; the link between 'strategy' and success is reiterated but instead of defining a rationalist, top-down route to the achievement of this goal, the authors emphasize the precariousness of achieving the sort of social consensus which makes for effective strategy. In effect, these authors take the 'truth' of strategy more deeply into the subjectivities of the actors than do the rationalist school because their analyses and judgements involve the ideas of political and cultural manipulation. In describing the ways in which successful outcomes can emerge from the strategy process, they emphasize the need to control and manage the 'hearts and minds' of people inside the organization. Whilst Pettigrew retains a scepticism about the degree to which this can be achieved (see for example his article 'Is Corporate Culture Manageable?') (1990), the whole thrust of the research agenda which he propounds is towards sensitizing top management to these social processes and thereby offering 'knowledge' of the 'truth' of strategy and knowledge of forms of power which follow from this.

In itself, however, the discourse of strategy can achieve nothing, even in apparently conducive circumstances. It has to be connected to some specific techniques, arguments and processes which managers can learn about and implement in order to achieve this sense of order. It must also be linked to a system of control, monitoring and surveillance which reinforce actions and processes directed towards these ends.

**Strategy as a Set of Frameworks**

What should the strategy-maker do? How should the organization position itself on the battlefield? At this point, the academics and consultants helpfully step into the breach and offer their solutions and frameworks. Whipp (1996) suggests that it is possible to discern an evolution – from a series of *ad hoc* analytical tools such as the product life-cycle model and the portfolio planning model, towards some broader consensus in the 1980s around Porter's five-forces and generic strategies framework (1980, 1985). As we have noted, in the early stages of the strategy discourse, strategy-makers were provided mainly with a sense of their own importance and distinctiveness from mere 'operational managers'. Their actual tools of analysis were rather limited, based on a number of simple models of how industries and products evolved. Thus, life-cycle models were used as a means to justify the need for diversification and, in particular, acquisition strategies which ensured that firms would not hang on in a declining industry. Simple models of the environment and the organization were developed into standardized acronyms. The STEP model (also known as PEST) asked the strategist to analyse the social, technological, economic and political aspects of the environment which would influence organization over a variety of time scales. The SWOT model turned this into a process of identifying the strengths, weaknesses, opportunities and threats which the organization faced in the environment. Boston Consulting Group developed their well-known matrix to illustrate the need to have a balanced portfolio of different types of businesses ranging from 'cash-cows' to 'stars' in order to provide companies with the flexibility to survive changing product market conditions (see O'Shea and Madigan, 1997).

In the 1980s, Porter's Five-forces model, drawn from industrial economics, offered an apparently much more robust framework (1980). It provided strategy-makers with a theory of how profitable a particular industry could be, whilst the generic strategies framework offered them a way of focusing the activities of their own organizations. The model appeared to be predictive in a more determinant sense than the previous frameworks that had been offered. It claimed to predict on the basis of particular configurations of the five forces, industries where profits would be high and others where they would be low. It also claimed to predict that failure to focus on one of the generic strategies and instead to drift between strategies or, more concretely, to mix a price-differentiation strategy with a quality focus, would lead to disaster. Porter's model picked up and developed the rational and voluntarist sides of the strategy framework. The strategist could decide which industry and which strategy and then move the organization there. Generally, this would be in addition to existing businesses, in which case, it was a further elaboration and justification for diversification and expansion through acquisition.

As well as these two streams picked out by Whipp (1996), it is clear that a third trend has emerged in what is variously called the 'resource-based theory of the firm' or the 'core competences' approach. This approach has been built on a growing scepticism of the relevance of the five-forces and generic strategies model. In this model, the key role for the strategist is to identify the resources *inside* the firm which make it different and unique. The voluntarist basis of Porter's approach leads to the conclusion that any 'strategy' can be copied; the only things that stop this leading to a downward spiral of competition between equally capable firms are barriers to entry. These may either be legal barriers or, more likely, economic barriers. The latter may consist of the high initial cost of setting up businesses in certain markets and/or the knowledge that, as more competitors enter a market, prices move down and the profits available decrease. These forces create an equilibrium which is only disturbed when some exogenous factor (e.g. technology or regulation) causes barriers to entry to fall. The resource-based theory of the firm rejects the idea that everything is in theory capable of being copied. Instead, the firm is seen as a bundle of competences and skills that have been built over time and create a unique pattern of what the firm is good at. The role of the strategist is to ensure that this uniqueness (the core competences and key resources) is developed and reapplied into new areas. In this view, barriers to entry can never be guaranteed long-term; they may be breached by some major technological innovation (as happened with the impact of personal computers on the computer industry as a whole and IBM in particular) or they may be simply made irrelevant by the opening up of new technologies (for example, in the way in which pharmaceuticals is gradually being transformed by biotechnology).

The role of the strategist, therefore, is not to find a position behind which to defend but to constantly move forward into new areas, 'leveraging' the core competences (see for example Hamel and Prahalad, 1989; also Kay, 1993). The issue is to find what these core competences are, how they can be sustained, developed and 'leveraged'. This in turn has led into the related area of knowledge management and the 'learning organization' (Nonaka and Takeuichi, 1995; Easterby-Smith, 1997) where the concern is to identify the underlying knowledge assets of companies and enhance the ability of managers to monitor and retain the results of learning processes. Whereas Porter and previous approaches look at growth through internal expansion and diversification, the resource-based theory of the firm is particularly interested in managing growth through cooperation and networks, where the issues concern maintaining proprietorial knowledge and unique competences while also learning from others. This brings the rationalist approach to strategy closer to the processual approaches referred to earlier as it begins to identify the social and organizational basis of success and the need for strategy-makers to make these explicit. Thus, strategy becomes concerned with making 'visible' certain underlying processes in the organization and through the effort of making them visible open them up to power and control.

Our goal is not to adjudicate between these approaches as to which is 'true'. They are all means of extending and articulating the 'truth' of strategy as a whole – in other words, extending the over-arching framework of strategy discourse into a set of specific concepts which structure the actors and their practices. Each of them provides a way of translating the broad objective of being 'strategic' into a meaningful vocabulary of action for firms and subjects. Each of them is both sufficiently positivistic in its approach to suggest solutions, and sufficiently vague in the weight it gives to particular factors as to allow discussion, negotiation, refinement as well as a sense of ownership of the actual details of the strategy. They therefore allow managers to move from one course of action to another whilst still claiming a rational, positivistic basis for what they are doing and, as we shall see, a sense of identity as competent and in control. They also provide the frameworks within which managers and shareholders can debate their differences. They become mechanisms of power in the struggle between different groups and the legitimation for forms of action which may involve the displacement of certain groups of top managers (as well as middle managers and other employees).

We should emphasize that our argument about strategic discourse does not depend upon a single or straightforward process of diffusion whereby, for example, academics 'invent' ideas such as theories of strategy, management consultants 'commercialize' them and managers 'implement' them. It is clear that the interaction between these groups and innovation dynamics are far more complex (see Guillen, 1994; Smith and Meiksins, 1995; Abrahamson, 1996; Sturdy, 1997a; Djelic, 1998; Kipping and Bjarnar, 1998; Tiratsoo and Tomlinson, 1998). It is often the case that what academics seek to turn into 'polished' theories are derived from observations and/or claims of what is occurring in 'successful' companies. Certainly, many recent popular books, written by academics for practitioner audiences, have been constructed in this style – for example Hamel and Prahalad (1989), Kanter *et al.* (1992) and so on. Similarly, the academic interest in networks and innovation which has evolved out of empirical research has led authors such as Kay (1993) to seek to formulate more rigorous definitions of key concepts which can then be applied to management practice. What managers do

in constructing strategy may be partially influenced by these more explicit theorizations of the 'strategy process', but this is not necessarily the
case. These particular frameworks and ideas are available either in a
'pure form' (i.e. directly from books) or in an adapted form (e.g.
through the popular management press and, in particular, management
consultancies). In general, they reinforce the notion that organizations
need 'strategies' whilst maintaining and encouraging a marketplace in
what this might actually mean. Organizations and actors can 'buy' strategies in the marketplace, 'make' or adapt their own and/or copy from
others (a form of 'clan control' or 'mimetic isomorphism' in terms of
institutionalist theory; DiMaggio and Powell, 1983). Whichever they
choose, the important point is that they increasingly orient their actions
through placing 'strategy' at the centre of how they operate. Strategy
becomes the lens through which all aspects of the functioning of the
organization are refracted.

**Strategy: Implementation, Measurement and Control**

Strategy discourse proceeds from frameworks and the identification of
goals towards the processes of implementation, measurement and control. This is one of the key areas where strategy discourse meets and
moulds other functions and discourses in the organization. Sitting on
top of the organization as the 'master builder', strategy translates into a
series of requirements for each of the different functions in the organization. Frequently, annual business plans will be constructed which set
quantifiable targets for particular aspects of the business which can
then be monitored regularly in order to enable early intervention or
remedial action when targets are not being met. Whichever specific
strategy framework is adopted, there will be a demand for information
and data. Porter's models, for example, set out to determine the profitability of industries based on the five-forces model. It requires the
application of accounting to interpret and analyse profitability data and
how they evolve and change over time as barriers to entry rise and fall.
Marketing data are also essential to assess how big markets are and
whether economies of scale make a price-differentiation strategy a viable
option, or limit the possibilities to a focused strategy. This demand for
information strengthens the role of Information and Management
Systems departments in organizations, but, more importantly, further
reinforces the significance of strategy since it becomes the point at
which all the various parts of the operation of the organization can be

identified, monitored, assessed and integrated. Despite this primacy, we shall see in relation to information technology, for example how the emergence of strategy within organizations may actually occur through concerns which have come to be seen as 'operational'. In the following chapters, we examine in detail this level of strategy discourse as it permeates and shapes organizations and subjects in often contested and uninteded ways.

## STRATEGY DISCOURSE: IMPLICATIONS

The argument which we have presented is built on the idea that organizations and actors have been transformed by their implication and involvement in what we have termed 'strategic discourse'. This transformation process cannot be understood as the unfolding of an inherent logic of progress and technical rationality. Strategy discourse does not identify a single mode of action. Rather, it opens up a field of actions within which organizations and individuals interact to produce specific outcomes. From our perspective, the central interest is to understand how this process relates to the structuring and break-up of existing organizational fields. These fields tend to have their own logic of action articulated in their own specific way, and strategic discourse can contribute to both the break-up and reconstruction of these fields. In general terms, it acts as an overarching form of response to change by offering organizations and actors a framework, a set of techniques and a system of control and monitoring which can be utilized and is attractive in times of uncertainty. Because this 'offer' is not a commitment to a certain way of doing things, but rather a means of access to an array of ways of working, it may open up the future rather than close it down. Once the basic framework is accepted, it becomes possible to move on from one specific set of strategy ideas and practices to another as circumstances change. Every failure can be explained as a failure not of the framework *per se*, but of its specific embodiment in a particular set of ideas and practices. Organizations can move on from one failing (or even successful) strategy to another without ever challenging the idea that they need strategy. Whether the same managers move on is more problematic, but even they will be able to find 'reasons' to legitimate what happened and in this way to partially explain away failure. Similarly every success becomes translated into a general principle of strategy, available for copying by others and a means of promoting the individuals involved as well as the organization itself. This is not to suggest that strategy is invulnerable to dissolution. As we suggest in the concluding chapter, a number of conditions present the possibility for other emerging 'post-strategic' discourses. However, here we are concerned with accounting for some of the ways in which it emerged as dominant in financial services. In the next chapter, we begin our exploration of this process.

# 5 Strategy Discourse and Financial Services: Enter the Management Consultants and IT

## INTRODUCTION

Our general argument about strategy can now be linked to the previous chapters. We have seen how, during the 1960s and 1970s, the organizational field which characterized the financial services in the UK began to break up. Actors within firms, aided and pushed by key outside interests such as shareholders, the government and management consultancies, began to search for ways of understanding what was happening and, in the process, of exerting some control over their futures. In this process, the 'need for strategy' began to loom as a central part of their transformation process. They began to articulate this new language and to work out its effects. In the process, old practices and languages began to fall by the wayside or to be reconstructed from the point of view of strategy. These processes were by no means painless. They involved the ejection of certain organizations and individuals from the industry, the repositioning of firms (which had implications for the status, rewards and careers of individuals within them) and the reconstruction of relations between the firms, the state and consumers (which had effects on the financial well-being of millions of people). These processes of change were neither smooth nor unidirectional. They proceeded more quickly in some organizations than others; they evolved in ways which were not at first predicted and they had outcomes which did not entirely match the expectations of many of those involved in this process of transformation. What we would argue became the common currency of these transitions was their 'strategic necessity'. This language, in turn, percolated down (and sometimes up) into the organization, reshaping practices and constructing new ways of working to such an extent that, by the late 1990s, it would have been difficult to find an organization which had not become dominated by this discourse and was not trying to work out its implications (though not impossible, given the continued existence of some small 'friendly societies' and building societies which continued to profess and values of mutual support).

Central to this process was the role played by management consultants. They acted as crucial carriers of strategy discourse into the financial services sector at the time when the conditions of stability were being undermined. Their importance was enhanced by their role in mediating for financial institutions the impact of information technology which became increasingly significant from the late 1960s (see Knights and Murray, 1994). In many cases, major financial institutions took the 'strategic' decision that IT was going to be the key to success in the future. As we shall describe, the meaning of this decision itself evolved through a variety of stages as the capacities of information technology were increased and consultants and managers identified new ways in which it could affect business. However, translating this into action was highly complex and frequently led to the employment of management consultants to aid in the process. For the consultants, IT sometimes became the bridgehead from which they sought to sell further 'strategic' services, thus enhancing and reinforcing the centrality of strategy.

In this chapter, we firstly examine the consultancy process itself before showing how financial services companies began to use consultants extensively to bring a sense of order particularly to their information technology systems. Consultants articulated this ordering process increasingly through the language of 'strategy'. Thus the link between strategy, success and order in a disorderly environment became articulated in the interface and interactions of senior managers and consultants. Our argument is not that this constitutes the initial 'cause' of the shift towards the discourse of strategy but rather that it played a crucial role in constructing the specific web of language, meaning and practices that increasingly encompassed the industry. In subsequent chapters, we show how this web of meaning was extended and expanded in an attempt to construct strategic discourse and practices.

As we saw in Chapter 1, there are an increasing number of accounts seeking to explain the historical and/or current influence of management ideas and practices. These typically highlight the important and growing role played by management consultants (e.g. Huczynski, 1993; Gill and Whittle, 1993; Abrahamson, 1996). A key focus in much of this literature (c.f. Guillen, 1994) is the apparent transience or, at most, temporary institutionalization of 'new' (usually repackaged) (Jacques, 1996;

Grint, 1994) ideas and the irony of continued demand for 'solutions'. Here, a common approach is derived from the psychodynamic interpretation of management whereby both the adoption and discarding of ideas are based on managerial anxiety over the uncertainty surrounding their careers, work role and organizational environment. This anxiety is seen to be played upon and reinforced by consultants and the ideas which they and others adapt and promote.

Whilst this focus on the psychodynamics of the relationships between managers and consultants provides valuable insights into the nature and use of managerial knowledge, it is more limited in scope than the concerns which we have for understanding the causes and nature of the transformation towards strategic discourse. This requires that as well as highlighting the insecurity and vulnerability of managers, their active role in the consultancy process and its interactive nature needs to be considered. For example, and as we have already suggested, managers may create or adapt new ideas and are often resistant to them and their purveyors. In turn, we shall see how consultants respond to and seek to anticipate such concerns. Also, by focusing upon why managers adopt ideas and on their anxieties, consultants tend to be portrayed as confident and 'in control' rather than being subject to similar pressures and uncertainties.

Another limitation of the purely psychodynamic approach is the frequent failure to contextualize fully managerial anxieties. Some accounts draw links with bureaucratic structures and pressures (e.g. Jackall, 1988) or those associated with broad economic trends and crises (e.g. Gill and Whittle, 1993). However, both capitalist and localized structures and associated tensions and dynamics are neglected or underplayed (Willmott, 1997). These criticisms and an alternative framework for conceptualizing consultancy are outlined elsewhere (e.g. Sturdy, 1997a, 1997b). Here, we are concerned with illustrating and outlining the role and interactive or dialectical process of consultancy in the particular context of IT strategy consultancy in the late 1980s and early 1990s in UK personal financial services companies. We draw selectively upon empirical work on the perceptions and experiences of clients (IT managers and directors in banks, building societies and insurers) and IT and strategy consultants regarding their work and interrelationships (Sturdy *et al.*, 1989, 1990, 1991; for other studies which reveal the degree of variation in consultancy projects, practices and 'styles', see Penn, 1995; Argyris, 1961; Garratt, 1981; Stevens, 1981; Bennett, 1990; Thrift, 1998).

THE RISE(S) OF MANAGEMENT CONSULTANCY

The UK consulting industry has experienced considerable growth since the 1980s and continues to prosper (Morrison, 1998). It is made up of multidisciplinary, often international, firms such as the accountancy-based companies and specialists. The latter range from the large functional (or sector) groups such as the 'strategy houses' and divisions of IT suppliers and the small 'boutiques' of individual operators (including academics) and specialist groups. It was estimated that in 1990 there were around 12 000 mostly small firms operating, with fee income of approximately £2.5 billion (Clark, 1995). However, in the UK in 1996, the top-ten firms accounted for half of the total fee income of £2.1 billion, and seven of them are also in the top 15 for strategy consultancy. Despite this concentration, there is some indication of a shift towards use of smaller, niche firms generally and in financial services (*Management Consultancy*, 1997a, b; Markham, 1997).

The multidisciplinary firms tend to be structured functionally, drawing consultants on to projects from different disciplines as appropriate. However, there might also be divisions by industry sector, such as financial services or local government. IT consultancy was divided into three activities: strategy, system design and implementation and facilities management (outsourcing) (Rassam and Oates, 1991), but is increasingly seen as central to all aspects of business consultancy. The activities of these large firms extend far beyond working on defined projects for individual clients. Considerable effort is put into researching sectors and companies sometimes as part of organized 'clubs' of firms wanting to share information. Research is part of the broad-ranging promotional activities which include 'making contacts' at local, national and international levels with potential clients, IT suppliers and government organizations. These activities are a crucial part of the consultancy process although little researched (Sturdy, 1997a).

The role of consultants is highlighted in many historical accounts of the emergence of different management ideas, practices and occupations (e.g. Rose, 1989; Hollway, 1991; Guillen, 1994; Armstrong, 1989; Djelic, 1998). While these might inform a specific history of the use of 'external' expertise (e.g. Littler, 1982), the few historical accounts of consultancy in the UK tend to focus on the activities of individual consultancy 'pioneers' (Cheadle, 1994: 8) or 'missionaries' (Tisdall, 1982: 1) and companies (c.f. Kipping, 1996). According to this literature, management consultancy emerged as a separate activity with the development and application of accounting and engineering (e.g. work measurement) practices, although, in the USA at least, lawyers were also involved in developing firms such as McKinsey (*In Business*, 1994). The first consultancy firms or partnerships were not established until around the turn of the century in the USA, and later in the UK, as manufacturers grew in size and American consulting experience, such as that of Bedaux and Whitehead was brought to Britain in the 1920s (Rassam and Oates, 1991; Cheadle, 1994; see also Littler, 1982). The depression of the 1930s boosted consultancy with, for example, the Bank of England referring ailing manufacturers to accountancy firms for reorganization. However, it was not until the 1960s and early 1970s that most of the large UK accounting practices formed separate consultancy arms as audit growth slowed and computer technology and corporate planning began to 'take off' (Tisdall, 1982; *Economist*, 1988). Price Waterhouse was the exception in establishing a management consultancy operation in 1948. By the late 1980s, income from consultancy in some of the large accountancy practices began to exceed that from auditing.

The Second World War and immediately afterwards saw the continued extension of work-study practices, supported by the government's Production Efficiency Board (Tisdall, 1982; Hollway, 1991; Guillen, 1994; Tiratsoo and Tomlinson, 1998). In addition, 'personnel' practices developed which increasingly identified the need for specialist skills in areas such as training. On the basis of claims to expertise in these areas of knowledge, particularly arising from the emerging field of psychology, management consultancy operations were established which sought to apply these ideas to industrial settings (Rose, 1989). At this time also, the first moves towards (limited) professionalization of the management consultancy role began, partly in response to government concerns in 1948 over sales staff posing as 'independent consultants' (Tisdall, 1982). Professional bodies were first formed in the 1950s at the start of what was described (before the 1980s) as the 'boom period' in consultancy (Cheadle, 1994). By this period, management consultancy in the UK was dominated by four firms (Inbucon, Urwick, PE and PA) who had three-quarters of the market between them (Tisdall, 1982), with the other 200 competing for the rest (IMC, 1986). A key part of this growth was the formation and expansion of specialist strategy consultancies such as Boston Consulting Group (known as BCG) and McKinsey (London office opened in 1959) (Tisdall, 1982; *Economist*, 1988). The use of such firms by large organizations itself helped boost the status of consultants generally, the companies which employed them and of strategy as a discourse.

While the use of strategy consultancy was to develop further and assume a high status, consultancy growth generally was severely interrupted in the early 1970s recessions. In contrast to the apparently stimulating effects of the interwar economic climate, this period saw a 'dramatic fall' in demand for consultancy (Cheadle, 1994: 9) and a corresponding drop in consultant numbers, including through redundancies. For example, the number of consultants employed by member firms of the Management Consultancy Association fell from 3200 to 1350 between 1970 and 1975 (Tisdall, 1982).

This pattern was reversed during the 'new' boom in consultancy in the 1980s where the corresponding figures for 1980–88 showed a growth from 1694 to 4773 (Grosvenor, 1988) and the consultancy market in Europe and the USA grew by 20–30 per cent per annum in the last three years of the 1980s (Rassam and Oates, 1991: 54; see also LRD, 1988: 2). Accounts at the time cited as important the shedding of middle-management (and therefore their expertise) in companies' moves towards 'flexibility' (Rassam and Oates, 1991; *Economist*, 1988). High unemployment, as in the 1930s, also strengthened the appeal and adoption of the 'new' ideas (Huczynski, 1993). Also, a recovery in profitability in certain client sectors coincided with new demands and developments in information technology which became core consultancy activities (36% of fee income in 1991, *Management Consultancy*, 1992b). The importance of IT has continued to the extent that while 'the 1986 top 30 [consultancy] firms contained only three or four popularly associated with IT; the 1995 top 30 contain about a dozen...And even among "traditional" consultancy firms, IT-related projects constitute at least half their revenue' (Markham, 1997: 50). Finally, government-led changes in the public sector and subsidies for consultancy use in small firms for strategy opened up new markets (see Sturdy *et al.*, 1989; Williams, 1996; DTI, 1991). Moreover, these developments were a condition and consequence of broader changes associated with renewed management interest in 'new' ideas (e.g., Byrne, 1986; *Economist*, 1994; Grint, 1994). While there may be some variation between sectors and functional areas of consultancy over time, IT and strategy have been central to the postwar expansion of consultancy generally, especially since the 1980s.

Currently, perhaps the single most important aspect of consultancy practice centres on the notion of strategy which has become a key element of discourse on organizations and IT. (Bloomfield and Danieli, 1995: 29)

Financial services companies have played a dominant role in this process and continue to do so. In 1996, they were the largest client sector in consultancy, accounting for approximately 15 per cent (£325 million) of all business, and with 'four in five of the top 100 [consultancies] report[ing] sales' mostly to retail companies (*Management Consultancy*, 1997b). In 1991, their contribution was even higher at 28.5 per cent of UK fee income (*Management Consultancy*, 1992b). Despite fluctuations, in both 1992 and 1996, IT, strategy and financial services companies together represented 45 per cent of all UK fee income (*Management Consultancy*, 1993, 1997b; see also Rassam and Oates, 1991).

## IT, STRATEGY AND INTEGRATION IN UK FINANCIAL SERVICES

In the current era, technology management and development cannot be seen as empirically distinct from other business concerns – both feed each other. This has, of course, always been the case, but not always in terms of how they were organized and talked about. For example, up until recently in financial services, IT was seen as an administrative function with little or no board representation and little or only periodic integration and interaction between practices and staffs. Now, business managers are expected to have, articulate and manage systems needs, and IT managers should be oriented towards the needs of the business and organization. In some ways this continues or even reinforces the subordination of technology to business. However, IT has come to be seen as more important. Part of this change is its connection to, or 'integration' with, the discourse of strategy.

Such a transition in IT is evident in many sectors. For example, Friedman and Cornford (1989) in their study of managerial strategies to control IS specialists identify three phases in the history of IT organization. In the first, the constraints of computer *hardware*, and therefore its selection and evaluation, were a central concern to managers. Raising the productivity of *software* developers then became the focus, despite severe skill shortages. In the third stage, from the beginning of the 1980s, attention shifted to *relations* between developers and *users* whose demands were becoming more varied and exacting. Moreover, they often conflicted such that responsibility for setting systems priorities shifted away from the IS function to senior management. This, combined with escalating costs, led to IS divisions becoming profit or cost centres which required clearer specification of demands. The possibilities for a fourth phase are also discussed. These involve a concern with the organization's *external environment* constraints based on a *strategically-informed* focus and concomitant growth in inter-organizational and decision support systems (*ibid.*). These phases are broadly apparent in UK financial services where the focus is perhaps also shifting away from IT to information more broadly. However, our focus is more specific in exploring the conditions of emergence of IT strategy, prior to the fourth phase (for more detailed discussions of these processes, see Knights and Murray, 1994; Sturdy, 1989 Knights, Morgan and Murray, 1991; Knights and Morgan, 1995; Scarbrough and Corbett, 1992; Scarbrough, 1992; Fincham and Roslender, 1995).

The managerialist perspective on the emergence of IT strategy is that it was a natural development to cope with increasing change and uncertainty in the management of IT – a tool to rationalize (control/prioritize) the use of, and internal competition for, resources in changing markets. Indeed, aside from market changes, a growing complexity was evident, itself partly fuelled by new strategic priorities and demands (e.g. for data and information). This transition is itemized in the form of interrelated developments by Knights and Murray (1994) in relation to financial services and insurance in particular.

Financial services, in general, is an information business. Accordingly, it has long been a dominant, large-scale and often progressive user of IT. In particular, it involves large volumes of data storage (e.g. policy and account details) and transactions (e.g. cash withdrawals, payments). Processing this data was achieved with paper documents – in the 'back office' – and, increasingly, large mainframe computers. These were located and staffed in data-processing centres, often in provincial locations. Access to the data and processing capacity was restricted geographically, technologically and in terms of expertise (i.e. programming). This was to change with the shift from batch processing of data (e.g. routine data input from policy forms, cheque clearance) to on-line access to databases from remote locations (e.g. branch offices) (see Knights and Sturdy, 1990). Nevertheless, for the most part this arrangement served well a sector in relative stability. Indeed, partly because of the huge volumes of data involved in financial services, the reliance on 'big' mainframes and systems persists (albeit, sometimes now outsourced).

However, a combination of *related* technological, ideational, organizational and market changes resulted in existing arrangements becoming seen as inflexible and increasingly costly.

In the 1980s, an increasing range of technological possibilities became available in terms of hardware, software and telecommunications. For example, mini and personal computers combined with new fourth-generation programming languages, tailored software packages (e.g. for assessing credit or underwriting risks) and networked communications were significant in eroding the restricted access to data processing. This coincided with and facilitated an increasing range of IT applications, particularly from the back to the front-office in terms of marketing, sales and distribution. At the same time, an increasing range of actors were demanding a share of IS resources and systems development projects, locally and centrally which combined to transform intra-organizational relations between IS and other specialisms. These developments created problems of integrating the different emerging systems and software packages and intensified the pressure to renew existing systems. A key issue here was the new market-oriented requirement to transform the huge existing databases from being based on policy/account numbers to being based customer names and addresses. This was all in the context of and exacerbated by rapidly changing and often growing markets (e.g. direct distribution and pensions and investments) and, in investment especially, uncertain regulatory parameters. The new markets had, in part, been made possible by earlier IT developments, but served to heighten the pressures on those responsible for IT management. In short, 'the old ways of managing based on technology and technologist-led decision-making and an often *ad hoc* approach to long-term planning were no longer sustainable' (Knights and Murray, 1994: 69).

These changes and attendant uncertainties, perhaps paradoxically, led to the strategic management of IT being seen by both the IT community and senior managers as crucial to the success and survival of companies. At the same time, new strategic ideas and demands contributed to the changes in technologies and applications (e.g. MIS and database renewal). Senior management (typically without an IT background) became increasingly critical (e.g. in consultants' reports) of IT 'not delivering' user requirements to budget or deadline. Moreover, in the early 1990s recession, attention became more focused on IT cost control. The new (corporate) 'strategic' emphasis on business (as opposed to 'administration') needs was reflected in the creation of decentralized, 'autonomous' business units and in IT strategy as being seen as derivative and supportive of business strategy. It was argued that IT management should become less operationally and technologically-led and more market-driven with developments linked to, or 'integrated with', long-term and other strategic business goals (see Watkins, 1989). Indeed, in some companies these demands even led to the dissolution of a centralized IS function (Knights and Murray, 1994: 70). The integration of IT and business strategies promised to solve the growing conflict between users and IT. This was supported by calls for more joint project teams, management development and communication programmes and hybrid (e.g. IT and user) senior managers.

Of course, in practice and as with business strategy, reactivity to constant change, short-term targets and sectional interests predominated. Far from resolving conflict, the changes and strategic organization often intensified it (Knights and Murray, 1994; Friedman and Cornford, 1989; Doorewaard and Van Bijsterveld, 1998). Moreover, the relationship between IT and business strategies may be reversed. While IT may have borrowed strategic management from the more general and dominant corporate strategy discourse (Knights and Murray, 1994: 67), in some firms it initiated the development of business strategy (see below). By presenting their concerns in strategic terms, IT managers influenced boards more effectively. Indeed, alternative perspectives to this process would highlight normative, existential and political dimensions. IT strategy was increasingly adopted as a badge of progressiveness in the IT field even if it was not always taken forward in practice – 'it was a big and rolling bandwagon and many managers felt compelled to jump on it' (Knights and Morgan, 1995: 68). Relatedly, strategy became associated with power and influence in organizations and thereby the adoption of a strategic approach to IT gave IS managers individually and collectively a medium to defend and/or advance their interests and identity, particularly as the discourse of strategy gave primacy to the market and therefore, business concerns. At the same time, the possibilities offered by developments in IT (e.g. new markets, distribution channels, cost reductions etc.) gave it greater importance 'strategically'.

Whatever the perspective taken, the growing cost of, and demand for, IT in a changing business context in financial services provided fertile ground for management consultants. Fincham and Roslender (1995) emphasize the reliance of financial services company boards on expertise from suppliers, users and IT management as well as consultants in the strategy process. Even in the late 1980s, the most senior managers in financial services companies tended to have followed a banking or actuarial career and saw IT as beyond their domain of expertise. Moreover, many companies did not have an IT director (Sturdy, 1989; Scarbrough and Corbett, 1992). IT strategy was 'offered' to boards and/or senior and aspiring IT managers as a tool to solve their control problems – conflicts, costs, uncertainties and prioritizing. For consultants, the sales approach would promote business and/or IT strategy – 'the one sells or recommends the other' (*Management Consultancy*, 1992c; see also Rassam and Oates, 1991: 32). Indeed, the role of consultants and their strategic discourse was not simply a *response* to the dynamic context:

> One of the main *conditions* leading to the possibility of a discourse and practice of strategic IT management came from . . . the rapidly growing field of business and IT consultancy. (Knights, Morgan and Murray, 1991: 20, emphasis added)

## BUYING AND SELLING STRATEGY

There are numerous accounts of why managers use consultancy and how consultancy can succeed and/or address their clients concerns (e.g. see Bennett, 1990; Huczynski, 1993). For example, for IT projects generally, typical reasons given include:

1. Executives wanting to exercise control over the management and investment of IT, but lacking the expertise.
2. A 'user' or IS department (manager) lacking the skills or resources for a project and/or, less explicitly, to compete with each other.
3. An individual or one of the above groups using the 'objectivity', fee and/or status of consultants to legitimate or influence a course of action.

The above conform to the conventional roles of 'experts, extras and facilitators' (Tisdall, 1982: 3), but also highlight themes of control, expertise and legitimation. Consulting techniques or approaches can be seen as ways of more or less explicitly addressing these problems and may vary depending on circumstances and preferences. Traditionally, two polar 'styles' are referred to – process and resource – although different terms are sometimes used. The latter can be likened to a doctor in terms of diagnosis and prescription while process consultancy is primarily facilitative, eliciting self-reliance and more like counselling (Bennett, 1990) although both are typically used in practice. Moreover, as we shall see, process techniques can be used in such a way as to obscure prescription and the creation of client dependence. Conflicts of interest between clients and consultants, such as securing repeat business or 'sell-on' from clients are sometimes recognized in mainstream literature. However, they are seen as avoidable if consultants behave ethically and, in particular, if clients know what they want and can manage the process effectively. Both these assumptions are untenable and certainly unrealistic in practice. In particular, they underestimate the commercial pressure on consultants and overestimate the rationality, knowledge and ability of clients (e.g. to be able to specify project objectives) and the transparency of project outcomes and accountabilities. The following demonstrates that an emerging practice such as strategy is promoted and bought through processes concerned with individual identities and anxieties as much as the contextual changes and organizational problems they are associated with. In particular, somewhat like the selling of life assurance, it is not simply a case of consultants playing on client insecurities, but the product itself (IT strategy) serves to exacerbate the problem.

**Providing reassurance**

Institutionalist theories argue that organizational structures and practices such as strategy are often adopted because of a concern to conform to industry norms or those of peer (e.g. leading/progressive) companies – isomorphism (e.g. Scott, 1987):

> Executives trade ideas and schemes and judge the efficacy of consultant programs not by any detached critical standards but by what is socially acceptable, desirable and, perhaps most important, current in their circles. (Jackall, 1988: 141)

Consultants are both fully aware and actively involved in this process. Indeed, the very use of consultants, either generally or in particular from prestigious firms such as McKinsey (which specializes in strategy consultancy), has, in certain contexts, become a norm or mark of status for the employing company Consultancies seek to capitalize on this by targeting high-status clients, especially when first entering a sector, so that they can then present these as 'role models' for prospective clients.

They also seek to address client concerns about not being 'deviant' in their publicity and sales practices whereby both problems and solutions are 'normalized' as the experience of competitors or peers and even, generally: 'We are all familiar with the problem of ... a problem that is common and constant' (consultancy publicity).

However, managers are concerned to be autonomous and innovative as well as 'current' (Huczynski, 1993). Accordingly and at the same time, 'solutions' may also be *presented* by consultants as specifically tailored to the sector and organization:

> Some consultancies will come in and say 'we are the XYZ firm, we know what's right, do it this way' ... that tends not to be our approach. Although we do have [strong] views ... we're also going to have to amend that to fit the culture. (Consultant)

> We use a wide range of methodologies but avoid their rigid application. (Publicity)

An important element in this process of reassuring or involving clients is the use of counselling-type techniques or 'active listening' (Sturdy *et al.*, 1989). The initial emphasis on listening is often preceded by research on the organization and its potential problems. Jackall also makes reference to this and the importance, prior to making any substantive comments, of identifying the key client managers, their definitions of 'the problem' and any hidden agendas. The aim of this is to avoid an early rejection by the client and to be able to present a case in keeping with the problem as defined – it 'implicitly promises nearly infinite adaptability' (1988: 142). There is always great pressure to accept, in broad terms, the clients' definition of 'the problem'. Indeed, a common observation in consultancy is the imperative of securing and maintaining powerful support within a client company for 'acceptability, legitimacy and impact' (Pettigrew, 1985: 478). However, this neglects the process of translating or redefining the 'problem' into a form compatible with the consultant's available or preferred solutions or approaches. As Bloomfield and Danieli argue, consultants 'do not so much target themselves at a particular niche as seek to create a niche and persuade clients that they are within it' (1995: 28; see also Bloomfield and Best, 1992). Thus, the 'listening' includes and is followed by more direction or guiding to 'bring' the client to an appropriate 'choice' or course of action such as developing a standard IT strategy:

We try and identify what the business issues are before we ever meet the company and draw out some IT implications of that. So we don't go in and say 'we've got a lovely IT strategy for you!' We say 'Is the fact that you are finding it hard to attract suitable labour an issue?' and 'Yes it is'... (Consultant)

...we actually start people talking and in the end, they just can't say enough. They find it totally therapeutic apart from anything else. (Consultant)

Apart from normalizing problems and solutions and selling 'ownership' of the latter, consultants provide reassurance in other ways at the same time, most conventionally through the objectivity and control promised by technical rationality. As we saw in Chapter 1, the appeal and political utility of this is well-established – the rationalized myths of institutional theory – and it is particularly significant in relation to IT (Scarbrough and Corbett, 1992; Bloomfield and Danieli, 1995). As one insurance client declared:

We're not sure exactly what we want, but we want to show whether current IT investment is right or wrong...We need figures...We need to convince them [the Board] that the investment [proposed] is not out of line with other people ... It is difficult to start to justify proposals, we need sound statistics as a basis for trends they are already seeing. (Client IT manager)

Consultants deploy and reproduce the familiar technical–social dualism in order to sell their expert services and offer reassurance to clients in different ways. For example, even IT consultants claim that 'technical' knowledge and skills are a very limited part of their work (Sturdy *et al.*, 1989; Alvesson, 1993). Rather, in addition to industry knowledge, 'political' and 'practical' skills are important to both parties (McGivern, 1983). Consultants market these strongly to potential clients, particularly in the area of IT strategy where they often see the main client need as being that of resolving IS-user conflicts:

We stimulate senior management's commitment to IT systems. (Publicity).

The other definition I have of IT strategy is that it is bloody war because within an insurance company there are so many different factions... There's a fantastic 'we'll go our way, you go yours' posture. So we're trying to merge together units of an organization. (Consultant)

An emphasis on resolving conflicts and on persuasion is central to Alvesson's study of 'knowledge intensive firms and workers' (KIFWs). Once again, contrary to the view of knowledge as a technical rational commodity, it is seen as 'credible stories about the world' (1993: 1018) and KIFs as 'systems of persuasion' (*ibid*.: 1011; see also Clark, 1995). It is not so much the validity of ideas or that techniques have been proven to work or emerge as the 'best', but that they are seen to be plausible (Gill and Whittle, 1993; Grint, 1994).

**Reinforcing uncertainty**

The foregoing discussion has introduced some of the ways in which consultants 'sell' ideas and techniques by providing or offering management reassurance. However, at the same time they contribute to or reinforce managerial uncertainty and insecurity. Indeed, this is one basis of their continuing popularity/influence. For example, their research of different sectors and technologies and their marketing and sale of 'solutions' does not only normalize 'problems', but elaborates them, and directs attention to new ones. They are actively involved in the construction and definition of 'problems'. Moreover, in providing 'solutions', new 'problems' and 'opportunities' are identified, particularly in the case of business and IT strategy. For example, it has already been noted how one sells the other and it is not uncommon for a small assignment, such as a review of growing IT expenditure, to lead to IT and business strategy projects:

The MD had an uneasy feeling that they weren't getting value for money from their IT and asked us to do a *quick appraisal* of essentially what was going on... Now, it was quite clear when we got there that... it was a pretty messy situation...[2 months later]... so the question is what was going to happen after that? So, obviously, the ideal thing to do was develop an IT strategy, but there was no business strategy and it was quite clear that developing one in line with an IT strategy was going to take some time. (Consultant, emphasis added)

'Sell-on' or 'repeat business' represents around two-thirds of revenue for some companies (Rassam and Oates, 1991: 25) and was regarded by consultants as a primary factor in defining a project as successful (see also Stevens, 1981). It also became a key performance indicator in the Department of Trade and Industry's 'Consultancy Initiative' (DTI, 1991). It may be achieved in similar ways to securing the initial project and client commitment as those described earlier although, in some ways, it is easier since greater trust and knowledge of the client company is likely to have developed. Ironically, securing user-involvement is justified on the basis of rendering them self-reliant or skilled in the new techniques as well as resolving internal conflicts. However, it also serves to reduce resistance to the use of consultants and, by 'active listening', induces clients to feel that they have identified the new problem and (consultant's) solution themselves: 'You need to present the information to the strategists in a way that they can't fail to draw out the message themselves' (consultant).

Thus, consultants' success is partly founded on their ability to provide/offer reassurance while, at the same time, reinforcing insecurities through the elaboration of problems. This double-edged quality is particularly evident with the practice of strategy. In terms of the classical, masculine and technically rational form of the strategy discourse as a way of knowing and controlling, then it clearly promises reassurance in terms of coordinating the organization and its changing environments:

> An insurance company is looking constantly at ways of buffering itself from the pressures of the outside world and planning is obviously one of the ways of doing that ... Strategy at least gives you some chance of arriving at the point you want to be at a certain point in time. (Consultant)

The limitations of this view, implied in the above quote are central to the processual view whereby strategy and reassurance are 'discovered' in action and 'any old map (strategy) will do' (Weick, 1987; see also Burnes, 1996).

> Strategy is a way in which managers try and simplify and order a world which is too complex and chaotic for them to comprehend. The regular procedures and precise quantifications of strategic planning are comforting rituals, managerial security blankets in a hostile world. (Whittington, 1993: 25)

This view is echoed by some practitioners who may also note the irony of the emergence of strategy during a period when planning became especially difficult: 'At least any order is better than no order at all . . . it's a problem because it's a complex world out there' (client strategy manager).

Overall, then, we have seen some of the ways in which consultants played an active part in strategy becoming an 'imperative' in the industry – a symbolic resource for companies, management functions such as IT and individual managers or 'strategists'. This status provided a sense of control for clients in terms of their personal careers and/or the importance of their discipline. Indeed, even within consultancy, practising in more 'strategic' (as opposed to technical or operational) areas is considered more prestigious and a position to be aspired to. However, for clients at least, uncertainties and anxieties are reinforced at the same time. This paradoxical process is evident generally in consultancy, particularly in achieving 'sell-on', but it is also inherent in the discourse of strategy. By drawing attention to the market environment, particularly during a period in which preexisting conditions and relations are breaking down, uncertainty is increased through strategy. Moreover and more generally, unpredictable and dynamic global and local markets have become defined as the norm in the 'excellence' literature of management 'gurus' (Huczynski, 1993). However, even in apparently stable contexts, the future, the environment and other actors are, of course, inevitably unpredictable and therefore control 'solutions' are bound to be limited. A recognition of this and the 'essentially contested and imperfectable' nature of strategy (Whittington, 1993: 1) may condition new discourses, but is not likely to result in the demise of consultants especially in UK financial services. Rather, managerial insecurity will continue to be associated with a self-defeating preoccupation with independent control and identity.

**Client resistance**

In showing how consultants sell their services and ideas by offering clients reassurance whilst at the same time reinforcing or creating 'new' uncertainties, a conception of management as vulnerable and insecure about job and career is presented. This might not seem wholly appropriate when considering managers' tactical use of consultants to legitimate prior decisions and pursue career objectives, and should perhaps be restricted to those who seem attracted to or who adopt 'new' management ideas or fads in 'good faith'. However, literature based on intensive or ethnographic research of managers (e.g. Jackall, 1988; Watson, 1994b; Kunda, 1991) emphasizes their ambivalence or equivocality towards new management ideas or initiatives such as corporate culture and to their proliferation (Markham, 1997; Ramsay, 1996; c.f. Huczynski, 1993; Gill and Whittle, 1993). For example, Watson cites the apparently typical case in the company under investigation, of a manager who had copies of all the 'big-name' management guru texts and had read them. However, their ideas had apparently not been applied in any direct sense 'Yes, I found them good for insights. I can't say that I've applied anything I've read in them. But they have often confirmed some of the things that I have worked out for myself . . . '.

Similarly, another manager, echoing themes in the literature (e.g. Jackall, 1988; Huczynski, 1993; Grint, 1994) recognized the lack of originality in 'new' ideas: 'It is all there. It has just been renamed a few dozen times by all sorts of people either writing books or trying to justify their consultancy tasks or whatever' (quoted in Watson, 1994b: 217).

As intimated above, criticism, scepticism and/or cynicism is directed not only at ideas in management texts, but also towards consultants and the ideas they promote. Indeed, this is common parlance and has long been recognized and documented in prescriptive consultancy literature (e.g. Tisdall, 1982; Wood, 1983; Bennett, 1990; Shapiro *et al.*, 1993; Mitchell, 1994; c.f. Mackay, 1987). Indeed, our research included companies which, for a number of reasons, did not use consultants at all (Sturdy *et al.*, 1991). Users of consultants tended to be ambivalent – both positive and critical. The types of concerns expressed include:

- cost/value for money
- 'sell on' – seek long-term relationships/dependency
- ambiguous/unfalsifiable techniques and results
- abstract and standardized models
- confidentiality/parasitic
- lack industry knowledge
- old/repackaged ideas
- senior staff sell but juniors sent to do work
- tendency to conservatism
- formulate, but don't implement
- insensitive to employees/arrogant

Such concerns are recognized by consultants and, as we have seen in relation to offering 'tailored' and 'practical' solutions, 'self-reliance' and the deployment of political skills, they are partially anticipated in marketing practices and interactions with clients. For example, the criticism of lacking industry knowledge may be re-presented as the positive virtue of an 'outside' or fresh approach. Similarly firms may be encouraged to develop long-term relationships with a consultancy in order to avoid the risk and uncertainty associated in selecting a new consultancy (Clark, 1995). Nevertheless, the criticisms suggest that management consultancies are not always successful in countering potentially negative criticisms of their activities and provide some counter to the apparent popularity of management 'gurus' and ideas in the UK. Moreover, they appear to at least temper the idea that management feel so vulnerable that they are always 'ripe' for the picking by consultancy firms. On the contrary, the fact that the consultancy firms have to seek to anticipate and deal with potential objections suggests that a more equitable or iterative process is involved in the production and diffusion of consultancy discourse (Sturdy, 1997a).

Criticisms of management ideas/consultants can be accounted for in a number of ways. The prescriptive consultancy literature tends to view criticism and conflict as a result of a lack of 'professionalism' on the part of consultants and, similarly, a lack of understanding or preparation from clients. Thus, conflict may arise where clients expect a facilitative and non-directive approach, but are faced with the opposite, and vice versa (see McGivern, 1983). As noted earlier, avoiding conflict is seen to be achievable through preparation and clarifying the nature of the problem and/or project objectives (see Shapiro *et al.*, 1993; Cash and Minter, 1979; IMC, 1995). Of course, this obscures or denies underlying conflicts (e.g. 'sell on'), inevitable uncertainty and the social construction of problems. Others explain criticism differently. For example, Gill and Whittle see management disillusionment as a part of the natural life-cycle of ideas which follows stages of enthusiasm and bureaucratization (1993). Similarly, Jackall sees the 'short-term ethos' as 'crucial in determining managers' stance towards consultants and their programs' (1988: 143). Whilst managers may sometimes be publicly enthusiastic, overall, their provisional or equivocal attitudes reflect a recognition of the temporary nature of their superordinates' commitment to new ideas. This was also evident in a UK company where individual managers who were seen to be embrace new ideas were mocked by their peers as 'guru groupies' or 'whores'. In addition, we have noted how attachment to preexisting or other competing (e.g. non-strategic) discourses may provide the basis of resistance. Relatedly, it can be seen as arising from the threat that consultants/ideas pose to managers' existing identities as competent and 'in control' – to their careers and job security.

Criticism may be most vocal from those who do not commission the consultants – for whom new ideas or solutions have not been personally adopted to support career ambitions (Watson, 1994a; Scase and Goffee, 1989; Sturdy *et al.*, 1990). As one questionnaire respondent commented: 'I like working with consultants (provided that they report to me and not my boss!!)'. Even the most senior management levels are vulnerable. For example, in one case in the insurance industry, the Board of Directors called in a consultancy firm ostensibly to examine the 'soaring' costs of IT. On the basis of the firm's assessment, the IT director was sacked and the senior consultant was asked to undertake the responsibility and implement new controls whilst still reporting to his firm. This sort of case supports Armstrong's (1989) thesis of trust substitution between management groups (Sturdy, 1997b) although it is usually more applicable to more junior levels. Here, as Jackall points out, managers cannot afford to be seen to refuse to cooperate with consultants and so publicly assume the relationship of 'a polite, arms-length embrace' (1988: 140) – 'they put up with us' (consultant). However, their fear or suspicion may also be reflected in subtle forms of resistance.

> The task, then, for the target[ed] group is to persuade the consultant that whatever problem might exist, exists elsewhere in the organization or, failing that, to negotiate with the consultant in an oblique way some amelioristic program that will disrupt ... [things] as little as possible. (Jackall, 1988: 140; see also Phills, 1996)

Even for those commissioning consultants, our research suggested that the threat posed may be very direct and recognizable – to job security for example:

> I mean it was risky in a sense. It's easy to let things go on because, you know, you bring in external people and the first thing they look at and say is 'your management is rubbish and you need to swap them' and so on. So there was a calculated risk in that ... There wasn't the perception by the then management team that it was important to have a new [IT] strategy. (IT manager, insurance company)

Resistance to consultants founded on their threat to expertise was also suggested in the case of a board with little knowledge of IT but, as one might expect, a strong claim to business expertise:

> They were very receptive. They recognised that some of their [IT] expenditure had been entirely wasteful and that they needed an IT strategy... However, when we got to the business strategy side, there is less accord... (Consultant)

Similarly, while consultants and new ideas can be used to enhance status, managers may underplay their influence (particularly in their own area of competence) in order to assert their identity and sense of control. Alternatively, the role of consultants may be highlighted in the case of 'failed' projects – scapegoating. The former is evident in the earlier quotation from Watson (1994b) and others, where the claim is that they 'confirmed' existing knowledge. Moreover, Watson continued by showing that despite his criticism, the manager had clearly taken on the new ideas (and language) and believed in their effectiveness (*ibid.*: 217).

If criticism of, and resistance to, management consultants and ideas is founded on the threat posed to managers' identities, jobs and careers, then the view of management as insecure and vulnerable is *reinforced* rather than tempered. Indeed, their recognition of the perceived limitations of consultants such as the likelihood of securing a dependent relationship, may further such anxiety. However, such apparent vulnerability does not preclude exercising power over consultants. Not only are consultants not immune from hierarchical and existential concerns (Sturdy, 1997a), but their market position may change individually and collectively. This is illustrated in the end of the long 1980s boom in consultancy business which led in the 1990s to over-supply and a fall in growth of consultancy business, related mergers of key firms and a decline in consultant numbers even in the hitherto buoyant strategy area and financial services (*Economist*, 1991; *Management Consultancy*, 1993, 1992c; Clark, 1995). Economic recession and regulatory/cost pressures on potential client companies combined with their increasing experience of, or familiarity with, consultants, strategy and IT combined to intensify the pressures, uncertainties and anxieties of consultants. As with other sectors before them (*Economist*, 1988; Rassam and Oates, 1991), financial services companies began to adopt a 'harder line' in the use of consultants, recognizing the need to keep them under 'tight control'.

Indeed, it was claimed that 'the financial sector had the most sophist-icated consultancy purchasers in Britain' (*Management Consultancy*, 1993) especially among the larger companies. In some cases they recruited their own strategists and internal consultants, often from consultancy firms. When using outside help, greater attention tended to be given to gaining 'good value'. For example, it was reported that more emphasis was being placed on strategy implementation as well as formu-lation (Rassam and Oates, 1991; *Economist*, 1991; Shapiro *et al.*, 1993). Also, the recession led to a stressing of cost-reduction and control (*Man-agement Consultancy*, 1992c) or accounting criteria in strategic planning. More recently, despite economic recovery, strategy consultancy has begun to decline as a proportion of consultancy business in financial ser-vices – from 13 per cent in 1992 to 9 per cent in 1996/7 (*Management Consultancy*, 1997a). This provides some indication of the extent to which it has become an established discourse in the sector.

Consultancies, of course, responded and contributed to these devel-opments. For example, direct financial benefits or savings are increas-ingly calculated for each of their projects as 'an incredibly good sales tool' for they can be compared against the fees charged. Indeed, some firms set fees partly as a percentage of identified savings or benefits. More generally, firms have responded, as in the past, by looking to other sectors (e.g. the public sector), geographical areas (e.g. Eastern Europe) and problems and/or 'solutions' (e.g. knowledge manage-ment). For example, in financial services, 're-engineering' became a new field of consultancy business (*Management Consultancy*, 1997a). Furthermore, as we have seen, IT if anything has grown in importance and the financial services sector remains a relatively buoyant, indeed the largest, market for consultancy (*Management Consultancy*, 1992a, 1997b). This both reflects and serves to reinforce the continued dynam-ism and uncertainty within its organizational field.


CONCLUSION

We have begun to show some of the ways in which strategic discourse gradually colonized key institutions in the financial sector. In doing so, it had to overcome resistance and promote itself as a solution to uncer-tainties and unpredictable outcomes. This process led to major changes in culture and practices which impacted on individuals at all different levels in the financial institutions. Strategy discourse became embedded inside these organizations as the central way of making sense of the world. But, in doing so, it did not necessarily overcome uncertainty. Rather it reconstructed the setting inside and outside the organization and created new forms of uncertainty and difficulty.

In particular, using the discourse of IT strategy we have seen how management's apparently persistent appetite for 'solutions' can be partly accounted for by the way in which consultancy practices and the ideas they promote provide clients with the prospect of a reassuring sense of control over organization and identity and yet simultaneously reinforce their insecurities. It was also argued that greater attention should be given to the interactive nature of the process and, in particular, to the active role and resistance of client managers. However, while strategy was initially contested within companies and sometimes introduced through the 'back door' of IT cost-escalation for example, over time, conflict and negotiation has shifted to its particular form and emphasis, such as cost control and implementation.

In the following two chapters, we continue the examination of how companies became more strategic. Firstly, we demonstrate that marketing techniques were largely absent from financial companies until the early 1970s. As they became embedded, they challenged previous conceptions of how financial institutions worked and replaced traditional notions of service and conservatism with ideas about selling products. Thus, financial institutions were encouraged to see themselves as just a distinctive type of retail service environment which had much in common with supermarkets or other mass retailers such as Marks and Spencer. Secondly, we examine what these changes meant for employment relations within firms. Here, a range of changes need to be identified in order to understand the ways in which employees within these institutions had to adapt to this process. Conceptions of what it meant to work in a financial institution had to be changed and this change had to be reflected in new patterns of work and career as well as in new sets of values such as customer service.

# 6 Marketing Discourse: Its Emergence and Contradictions

## INTRODUCTION

In the previous chapters we argued that financial services organizations and those who worked inside them gradually began to reconstitute themselves from the point of view of strategic discourse. As the old field of relations which had connected the state, financial institutions and consumers together began to fall apart, managers began to evolve new ways of looking at their world and intervening in it. Strategic discourse provided a framework and techniques for this at a high level of generality, but in order to be effective and powerful it needed to be translated into more specific and penetrative mechanisms. These involved ways of categorizing and measuring the world which could provide the basis for instituting specific forms of practice, control, monitoring and disciplining. We have already seen how strategy emerged alongside the development of IT and came to provide a core, but contested, framework for its management. However, one of the most important of these mechanisms was associated with the establishment of marketing within financial services. In what follows, we explore the process whereby marketing became established within financial services. This is not simply an issue to do with the functional structure of firms such as the establishment of marketing departments. As with strategy, it concerns the evolution of a particular way of looking at the world, the incorporation of a range of techniques and methods of analysing and acting upon the world. Finally, it involves the interactive production and reproduction of the social world in new ways to make sense of the power of strategic discourse. Thus marketing and strategy became increasingly strongly linked.

In the first section of the chapter, we examine the nature of marketing discourse, what it is and how it is differentiated from other discourses about the relationship between the organization and its environment. From this, we turn to often prescriptive discussions within the literature on financial services marketing. Many of these contributions note and promote the emergence of marketing under changing market conditions. They also associate the failure of organizations to adequately understand and appreciate the role of marketing with processes of organizational conservatism and decline. We explain this partly in terms of conflicts between marketing discourse (and marketing professionals) and other ways of looking at how organizations work. In particular, we note that as financial institutions evolved from their cosseted and state-supported position towards a more competitive environment and uncertain organizational field, the characteristic battles within the organizations were initially between the traditionalists and the modernizers over the issue of selling. Selling was used as a very blunt tool to characterize the difference between the old orientation and the new one. However, whilst it was a highly effective rallying point for those seeking change, it was difficult to integrate with strategic discourse without the mediation of a more complex and legitimating set of ideas and practices. Marketing became the means for that integration and in the process began to subordinate selling. This had significant consequences for the discourses and practices of financial institutions as they sought to stabilize the interorganizational field during the 1990s under the challenge of new regulations and new distribution technologies which we explore in later chapters.

In the final section of the chapter, we draw attention to contradictions and tensions within marketing discourse and their specific consequences in financial services. In particular, we show how consumer interests are *at odds with* cost containment and profitability requirements. This is reflected in both strategic market segmentation and product design practices and reinforced by consumer inertia. In this way, our analysis shifts from the internal political dynamics of the organization to the issue of how this is related to the constitution of consumers. As a discourse and set of practices, marketing implied a particular understanding of consumers. These interrelated in various complex ways with the expectations of the state, others within the financial institutions and consumers and their representatives. What seems to be emerging is a new consumer in embryo – not yet fully developed but distinct from that of the pre-1970s period – because, in part, of the actions which marketing have undertaken to create such a new consumer. We therefore reject the view that marketing simply reflects and reproduces existing social reality. As with other discourses and practices, it changes and reshapes that reality in ways that are partially deliberate but also in ways that are unanticipated. The 'truth' of marketing is created through these discourses and practices which are crucially linked to the notion of strategy within the financial services industry. Thus, the initial processes of constructing strategy discourse and practices around information technology and through the intervention of management consultants is reinforced by the emerging role of marketing.

## THE EMERGENCE OF THE MARKETING CONCEPT

In this section, we adopt a similar perspective to our previous discussion of strategy. We are not interested in 'naturalizing' marketing – imputing it to any exchange, whatever the time or context, which has been the approach of some marketing theorists. This de-historicizes the formation and development of knowledges and practices. As Alvesson and Willmott state, the dominant view within marketing is one which 'pays little regard to the relationship between knowledge and wider issues, including history, culture and power' (1996: 120; see also Morgan, 1992). On the contrary, our interest is in how marketing becomes constructed and produced in particular contexts and what effect this has on particular patterns of social relationships.

From this perspective, we can note that the term marketing began to be used in the UK in the late 1920s (Walker and Child, 1979). In the US context, marketing developed slightly earlier though the conditions of its emergence have still not properly been documented (see the discussion in Morgan, 1992). In general terms, marketing justifies its own existence in terms of creating a body of knowledge and practices which enable organizations to serve customer 'needs' through the production of appropriate goods and services. Alvesson and Willmott quote one defence of marketing which states that 'it is all about mutually satisfying exchange relationships for which the catalyst is the producers attempt to define and satisfy the customers need better' (1996: 120).

It is clear that there has been debate in marketing literature over the nature of the 'marketing concept' and what marketing *should* be. One, often cited definition is that marketing is a process 'to create exchanges that satisfy individual (i.e. consumer) and organizational objectives' (Hooley *et al*., 1990: 7). This overly broad 'de(pre)scription' does not contradict the version used here which is drawn from practitioners and financial services and other marketing literature. However, it does depart from Houston's more considered and critical discussion (1986). Here, the concept is defined in terms of a *willingness* both to understand

and respond to consumer needs. Under certain conditions, such as consumer passivity, it is entirely appropriate and consistent with the marketing concept for organizations not to design goods and services in accordance with existing consumer needs. As in this chapter, Houston is critical of those who assume that responding to needs is an 'optimal' approach (*ibid*.: 86). However, his account neglects the issue of power in terms of the role of organizations in shaping consumer preferences except in the apparently neutral sense of educating potential buyers (c.f. Dixon, 1992; Brownlie and Saren, 1992; Grafton-Small, 1987; Alvesson and Willmott, 1996).

The emergence of the marketing concept, of establishing and satisfying consumer needs *profitably*, was described and also reinforced by Smith in 1956 through his influential article on 'product differentiation and market segmentation as alternative marketing strategies' in the USA (see also Keith, 1960; Dixon, 1992). He echoed the formal recognition in the economic theory of the 1930s (e.g. Chamberlain, 1933) of a diversity or heterogeneity of market demand. The crucial step in the construction of a space for the discourse and practice of marketing was the claim that hitherto, at least theoretically and with mass production goods, product differentiation had predominated. This 'in its simplest terms . . . is concerned with the bending of demand to the will of supply . . .' (Smith, 1956: 398) through hard selling for example. In other words, from the point of view of the relationship between the organization and the environment, the claim that was being made was that organizations tended to just produce what they were good at with very little initial concern for whether anybody wanted to buy it.

As a proposed academic discipline and set of professional practices, what marketing sought to do was to establish first of all the claim that the environment (in terms of the 'needs' of the consumers) could be known and that this information could become a central part of an organization's development and activities. The general claim needed to be supported by a set of techniques and practices which could measure the market and, in particular, could segment it into groups to whom particular marketing offers (i.e. a combination of product, price, promotion and place) could be made. This therefore went hand in hand with a market segmentation strategy which is 'based upon developments on the demand side of the market and represents . . . [an] . . . adjustment of product and marketing effort to consumer or user requirements' (*ibid*.). Thus, defined in this way, a segmentation strategy is almost synonymous with the marketing concept (c.f. Brownlie and Saren, 1992).

For example, it coincides with Levitt's contemporaneous and similarly influential prescription of the competitive value of (profitability from) asking customers what they want to buy and making it, rather than continuing to sell what one wanted to make (1960; c.f. 1983: 94 and 102).

Smith acknowledged that there was nothing new about a recognition of diversity in demand, particularly to sales managements and in industrial markets where production to order was the norm. Indeed, targeted advertising was common and even central to product differentiation. However, as a strategy, segmentation was seen to be emerging at this time and 'many examples' (1956: 398) were available such as the marketing of fridges without an ice box for freezer owners. Such developments coincided with, and gave a sharper focus to, the application of social science concepts and techniques in North American marketing literature especially, which mushroomed in the 1960s and 1970s (see Engel *et al.*, 1972; Sturdy and Knights, 1996). The different bases of classifying consumer differences and similarities and their relationship with market demand or purchasing behaviour were developed. For example, 'demographics', including the family life-cycle concept, began to be applied to different market sectors from the 1950s (see Clark, 1955; Wells and Gubar, 1966). Similarly, psychologically-based studies on consumer personality and motivation were combined in the development of 'lifestyle' or 'psychographic' segmentation concepts in the 1960s (Wells, 1975). More recently, 'geodemographics' (classifying small areas according to inhabitants' characteristics) emerged. Many of these ideas were derived originally from nineteenth century survey work in the UK on poverty (Booth, 1889; Rowntree, 1901) and subsequently developed in postwar town-planning surveys (Moser, 1958; see also Bulmer, 1982). However, their application to marketing was facilitated and stimulated by concomitant developments in data gathering and computer technology (Rothman, 1989).

As a set of discourses and practices, marketing sought to establish its legitimacy in opposition to another particular view of the world. The dominance within organizations of a production-focus was presented as outdated and irrational. Clearly, this critique can be overdrawn and simplistic. In market systems, such organizations could not survive for long without also considering how they were to sell their goods and services. This process of selling might not be clearly articulated or formalized, but a matter of tradition or 'intuition' without the use of formal systems of measurement and knowledge. Indeed, such forms of practical knowledge may have worked well in particular circumstances, but as a discourse marketing poured scorn on such amateurism in the name of professionalism, science and efficiency as well as consumer 'needs' (see also Sturdy and Knights, 1996; Rose, 1989). The notion of the marketing concept including all these 'technical' aspects could be used as an additional weapon to undermine other ways of linking the organization and the environment which could be labelled as production-focused and lacking a marketing orientation.

As with strategy, this must be seen as a claim made in specific circumstances, drawing on specific legitimatory languages, that can become embedded in organizational practices and meanings. Marketing's claim had to be made successful by the actions of individuals and groups and by incorporating it into their way of looking at the world. Once this is achieved, it is difficult for the general claims of marketing to be disputed, so deeply ingrained do they become. It is, of course, possible to dispute specifics such as the most appropriate techniques for measuring and assessing markets. But this serves to reinforce the legitimacy of the *general* claim of marketing. The establishment of this is, however, historically specific. It occurs in different countries, sectors and organizations at distinct times according to the social processes of creating and diffusing knowledge and professional practices. In the next section, we try to identify some of these specificities in relation to marketing in British financial services.

## THE MARKETING ORIENTATION IN UK FINANCIAL SERVICES

Within UK financial services, commentators have frequently noted what might be termed the under-development of marketing and, indeed, the reluctance of the industry to adopt the marketing concept (Channon, 1988; Ackrill, 1993; Morgan and Piercy, 1990; Newman, 1984; Egan and Shipley, 1995). For most of the last 30 years these concerns have been articulated, and at each stage some optimists have argued that marketing is at last beginning to dominate financial services whilst others have been more sceptical. The reasons for the difficulty in achieving a marketing orientation are seen to lie in the domination within the sector of a supply-side focus that led to firms being principally concerned with operational and finance issues and being, in marketing terms, 'product-led'. A range of mainly established products would be sold, 'hard' in some areas such as life assurance, or left to be 'bought' (Egan and Shipley, 1995; Thwaites and Lynch, 1992; Ennew *et al.*, 1990; Morgan and Piercy, 1990; Hooley and Mann, 1988). This supply orientation coupled with an emerging emphasis on selling acted as a barrier to the establishment of marketing ideas. Commentators noted that marketing activities, ideas and departments within financial services companies were limited in their scope and afforded low status in relation to other business 'disciplines' (Davison *et al.*, 1989). Specific ideas and practices such as those arising from notions of market segmentation were only applied in a limited and crude form, using income and wealth and financial and product life-cycles (Stanley *et al.*, 1987; Speed and Smith, 1992).

In the competitive climate of the late 1980s and early 1990s, a number of authors claimed that a *real* transition was occurring from the supply orientation towards a focus on consumer needs. Such a change was seen to be leading towards the reevaluation of existing products and services and the development of new ones which were better tailored to customer needs as identified by marketing techniques (Hooley and Mann, 1988; Clarke *et al.*, 1988; Joseph and Yorke, 1989). The transition appeared to be a recent and rapid one. For example, a survey of companies' self-perceptions recorded 53 per cent as being 'market-driven' compared with 2 per cent five years earlier when the dominant approach was to provide '. . . [a] traditional range of products/services for whoever will purchase (them)' (Hooley and Mann, 1988: 490). Similarly, another survey found that 48 per cent of the sample companies had established their marketing departments in the last five years (Davison *et al.*, 1989). Such findings, as with many other postal surveys (e.g. Hooley *et al.*, 1990; Egan and Shipley, 1995), do not necessarily establish that the professed marketing orientation has been put into practice. However, it is also said that the use of market research and segmentation techniques in product development (i.e. tailoring) has grown in recent years (Ennew, 1990; Thwaites and Lynch, 1992). For example, more companies are integrating and expanding their client databases and using 'non-traditional' forms of segmentation such as 'lifestyles' in focusing on customer needs (Joseph and Yorke, 1989; Lewis, 1990). Speed and Smith claim that 'market segmentation has become *accepted* and followed as a *strategy* in the financial services industry' (1992: 376, emphasis added). More specifically, banks and building societies in particular, have been expanding their product range and distribution channels beyond traditional core areas and aiming to maintain and develop their relationships with the existing customer base by cross-selling tailored, targeted and, often, branded products and services (McKechnie, 1992; Lewis, 1990; Thwaites and Lynch, 1992; McGoldrick and Greenland, 1992; Sturdy, 1992b).

As noted earlier, claims similar to those documented above have been made before. For example, Newman's comprehensive study of the nature and emergence of financial marketing notes that, after a slow start, the *subject* of bank marketing in the UK had 'fully come of age' by 1980 (1984: 296) and observes the banks' entry into a new era following their establishment of marketing departments in the late 1960s (Watson, 1982; see also Lewis, 1984 and Clarke *et al.*, 1988). Similarly, building societies began marketing in the 1970s. Recognizing that there was room for further development, Newman nevertheless claimed that 'the belief that products should be tailored to customer requirements has now become an *accepted tenet* of building society thinking' (1984: 273, emphasis added). Equally, examples of strategic segmentation in insurance are provided from the 1970s and early 1980s after marketing had become a 'fashionable' concept (1984: 337).

Like Newman, many of the recent observations of a marketing orientation in financial services are qualified (see e.g. Ackrill, 1993; McKechnie, 1992; Morgan, 1990; Hooley and Mann, 1988). For example, McKechnie argues that marketing literature in the area remains undeveloped particularly in relation to consumer behaviour (McKechnie, 1992). Knowledge and use of strategic and other marketing techniques, including segmentation, continues to lag behind other sectors (Ennew, 1990; Hooley and Mann, 1988; Egan and Shipley, 1995). In addition, some authors have noted that there was little use of market research in new product development in some areas. Indeed, in Davison *et al.*'s survey cited earlier, 72 per cent of the sample had no market research function, and 16 per cent no marketing department (1989). While a lack of market research may be partly accounted for by the relative ease of copying products in financial services, such findings suggest some variation in the extent of marketing development and practice. For example, some authors claim that larger companies may be more likely to be more 'advanced' (Morgan and Piercy, 1988 c.f. Hooley *et al.*, 1990), but this is by no means the only, or even a sufficient, factor.

Thwaites and Lynch (1992) constructed a typology of companies according to their approach to marketing and distinguished four stages in an 'evolutionary' pattern among building societies from 'marketing myopics', 'departmental promoters' and 'advanced functionalists' towards the 'ideal' of 'guiding philosophers'. The latter group, 40 per cent of respondents, viewed marketing as both a functional activity and a guiding philosophy throughout the organization allowing the identification and satisfaction of consumer needs (1992: 440; see also Hooley *et al.*, 1990 and Keith, 1960). This broadly corresponds to the 'final' stage or 'era' of 'strategic marketing control' outlined by Clarke *et al.* in their account of postwar changes in bank marketing (1988: 10), though similar ideas were promoted much earlier. For example, Ackrill quotes the advice of a Public Relations consultancy to National Provincial (now NatWest) bank in 1965 concerning the improvement of its image: '(What) has to be changed is the attitude of your own people towards their jobs, the customers and the public ... we would say that you are considered nice people but old fashioned' (1993: 158).

Despite their conflicting claims, what all these discussions share is a recognition of the problem of establishing the marketing concept inside financial services organizations. What they fail to provide adequately, however, is any sort of systematic analysis of why this has been the case beyond references to deregulation and IT developments. In our view, the answer to such a question is provided at two levels. Firstly, this process has to be understood in broader terms relating to the collapse of the particular interorganizational field and its associated modes of relating financial institutions to their environments. Secondly, and more provocatively, the process has to be understood in terms of some of the internal contradictions within marketing discourse.

### Marketing and the interorganizational field of financial services companies

In earlier chapters we described how, up to the 1970s, financial services organizations had existed within a highly stable environment in which there were a limited number of products, the prices of which were set in cooperation between the state and the financial institutions acting in concert. The financial institutions did not, in general, have to go out searching for customers. Customers came to them. Various trends in the 1950s and 1960s, such as growing disposable income, higher propensity to save, increased home ownership, wider availability of sources of consumer credit and the payment of wages and salaries by firms directly into bank accounts, drew more and more people into a direct relationship with one or more financial institution. Although financial institutions recognized that there was an element of competition in their environment, so great was the increased demand for their products that incentives to change fundamentally what was being done (as opposed to ensuring that the same things could be done for a much larger population) were minimal. Thus the conditions for accepting the challenge to change which was being put forward by the proponents of marketing were, at first, not propitious. At the local level, managers and employees were 'conservative' in their orientations and not interested in new products or new techniques for identifying and segmenting their customers. As we shall see in the following chapter, the rhetorical nature of claims to prioritise customer needs as well as career structures and reward systems encouraged this conservatism. More senior levels of the hierarchy tended to share this orientation and continuing success seemed to undermine any necessity for major change.

As this context began to break apart, such attitudes could no longer be unproblematically reproduced. This does not mean that they disappeared. Rather, they became less legitimate as articulations of how financial institutions could grow and develop, whilst still remaining central to the understanding of many within the organizations as to how they should work. The idea that outsiders from marketing could tell bank managers anything about their customers was always likely to be resisted by those who had grown up under the old system. Also the idea that product design had to become much more closely aligned to what customers wanted as opposed to what the organization could produce easily and profitably was resisted in various head office functions. Nevertheless, it was increasingly difficult to pretend that nothing had changed and that financial institutions could continue as before. As we have shown in earlier chapters, the conditions which had made for a stable and profitable market for companies had disappeared. Moreover, this situation was being made more visible, and thereby reinforced, by those promoting change such as consultants.

Within these changes, marketing became an aspect of the emerging strategic discourse and set of practices which sought not just to overcome traditional attitudes towards customers and the market but to frame the future for financial services institutions. This framing involved considerable conflict with other potential orientations to the future, of which the most important was a selling orientation. As we have seen, this builds upon a product or supply-side orientation to the world. The company continues to produce the goods and services which it has always done, but because it is finding it less easy to sell them, it focuses on the selling process and seeks to increase the effectiveness of the sales function so that more products are sold. This orientation is distinct from that of marketing although it is often similarly clothed in consumer-oriented language. It is not built on techniques and practices for identifying customer needs and developing products and modes of delivery which can meet those needs. Rather, needs are taken for granted and the task for the organization concerns making contact with customers and getting them to recognize their 'needs' and buy the products.

**The development of a sales orientation**

Establishing a sales orientation may be considered as an organizational reaction to the perceived requirement to move away from being conservative and traditional. It raises a relatively simple idea which can be rapidly understood by most people in the organization. In implementation terms, it also provides a framework for developing new skills and reward systems either in the old workforce or in a new one. Meanwhile, much of the rest of the organization can continue as before, producing the same products and services which are now being delivered in a new, more aggressive, sales-oriented manner. Shifting to a sales orientation has characterized many organizations over the last century as they have begun to find market conditions more difficult (e.g. the development of the US car industry by Sloan and Ford as they sought to expand the market for their products). In response to these market difficulties, firms develop sales forces supported by advertising and promotion campaigns to generate new business for them.

Just such a move characterized a number of the modern or modernizing financial institutions during the 1970s and 1980s. Burton has characterized this process of change in banks in terms of the shift from 'tellers to sellers' (Burton, 1994). Such a characterization, however, tells only part of the story because it neglects to clarify fully the interrelationship between selling activities and marketing. In this period, increased emphasis on the selling process began to emerge, particularly around the area of life insurance and long-term investments. However, it was often not explicitly linked into marketing. In fact, as we have seen in relation to the production orientation in the postwar USA, marketing was partly defined in opposition to it.

In part, the move to hard selling in banking was an extension of, and drew on, a long sales tradition in the life assurance sector. The nature of the product – its associations with death – had traditionally been seen as requiring a more proactive approach to customers. Thus, many of the old established companies had their roots in local organizations which had employed so-called collectors to visit existing and potential clients in their home either to collect premiums and savings on a weekly basis or to seek to persuade people to buy new policies. Selling was therefore endemic in the insurance side of the financial services industry, unlike in banking where most clients had been expected to come to the bank rather than vice versa. However, the range of types of sales forces grew rapidly from the 1970s onwards. In particular, a number of life assurance companies moved from the 'collector' notion (in which selling and administration/collection were combined) towards specialist sales forces which were rewarded entirely according to what they sold. The elements of collecting and so on were entirely separated and administered through back office systems dependent on setting up bank standing orders.

The new sales forces were required to be more aggressive and instrumental in selling life insurance and investments; the sales people learnt all about opening and closing deals and the tactics which could be used to overcome resistance. Such sales forces tended to have a limited number of products which were deemed to fit everybody, but in reality this was impossible. From a marketing point of view, customers had different requirements based on different levels of income, attitude to risk, stage in the life-cycle and so on. However, these variations were in the main unexplored as the sales people had a particular product to sell which was priced on making a profit for the company in a particular way (this issue is explored in more detail in Chapter 8). This view of the world clashed with that of marketing.

Marketing's claim to power and influence rested on the idea that it could represent and provide an understanding of the needs of customers and, crucially, that in doing so greater and longer-term profitability would result. Unlike sales, it was open to the idea that customers had different requirements and that companies had to adapt and shape their products and forms of distribution in order to fit these demands. In this perspective, direct selling was only one such channel amongst a number of others – such as direct mailing, telephone selling, the use of other types of staff and so on. The marketing mix had to be constructed according to the sorts of customers and products which were being sold and their most effective forms of delivery. It therefore had the potential to link to strategic discourse and arguments about how the firm could and should evolve in the future, in a way which a selling orientation did not.

Nevertheless, this interaction between traditional conservatism, a selling orientation and the marketing concept was not always or easily resolved inside firms. Two aspects were crucial. Firstly, the hard sell had worked when there were a high number of potential customers to each sales person. However, as more and more banks switched from their traditional conservatism to open up specialist sales forces, the supply side grew. On the other hand, from the late 1980s demand began to flatten out with the recession, the collapse of the property market and a growing wariness of sellers resulting from adverse publicity (e.g. over personal pensions). Thus, by the early 1990s, more and more sales people were chasing less and less business and the hard-sell approach was increasingly unsuccessful. Secondly, the economics of the hard-sell approach was being undermined by regulatory changes. As we saw in Chapter 3, from 1988 onwards the regulatory system began to institute a series of rules which, combined with associated media attention, affected the ways in which sales forces worked. Firstly, the regulators placed on sales forces an obligation to 'know your customer' and provide 'best advice'. These requirements meant that sales people had to record the details of their clients' financial positions and demonstrate that any products sold fitted that profile. Although it is still difficult to estimate how effective this has been, it was a substantial change which undermined the old attitude of sell, sell, sell. Every investment sale now had to be justified in terms of the particularities of the case.

Secondly, in order to be authorized to sell at all, a sales person now had to demonstrate that they had undergone training. Although this was not particularly arduous, it increased substantially the amount of money which firms were investing in their sales force. Thus high levels of turnover such as had occurred before regulation were seen as increasingly wasteful. Thirdly, the new regulatory system began to reveal that a number of companies, both 'modern' and established, were so intent on the hard sell that they were transgressing the boundaries which the regulators were trying to put in place. This could result in adverse publicity and/or a fine for the company and, in very serious cases, the suspension of the entire sales force, thus stopping the company doing business for a period of time (these issues are explored in more detail in Chapter 8).

On the one hand, all of these factors made it increasingly difficult for firms to continue to allow hard selling to dominate; on the other hand, they were all factors which enabled marketing to push its claims as a way of overcoming the existing difficulties. Marketing could be used as a means of continuing the modernization process but within a framework that was more sensitive to the customers, the regulators and the need to identify specific forms of competitive advantage. One recent textbook on financial services marketing, for example, claimed that the recent climate of regulation and competition meant that, for the first time, financial services needed to be proactive (i.e. customer-oriented) in their marketing efforts (Ennew *et al.*, 1990: xii). The experiences of the 1990s can be said to endorse this argument in the sense that marketing has now assumed a much more dominant position within financial services organizations. It has achieved this for the following reasons.

Firstly, most of the traditionalists within financial service organizations have either left (through retirement or redundancy) or been placed into a situation where they have little choice but to go along with the new system. Secondly, the attempt to modernize through turning themselves into selling organizations has failed most financial institutions. It has failed not in the sense that they are not still concerned centrally with selling. Clearly they are and they may justifiably think of themselves as retail organizations (McGoldrick and Greenland, 1994). What has failed has been the attempt to run large parts of the organization on the basis of a sales mentality which was, in effect, nothing but the old production/supply focus turned outwards and aggressively onto the customer. This has failed because of the conflicts it generated internally between the different parts of the organization and the conflicts it generated externally with the increasingly powerful or, at least, vigilant regulators. It has also failed because there are now many more channels of distribution for the sale of products than there were previously (e.g. telephone, internet, direct, off-the-page advertising etc.). Firms face complex decisions about which channels to use and what are the factors to consider in this choice.

These very questions are made possible by, and are the outcomes of, marketing and strategic discourses. The selling mentality does not have the methods, techniques or concepts which can help companies answer these questions. Instead, marketing has been able to link to the emerging strategic discourse in a very clear and direct way. Marketing provides mechanisms for understanding consumer needs, for segmenting these needs, for designing products and offers which analyse the relative efficacy and efficiency of particular distribution channels. It contributes to strategy formation in a direct way adding market data, information and concepts to this process. Similarly, it provides means for overcoming the weaknesses of the old sales orientation by designing products which are more related to specific customer needs (even if often only slightly). In so doing, it is able to reduce some of the tension between sales practices and regulatory requirements.

Marketing provides a language and a way of understanding the role which the company and its employees are playing which is much more legitimate and palatable both inside the organization and outside. The language of marketing emphasizes the needs of the customer and meeting those needs. Thus the role of marketing is to identify the needs and link them back to the products and services which the organization offers. It links in a powerful and subtle way with the discourse of the 'sovereign consumer' and the cult of the customer (du Gay and Salaman, 1992; du Gay, 1996). Employees learn this language when they enter the organization whatever their particular role (Sturdy, 1998; see also Chapter 7) and through this, may learn to see their subjectivities in terms of this moralized discourse of the market and the consumer.

This discourse goes beyond the pragmatic acceptance of the workings of the market into its positive moral evaluation as a source of 'freedom' and identity for the individual (Keat and Abercrombie, 1991; Featherstone, 1991). Although marketing can be and has been accused of manipulation and the construction of 'false needs' since at least Packard's *Hidden Persuaders* (1956), it still manages to escape the opprobrium which is attached to 'selling'. Selling tends to be seen in a more coercive manner – the 'hard sell', the 'foot in the door approach'. This is at least partly because marketing is more about constructing what du Gay *et al.* (1997) refer to as the 'identity' between the consumer and the product; in other words getting people to 'desire' the product through identifying the 'necessity' of its purchase with their own style of life. Thus, marketing aims to get the consumer to willingly go out and buy the product, whereas selling suggests the company is going to get to the consumer either literally (through sales people) or metaphorically (through grand gestures of price cutting or other incentives to buy).

This view is also reflected in the concept of *internal* marketing where fellow employees are required to be seen and treated as customers (Gronroos, 1981). Indeed, in some prescriptions, the presence of a *separate* marketing function in organizational structures suggests that marketing may be marginalized and not yet fully developed as a 'guiding philosophy' throughout the organization (Thwaites and Lynch, 1992). Financial institutions increasingly claim this, that they are market-driven, customer-focused organizations. It legitimates their internal practices (including sales) as well as presenting an acceptable face to the outside world where consumer sovereignty is increasingly deemed to be a value in its own right. Abercrombie, for example, describes this more general transition as follows:

> Producers of commodities have, it is said, a greatly different view of their activities. Instead of producing what they think ought to be produced, or what is most technologically advanced, they produce what the consumer wants or is assumed to want. Even more important, this prioritisation of assumed consumer preferences is extended ... to the provision of professional and public services. (Abercrombie, 1994: 44)

In short, ideological conditions towards neo-liberalism (c.f. 'New Left', see Miller, 1987) have raised the value and profile of consumer sovereignty in society. This has helped to increase the managerial legitimacy of marketing, as a discourse if not a management function, in relation to those of other managerial/professional groups (du Gay, 1993 c.f. Whittington and Whipp, 1992; Walker and Child, 1979). Such a discourse is disseminated, mediated and enacted in a number of formal and informal ways. In terms of particular management or marketing approaches and techniques, the prescriptions of literature (such as that documented here), business schools and consultancies which highlight 'good practice' and describe apparently evolutionary trends (e.g. Thwaites and Lynch, 1992; Clarke *et al.*, 1988) have been significant. Inside the organization, this approach is legitimated and implemented in a variety of ways, not least in what are termed customer care programmes (which will be discussed in the next chapter).

In conclusion, we have argued that after a long period of uncertainty and insecurity, marketing has become largely embedded within financial services organizations. It achieved this through gradually ousting both traditionalists and those propounding a sales orientation. By emphasizing its own ability to construct mechanisms for understanding customers and reaching them through the design of products and the effective utilization of different distribution channels, marketing established for itself a close connection with strategy-making inside these organizations. Moreover, the way in which its purpose and function was articulated gave it heightened legitimacy with key external stakeholders such as the regulators as well as providing a means of socializing new employees into the organization. This legitimacy was reinforced by the emphasis on consumer sovereignty in the broader cultural domain and the intensive efforts of marketing consultants, academics and gurus to establish the centrality of marketing to organizational success. However, the emergence of marketing as a dominant discourse is by no means unproblematic. It creates or renders visible new tensions and uncertainties to which we now turn.

## INTERNAL CONTRADICTIONS OF MARKETING DISCOURSE

In much of the literature cited above, examples are presented of how in response to increased competition products and forms of service or distribution have been developed or modified in accordance with a prior assessment of wide-ranging consumer needs or preferences (e.g. see Newman, 1984: Watkins and Wright, 1986; Ennew *et al.*, 1990). These examples are seen as expressions of the successful implementation of marketing within financial services. However, as Smith noted, considerations of cost and profitability clearly limit the possible diversity of the 'offer' (1956: 401) – an organization cannot possibly respond to all needs or preferences, particularly given their apparently increasing differentiation. This side of the marketing concept – the requirement for profitability – is obviously of great importance to marketing practitioners and management in general, especially in periods of intense competition. For example, it is reflected in Clarke *et al.*'s, albeit fine, distinction between a 'marketing orientation' and the emerging and more volatile period of 'strategic marketing control' (1988). In the latter and more comprehensive form of marketing, greater attention is paid to monitoring and control. Nevertheless, even here and in marketing literature generally (c.f. Houston, 1986), the extent to which considerations of cost or profit limit the capacity and incentive to respond to consumer needs is denied (Speed and Smith, 1993), neglected or, at least, underplayed (e.g. Marshall, 1985). It is interesting to note the observation by Walker and Child, in their account of the professionalization of marketing in the UK, that 'since the requirement to make profitable deals is always prominent in its [the company's] relations with customers, the role of ethical standards is always likely to be problematic in marketing' (1979: 47).

The competitive climate of financial services reinforces managerial concerns with costs and profitability as well as stimulating the maintenance and expansion of 'relationships' with consumers, thus creating a tension within the organization and the marketing department in particular which may partially account for why, despite the many claims of (and prescriptions for) marketing 'advancement' cited earlier, one quite recent and sympathetic survey of financial services found that: 'marketing myopia may be masquerading as marketing orientation' and that, once again, 'the marketing challenge has only just begun... and now needs to progress to a more structured approach to market segmentation...' (Egan and Shipley, 1995: 807 and 813). These tensions are revealed in respect of two processes – selecting profitable consumers and selecting profitable products.

## Selecting profitable consumers

Market segmentation typically involves an assessment of the cost/profitability of particular customer types. Indeed, in basic segmentation 'theory', segments should be 'substantial' (profitable) (as well as 'accessible', 'measurable' and 'actionable') (Kotler, 1988). In a more 'advanced' or 'strategic' form and aided by the development and use of information systems, such analyses are more penetrating and sophisticated, extending to individual customer (and product) profitability. The process necessarily involves a form of selection whereby, even in a crude form, relatively costly or unprofitable options are typically selected out. As Clarke *et al*. state 'Each market segment must justify *exploitation* in terms of return on investment. This may not be achieved for a variety of reasons ... too small, too competitive, too volatile or too financially weak' (1988: 15, emphasis added).

   The clearest example of this is the extension of risk segmentation in insurance whereby competitive pressures have led to increasing selectivity through pricing and other means which has excluded certain groups. This trend was acknowledged by one bank insurance director in an interview with the authors:

> We are actually encouraging – largely as a result of targeting – this search for the 'holy grail', the good customer who never makes a claim – we're giving him [sic] such competitive premiums but what's it doing at the other end of the book? ... we're seeing cases now where the choice is not which insurer but do I insure? The premium increases are such that it is becoming beyond some people's means.

Discounting 'good' risks and selecting out others appears to be good 'business sense' and insurance practice in that premiums are related to perceived individual risks. However, as the selectivity increases, the more the competing insurance principle of sharing risk is contradicted. It is not simply a question of excluding certain minority groups such as low-income drivers with convictions in the case of motor insurance. Rather, the 'needs' of a wider population among the poor are being 'selected out'. This is also evident in the recent development of banks' increased selectivity in accepting new account customers. It is somewhat ironic that some of the statistical techniques used in deselection were, as noted earlier, developed in studies on the plight of the poor.

**Selecting profitable products**

As intimated above, management concerns over costs and profitability and their related 'strategic' use of IT have led to the selection of profitable products and distribution channels as well as consumers. This is most evident in the life insurance sector which has long been criticized for encouraging, through variable sales commission rates, the sale of particular products irrespective of consumers' particular needs (Knights and Morgan, 1990). Indeed, we have seen how the Financial Services Act was introduced partly in recognition of this problem (see Chapter 8 for a more detailed discussion). Well-publicized cases whereby the authorities discovered malpractice suggest that the legislation has not been totally effective (OFT, 1992; Knights *et al.*, 1993). Moreover, companies may simply withdraw less-profitable products from their range whether or not certain customers' needs would be better served by them. This represents a product, rather than market-led approach, albeit with due regard to the profitability of the 'offer'.

The selection of 'profitable' products and consumers and the concomitant 'selecting out' of others can, in part, be attributed to managerial short-termism (Speed and Smith, 1993) or the continued predominance of 'non-marketing' professional groups' priorities and discourses within organizations (Hooley and Mann, 1988) such as those of strategists, financial accountants, actuaries, underwriters and sales managers (Whittington and Whipp, 1992; Morgan and Knights, 1990; Burton, 1994). This was certainly the view of one senior marketing executive in an interview with the authors:

> I like to think that I am the customers' champion within the organization ... Our underwriting colleagues are always wanting to pin it down to the street in which you live – I mean talk about segmentation – it's virtually individual risk ... Marketing segmentation is somewhat different from risk segmentation and the question is which one is going to prevail at the end of the day. With accountants driving companies these days, you know – I think I should have been an accountant! We'll have our day again one day!

This view of marketing as the customers' champion echoes claims reported earlier that marketing was considered by some as having greater prestige and social value by articulating consumer preferences and recognizing consumer dominance (see Walker and Child, 1979: 31 and 37). However, the reality is that the marketing orientation is hedged around with limitations. Meeting the needs of the customer only works as long as they can be met *profitably*. Indeed, within the financial services sector, these contradictions go even further because of the particular and continuing difficulty of specifying customer needs.

**The active consumer?**

The concept of the 'sovereign' consumer is central to the theory of a market economy – in this perspective, companies' competitive success in a free market is ultimately determined by their ability to address consumer needs or preferences cost-effectively. Keats explains this ideology in the following terms:

> Consumers are free to choose between the producers . . . and thus a failure of any producer to satisfy these preferences is typically met by the 'exit' response of taking their custom elsewhere . . . What is required of consumers though, is that they should know what their preferences are, and whether they have been satisfied by a particular purchase. But such knowledge, it is typically assumed . . . is something of which every consumer is capable. (Keat, 1994: 28–29)

This theme is echoed in, and reinforced by, marketing theory, though without any sense that these conditions are fundamentally problematic. As Dixon observes, the association of consumer sovereignty with the marketing concept 'remains one of marketing's myths, probably because one of the "wants" of the marketing discipline is a justification of marketing activity beyond that of attaining organizational goals' (1992: 121). For example, Clarke *et al*. note that the '"consumer is king" reflects the marketing orientation . . . [and] . . . the historical transition from the production to marketing control stage is also one from a sellers' to a buyers' market' (1988: 9 and 10). Similarly, in financial services, Speed and Smith claimed to have established a link between financial services companies' financial performance and their consideration of both customer needs and costs/profitability (1993).

Relatedly, the 'sovereign' consumer is also evident in recent debates in social theory concerning post/late modernity. Here, it is claimed that the power or authority of the consumer compared with that of producers (or, in some services, professionals) is growing (Keat *et al.*, 1994) and, as noted earlier, a form of freedom is exercised in choosing and adopting personal identity through consumption. These, albeit distinct, ideas have been subject to considerable criticism, even within marketing literature (e.g. Smith, 1987; Dixon, 1992). In particular, consumers' power to shape 'producer' activity is seen as limited by monopolistic and oligopolistic markets and companies' power to control consumer access to relevant information. Most significantly, and as intimated earlier, 'producers' are active in influencing the formation and nature of consumer preferences themselves. As Warde explains:

> The use of the term 'the consumer' signifies an undersocialized actor; it exaggerates the scope and capacity for individual action. In doing so, however, it authorises the view that consumers choose freely simply because they are not forced to purchase anything in particular. (1994: 66)

There is also debate over the 'motives' or meanings of consumption, with increasing attention given to the 'sign' or 'identity' value of goods and services as opposed to their 'use' or 'exchange' values (c.f. Knights and Morgan, 1993; Gabriel and Lang, 1995). Here, both market segmentation theory and social theory coincide in their recognition of multiple types of consumer/consumption. In certain contexts, for certain people and/or products and services, a more active and/or economically rational form of consumption will occur (i.e. closer to economic and marketing theory) (Smith, 1987; Winward, 1994) though it could be argued that this has been and, to a large extent, remains atypical, especially in financial services (see also Burton, 1994; Egan and Shipley, 1995).

There is some consensus in the literature that for the vast majority of financial services consumers in the UK the key factors in purchasing are *confidence* in the security of the organization and *convenience* of purchase (Carter *et al.*, 1986; McGoldrick and Greenland, 1992; Mitchell and Weisner, 1992: 74). For example, McKechnie, in her overview of consumer buying behaviour literature in financial services noted that 'the personal customer is more interested in the functional quality dimension of financial services (i.e. how the service is delivered) rather than the technical quality dimension (i.e. what is actually received as the outcome of the production process). ... ' (1992: 7).

Even in the relatively transparent market of general insurance, such as motor, where products are simpler, relatively well-known and more price sensitive, convenience of supply is the primary consideration for the majority (Evans and Gumby, 1992). With life insurance and investment products, the convenience of supply of branded products from a trusted organization appears to predominate over 'independent financial advice' where sales staff are legally required to give 'best advice' from a review of products across the market (Ennew, 1992). Indeed, if consumer needs are primarily concerned with service delivery, then companies can be said in many cases to be responding to or, at least, reinforcing them. For example, banks and building societies offer the convenience of high-street branch networks and bundled or packaged and branded products from a largely financially secure base (Sturdy, 1992). Similarly, insurance companies' and banks' development of direct telephone services is founded partly on the provision of a convenient service. Moreover, as in the examples of varying distribution channels cited earlier, service delivery (c.f. product qualities) can be segmented (Lewis, 1989) according to perceived variations in consumer preferences.

The primacy of service over product for consumers is typically explained by reference to the complexity of financial services. They are difficult to evaluate because of their 'intangibility, inseparability and heterogeneity' particularly in the case of long-term investments (McKechnie, 1992: 7). However, an alternative account of an interest in confidence and convenience is that it reflects a lack of interest in, or even indifference towards, financial service products which is reinforced by their complexity. They are not factors in thinking through a purchasing decision but of *avoiding* doing so. Indeed, as we shall see, the relatively 'inert' (c.f. 'active') nature of consumers (in marketing terms, their low involvement in purchase decision-making) is evident even with regard to service quality.

Despite an apparent increase in consumer 'sophistication' ('activity'), which is partly a consequence of heightened marketing activity, they do not typically 'vote with their feet' or 'shop around' (Mitchell and Weisner, 1992; Burton, 1994). As Watkins notes, with some exceptions, such as consumers' switching from bank accounts to interest-bearing building society accounts in the 1980s:

> There is little hard evidence of substantial shopping around by the majority of buyers in choosing financial services, nor of switching between suppliers on a large scale...Convenience of access to branches...and to provision of financial services in the home have been found to account for a significant proportion of supplier choice decisions (Watkins and Wright, 1986). (Watkins, 1990: 48)

This is particularly evident in insurance (Evans and Gumby, 1992; Campbell Keegan, 1984). Indeed consumers' lack of interest in insurance is given as one reason why there is little use of market research (an inherent part of the segmentation strategy) in this area (Davison *et al.*, 1989; see also Watkins and Wright, 1986: 146). In life assurance especially, despite years of successive education campaigns from the industry and increased marketing activity and media attention, the adage that it is not bought but must be sold because of 'ignorance of the product and distaste for the message' remains relevant. At the very least, widespread consumer inertia reduces the incentive for companies to design products primarily on the basis of prior needs analysis; as one senior bank manager told the authors:

> The classical product development step process you go through is really not all that relevant in financial services because you can't have an intelligent conversation with anyone [consumers] about what their requirements are. (Senior marketing manager, bank)

The most frequently cited example by practitioners of responding to needs in product design is merely simplifying the language and presentation of the literature. Designing products tailored to the needs of diffuse segments is even more limited. For many companies there are still only the 'mass' and 'high net-worth' markets and life-stages within them. Instead, particularly with the product diversification associated with 'bancassurance', traditional or standard products are packaged for convenience and presented and sold *as if* they specifically meet the consumer's needs. Indeed, the emergence of hard selling was often claimed as a customer-oriented development as it provided the convenience of 'one-stop' or one supplier 'shopping'. One bank insurance director described this 'mass marketing to units of one [consumer]' as an ideal to be sought. Indeed, such an approach conforms to one part of Smith's account of the segmentation strategy in the sense that associated promotional activities should '... inform market segments of the availability of goods or services produced for *or presented as* meeting their needs with precision' (1956: 399, emphasis added).

The complementarity of market segmentation and product differentiation strategies is noted by Smith, albeit without elaboration. However, it is difficult to distinguish the presentation of products *as if* they are tailored by design with his definition of the supposed 'alternative' product-led or differentiation strategy whereby 'variations in the demands of individual consumers are minimised or brought into line by means of effective use of appealing product claims designed to make a satisfactory volume of demand converge upon the product or product line being promoted' (*ibid.*: 397).

Thus, consumer inertia over product characteristics allows for, or even encourages, the continuation of a (profitable) product-led or sales approach and certainly qualifies the competitive imperative claimed for market segmentation strategies, except perhaps in terms of service delivery. Even here though, the apparent 'need' for convenience, that is, the wider inertia reflected in a reluctance to shop around or switch supplier, is open to abuse especially when cost pressures are heightened. Banks in particular are still conscious of the 'demonstrable fact that, once caught, a ... customer very rarely transfers his [sic] allegiance' (Newman, 1984: 306), and market aggressively to certain groups of people accordingly. Their strategy to 'farm' the captive customer-base by cross-selling and following customers' life-stages is informed more by the resulting cost savings (claimed to be as much as 3–7 times cheaper than selling to new customers) than responding to diffuse needs. Cross-selling is often achieved by bundling products together or product tie-ins such as the provision of building and contents insurance and other services with property loans. Such 'one-stop' packages may, as we have noted, conform to the 'need' for convenience, but they do not necessarily give 'better value' and serve to lock-in the consumer further (Eaglesham, 1992; Sturdy, 1992b). As one bank insurance marketing manager told the authors:

> You need to really aggravate the customer before he [sic] does go. I suppose from the organization's point of view, the more you bundle things together and tie them up, the more difficult it is for the consumer to leave ... There is a danger that we tie-in a customer so much that we can then just rip him [sic] off.

This is not to argue crudely that banks and other companies are omni-potent – the failure of most attempts to sell life assurance in face-to-face interactions suggests some consumer resilience (Knights *et al.*, 1993; Smith, 1987). Nor are we saying that companies always simply exploit customers. Rather, we raise questions about the claims that competitive pressures have led companies to respond to consumer needs in terms of products and service delivery. Competition is also a condition of the 'selecting out' of 'costly' consumers and products. The latter, product-led approach, is facilitated by consumer inertia (see Houston, 1986) which also allows the emphasis to be placed on cost containment and profitability rather than the other side of the marketing concept – responding to needs. Indeed, it opens up oppor-tunities to shape further the needs and preferences of consumers. As one bank senior manager commented, 'a lot of people are happy to be spoon-fed'.

As intimated earlier, the power of companies over consumers is also shaped by the extent of market concentration. In general this can result from the construction of 'entry barriers', through links with suppliers for instance. It is reflected in the business phrase: 'secure the distri-bution and you have got the sales'. Nevertheless, and as we shall see in Chapter 8, with banks seeking and taking an increasing share of some insurance markets (Shelton, 1991) and sector concentration increasing in general (Burton, 1994) one can see how:

> Much marketing is about avoidance of competition and the domin-ance of markets – i.e. marketing benefits the firm *not by satisfying customers* but by establishing quasi-monopolistic power over them. (Whittington and Whipp, 1992: 19–20, emphasis added)

**Limitations of the marketing orientation: the example of disclosure**

One of the most interesting and obvious examples over the last few years of how these contradictions around the active consumer reveal themselves has been the discussion about the disclosure of charges on long-term savings products (see also Chapter 8 for further discussion). As has been referred to earlier, consumers have generally been disinterested in the details of these products. The argument that these details are highly technical and difficult to understand was presented for years by the industry as an explanation of why consumers were not interested. Marketing information was confined to very limited 'feel-good' messages based on the belief that the consumer required confidence and security. Lury, for example, states that

> if you ask people what makes a 'good' financial services advertisement…they will tell you that it is [one]…that tells you that the organization is 'big, warm, friendly and careful with your money'. Why is this? Is it because people want financial institutions to project an image of being big, warm, friendly and caring or is it because financial institutions have spent the last ten years telling people that they are big, warm, friendly and caring? The answer is both. (1994: 96)

The argument that everything is too complicated for the lay person to understand is, of course, characteristic of organizations and groups which are trying to defend themselves against outside scrutiny. In the case of financial services and long-term savings products, the reasons are not too difficult to find. The characteristic product pricing structure for long-term insurance and investment products was based on ensuring that the sales person's commission and the company's expense in setting up the business was taken out of the premiums in the early months, even though the product might be sold on the basis that the customer would be paying into it for twenty years.

There is little doubt that the sellers of these products were concerned that customers would be scared away if they knew the amount of their supposed savings which were being lost in the early years. They were also concerned that if these costs were revealed, customers would tend to shop around more and see whether they could get a better deal at one company rather than another which, in fact, they could because these costs and their effects on both early surrender values and final values could be tremendous, but varied. Companies resisted commission disclosure for years on the grounds that, firstly, customers would never be able to understand it and, secondly, even if they did they would be misled because, the companies argued, final values were affected much more by investment performance than by charges. However, since as they themselves acknowledged, investment performance in the past was no guaranteed guide to investment performance in the future, the only firm (financial) evidence which customers were likely to have was derived from project surrender values based on existing charges (using a standardised investment return ratio).

It is important to note, given the prominence of consumer-oriented marketing rhetoric from and within firms, that the only reason why they eventually moved to a system of disclosure is because they were *forced* to do so by outside bodies. Successive investigations by the Consumers Association, the Office of Fair Trading and the Securities and Investment Board produced evidence that customers did want this evidence, that they could understand it if it was presented in a reasonable manner (free of deliberate technical obfuscation), and that they did intend to act on this information when choosing where to buy their long-term investment products. Thus, by the mid-1990s a disclosure regime had been introduced by the regulators which required companies to state their charges in a way which was simple and clear. This information revealed the impact of early surrender on the values which customers would retrieve from their initial outlay.

In short, in spite of claiming to be 'customer-focused' and 'market-driven', companies did their best to conceal information about crucial aspects of their products. However, their legitimations were swept aside. This raises the interesting question of how companies and consumers will interact in the future. Now that the information has to be revealed, there is a general expectation that two things will follow. Firstly, some companies will use this as an active marketing tool by structuring their costs in ways which reduce the impact of early surrender and show that they are better value than their competitors. This is indeed beginning to happen in certain segments of the market and is encouraging new entrants such as Marks and Spencer, Tescos, Sainsburys and Virgin to advertise themselves and their financial products as good value compared to the traditional companies in the industry. In turn, this is leading some companies to respond by improving their cost structure, partly through mergers and takeovers which create economies of scale (these themes are once again taken up in more detail in Chapter 8). In doing so, the companies themselves are stimulating further the emergence of a new type of consumer, one who is more concerned with issues of value rather than simply image and convenience. This emergence is also encouraged by the regulators who wish to improve competition on the basis of cost within the industry through revealing more information to more active consumers. This reinforces our previous arguments about the tensions within the marketing concept and that it is important to distinguish between the rhetorical claims of marketing and what this actually means in practice for how organizations in markets work. In real terms, what has actually brought about increased customer focus has not simply been the influence of marketing and its campaigns, but that of politicians, regulators and consumer groups.

## CONCLUSION

In this chapter, the aim has been to critically examine claims of an increasingly market-led approach within UK retail financial services. In the first part of the chapter we examined the general claims which marketing makes about itself; in the second section we looked at how marketing had become adopted inside financial services organizations. The main argument was that marketing met with resistance from a combination of traditional cultures and challenges from an aggressive sales orientation. We argued that hard selling became incorporated or enlarged in many financial organizations as they sought to transform themselves. Selling became the new language and mantra, but this was simply a development of the production/supply driven approach to the world which marketing sought to displace.

The dominance of hard selling was short-lived, even if a concern with sales levels was not. Its limitations as a form of modernization of financial services organizations were exposed by two processes. Firstly, heightened levels of competition brought even more suppliers into the marketplace whilst the number of buyers remained limited and indeed declined during the late 1980s and early 1990s. The sales orientation had little to offer in terms of ways of dealing with these competitive problems other than by exhorting more and more sales. However, this led into the second problem which was that within financial services, increasing regulation was making it increasingly difficult to sell more. Regulation was setting higher standards as to what could be regarded as proper selling, and failure to meet these standards led to a range of punishments. The call to sell more therefore met a regulatory barrier where the demand was to sell better, that is more appropriately.

These developments, combined with the wider emergence of a discourse of the sovereign consumer, meant that by the mid-1990s marketing was being increasingly placed at the centre of the operation of financial services organizations. Marketing discourse, practices and techniques could also be fitted well into the context of strategic discourse which has been described earlier. Marketing legitimated itself in terms of its customer-focus which could be demonstrated through its analysis of customer needs which fed into the product and distribution development and costing process. In strategic terms, this helped reinforce both the sense of control over a complex environment which was being lost and the sense of legitimacy for the organization and its role. Serving the customer through a long-term relationship became a binding slogan throughout financial institutions. It legitimated their role to the outside world by attempting to separate them from the old, unfriendly image of the bank or insurance company and, as we shall see, it became a way to bind their employees together in a more coherent or at least business-oriented way than previously, as well as in a language which accorded with more general notions of consumerism.

However, we argued that there were significant limitations and tensions in the way in which marketing conceptualized its role and that of the consumer and in how it acted within the financial services organizations. Serving the customer was interpreted within a framework where the overriding interest was in cost control and short-term profitability. Increasingly, this meant that certain customers would not be served as the companies could not expect to make a profit out of them. It also meant that certain products might be withdrawn, regardless of consumer needs, if they no longer delivered profitability. Finally, it meant that certain types of information would not be revealed to the customers because to do so might upset the established way in which the companies worked and achieved their profit. Some of these limitations have been exposed by the actions of new entrants, consumer associations, the Office of Fair Trading and the regulators. These actions, which are ongoing, began to push companies to reveal more information to customers in the expectation that this will work to increase competition, reduce consumer inertia and produce better value products.

Marketing, can claim these changes as a vindication of their overall goal of serving the customer (albeit within the parameters of organizational goals of profitability or survival). The sections of the organization which have taken the brunt of the blame for resisting these changes tend to be the financial and actuarial departments which are accused of making things unnecessarily complicated, and the sales department for not being concerned enough about how to serve the customers. The strategic level and the marketing function may have received some criticism, but it is mainly in a form with which they can work in order to extend themselves and reinforce their domination. Their claims are still strong in that they can assert that it is only through a greater attention to strategic and marketing issues that companies can succeed in this new environment. Thus they are able to feed on the problems of the industry and in the process become stronger. In the next chapter we examine how these changes and their contradictions have been reflected in changing patterns of work, employment and management control in the industry.

# 7 Changing Work Experiences and Practices: From Black Coats to Service Smiles

## INTRODUCTION

In this chapter, we explore the ways in which companies have sought to reshape and control employees in accordance with strategic and consumer discourses. Some observers have linked these changes to certain dimensions of the discourse of 'strategic HRM (human resource management)' (e.g. Storey, 1995; Cressey and Scott, 1992). Indeed, Personnel practitioners in the industry have, like those in IT and marketing discussed earlier, sought to transform themselves into 'strategic' (HRM) actors. However, this is not our main focus here (see Boxall, 1996; Purcell, 1995; Watson, 1995). Rather, we wish to draw out in more detail the organizational changes discussed in the previous two chapters and what they mean for the nature and experience of employment in financial service companies. In doing so, we consider the ways in which subjects respond to new and emerging discourses. In particular, we explore what is probably the main aspect of change and, given some variation across organizations and sectors in the field (Egan and Shipley, 1995; Storey *et al.*, 1997), one that appears to be more or less common – the shift to the employee as market/consumer-oriented and associated changes in forms of management control.

There is a long tradition in the UK of studies of the transformation of clerical, 'white-collar/blouse' or non-manual labour, mostly out of a concern with social (e.g. class and gender) stratification and *occupational* change – often based around the question of whether this group constitutes part of the service class or is becoming proletarianized (Klingender, 1935; Lockwood, 1958; Blackburn, 1967; Crompton and Jones, 1984). This debate continues today with the increasing focus on the plight of middle managers in de-layered organizations (e.g. Scarbrough and Burrell, 1996; Herriot *et al.*, 1996; Casey, 1995). Until very recently, the case of financial services was typically regarded as special, at least for male employees. For example, Storey argues that employment practices in banking had been 'out of step' with those elsewhere in the UK (1995: 24). The relatively protected and regulated form of the sector and mostly steady postwar employment and business growth had allowed the maintenance of an 'aristocratic' status among male clerical employees. This privileged position has been attributed to insurance and banking clerks in studies of non-manual labour from the nineteenth century onwards (Lockwood, 1958; Anderson, 1976; Crompton, 1979):

> The banks offered life-time employment, structured careers and paternalistic welfare-oriented personnel policies. Above all, the banking scene had been one of order, predictability, hierarchy and bureaucracy. Deference and 'gentlemanly' values were perpetuated during a period when these values had long before collapsed in other industries. (Storey, 1995: 24).

Of course, there is a danger of romanticizing and generalizing the nature of clerical work in financial services and, as Storey (1995) points out, of understating historical discontinuities. Even at the time of the recent acceleration of changes in employment in the late 1980s, it was well-established that the vast majority of jobs were highly routinized and that for women (a growing majority since the 1960s), and increasingly men, without professional qualifications, career opportunities were non-existent or limited (Crompton, 1979; Crompton and Jones, 1984). Nevertheless, as we shall see, there have been significant changes in the nature of financial services employment recently which are contested, continuing, piecemeal and with uncertain outcomes. Apart from the continuing decline in employment in a number of large companies and its consequences for organizational/occupational commitment and the geographical shift in some of the most routine jobs, the key dimension of the changes is in terms of the personal characteristics required of, and organizationally valued in, employees. As implied from our analysis in the previous chapter, this can be summarized as a shift from an administration to a sales and/or marketing *culture*. Once again, Storey summarizes this well although he does not adopt our distinction between sales and marketing discourses:

> Loyalty, caution, conformity and accuracy in every detail were qualities highly prized under the old regime. Under the new, the 'human

resource' was expected to be performance driven, competitive, sales-oriented and non-risk averse. (1995: 37)

Moreover, as Halford *et al.* emphasize, this change is gendered, in the deployment of both femininity and a transformed (i.e. more competitive) masculinity. In banking for example:

> this [restructuring] has involved re-evaluating the traditional masculine ethos of banking, including downgrading the branch manager who was previously the (literal) embodiment of all that was valued in traditional banking (the remote, austere and judgemental father figure). (1997: 74)

Whether one sees these developments as representing a 'sea change . . . crisis . . . [or] paradigm shift' in employment relations (Cressey and Scott, 1992: 87 and 95) or, more cautiously, that it is premature to claim the arrival of a new, coherent or 'HRM model' (Storey, 1995), is a matter for debate. Nevertheless, the new employment practices compare with (both lag behind and exemplify) broader patterns elsewhere – loosely, 'strategic HRM'. However, as we have consistently argued, such changes should not be seen as having clear start and finish points. Nor should they be regarded simply as a rational managerial response to environmental shifts such as sectoral (de)regulation and cost pressures (e.g. bad debts in banking), the late 1980s economic recession and developments in IT (see Cressey and Scott, 1992). Rather, we see the changes as part of the wider, longer-term and complex dynamic within the field of financial services through which actors have sought to come to terms with and control their worlds in new and sometimes competing and internally contradictory ways. These changes as a whole are summarized in Table 7.1.

The rest of the chapter examines the significance of these changes in relation to our argument concerning the shift to strategic discourse. We first of all examine changes in the career structure of employees and the shift towards customer service. We secondly illustrate this by reference to a case study of training for a telephone selling operation in financial services. Our argument is that these changes are part of the process of creating the 'truth' of strategic discourse. This 'truth' lies in its power to construct organizations and subjects in particular ways. In organizational terms, bureaucratic hierarchies are gradually scaled down in order to produce more streamlined and cost-conscious forms of management control. This drive towards organizational restructuring is part of the process of implementing a marketing orientation where (profitable) customer service is articulated as the highest priority. Strategy discourse identifies the necessity for organizational restructuring from the analysis and claims of marketing information and perspectives. At the individual level, this restructuring requires new orientations on the part of employees – a recognition of uncertainty, instability and the importance of customer service.

*Table 7.1*   Changes in retail financial services

| 1950–60s | 1980–90s | Processes |
|---|---|---|
| Male career, mainly 2-tier school leaver entry and no poaching (full-time staff) | Occupational insecurity and horizontal 'career' strategies, multi-tier and sector entry including graduates (growth in part-time and casual staff) | Strategic discourses |
| Seniority pay and annual increments | Job-evaluated and differentiated pay, including performance targets and profit links | New and increased competition |
| Technical primacy and division of labour ('tellers') – banks and insurers with account and policy numbers | Strategic-service/sales link ('sellers' of product range) – bancassurers with customer profiles | Demise of paternalism, continued bureaucracy and then rise of HRM with flatter structures |
| Producer authority – e.g. underwriting and credit risk assessment (unhurried) | (Regulated) consumer authority and rhetoric (pressure to sell/serve) | Continued feminization |
| Branches at core plus central administration | Admin/service centres plus multi-distribution (retail branches) | Marketization |
| Middle-class unions/Staff Associations | Resurgence of union interest; decline in internalism | Automation front and back – Taylorist? |
| Market stability (cartel) and simplicity | Market change and complexity | Continued, but fluctuating, unionization |

*Table 7.1   ( contd.)*

| 1950–60s | 1980–90s | Processes |
|---|---|---|
| Paper-based work | Keyboard and telephone-based | Credentialism |
| Managers and clerks | Service and 'manufacture' | De/re-regulation |
| Local autonomy (e.g. branch) | Central (IT) control with delegated autonomy | Strategic control and integration of functions |
| Employment growth | Employment decline | Rationalization |
| Male-dominated and strict gender segregation | Female majority and complex segregation | Repeal of Truck Acts 1987 |
| Banks' and insurers' images as solid and austere | Image of openness/ accessibility | Twin proletarianization and polarization? |
| 'Feminine' (office/male) support and paternalistic management | 'Feminine' service staff and competitive 'masculine' management | Business growth and recession |

## CAREERS AND SEGREGATION

In the nineteenth century, there were waiting lists for clerical jobs in banking and insurance. Positions were filled by the sons of the clergy, military and medical profession as well as from the sons of those already working in the companies. (Lockwood, 1958: 27). This was to change with the expansion of education and non-manual employment. Unlike in the civil service, entrants from public schools and universities were not particularly important in this sector except, as we saw in Chapter 2, at the very highest levels – almost all promotions were from within. In banking for example, boys from lower-middle-class backgrounds could start from school and, with favourable reports, rise through senior clerical and junior-appointed posts into the socially respected and secure position of branch manager. In 1956, the Westminster Bank asserted that 'one out of every two or three young men [recruits]...*must* reach Managerial or high Executive positions' (*Manchester Guardian*, 28 March, quoted in Lockwood, 1958: 65), although there were very few opportunities or, until recently, even managerial posts beyond branch manager levels (Blackburn, 1967: 74; Halford *et al.*, 1997). Despite

*Table 7.2*   Average weekly salaries of banking and insurance clerkss, London 1929–30

|        | Under 25 | 25+  | All   |
|--------|----------|------|-------|
| Male   | 42s 6d   | 105s | 82s 6d |
| Female | 40s      | 65s  | 50s   |

rationalization of work in financial services generally, especially since the 1960s, some form of male organizational career has persisted. This has been achieved by employment growth, a reliance on the internal labour market (i.e. school leavers) and, in particular, by the employment of women over the same period.

Compared to other non-manual sectors, there was initial employer resistance to the recruitment of women to financial services at the turn of the century, especially in banking (Supple, 1970; Lockwood, 1958: 122). In the subsequent feminization of clerical work, the sector continued to lag behind numerically until quite recently, reaching 50 per cent of employees in the late 1980s (*Employment Gazette*, February 1989). As elsewhere, women were recruited into different jobs to men (e.g. secretaries, typists, receptionists, telephonists, machine operators). There were also forms of horizontal segregation that were specific to the sector such as that between life insurance sales/building society branch managers (men) and office 'support' (women) staffs (see also Crompton and Sanderson, 1990). However, in some cases, they would receive similar salaries *initially* and perform the same tasks as men, for example in occupations such as bank cashiers (from the 1950s) or insurance underwriting clerks (Blackburn, 1967; Halford *et al.*, 1997). Generally this 'equality' would only last for a short time because men would move onwards and upwards into more 'technical' and/or supervisory/managerial and better-paid positions. This is illustrated in Table 7.2 from Lockwood (1958: 47; reproduced with permission of the author).

This segregation was achieved through direct discrimination, including the expectation, until the late 1960s, that women would leave on marriage – the average length of stay was four years in banking (Blackburn, 1967: 74; Halford *et al.*, 1997) – as well as indirectly through recruiting women with fewer and/or inferior qualifications. Even as recently as the 1980s, 7 per cent of 16-year-old female school leavers (i.e. with only minimal educational qualifications) were recruited into financial services compared to only 2 per cent of males (Povall, 1986). Moreover, women were not encouraged or expected to study for professional qualifications (an increasing important condition for hierarchical progression) (Rajan, 1984). However, partly as a result of equal-opportunity legislation, related EOC investigations into financial services companies in the 1980s (e.g. Barclays) and an expectation (largely unrealized) of staff shortages, employment policies began to change. Moreover, by the 1980s increasing numbers of women were taking and passing the CII (Chartered Insurance Institute) and IOB (Institute of Bankers) exams (e.g. women represented 3 per cent of ACII passes in 1970 and 26 per cent in 1983) (Crompton and Sanderson, 1986) and entering management levels (e.g. 18 per cent of managers in Halford *et al.*'s bank case study were women – 1997; c.f. Kerfoot, 1993). However, by this time a third, graduate-entry, recruitment tier was being developed which restricted progress for others (Crompton and Jones, 1984). Also, there was an increase in management grades in specialist head office positions which were not always open to branch staff. Thus, combined with more recent changes (see below), Halford *et al.* question whether the large and growing number of women at senior clerical levels in branches are about to make a career breakthrough or are in grades being constructed as alternative (i.e. final) 'career positions' (1997: 48–9).

## REPRESENTATION

Contrary to popular conceptions and to the once 'aristocratic' status of banking and insurance employees among non-manuals, there is a long history of unionization in financial services. For example, the Guild of Insurance Officials (for clerks) was formed in 1917 and affiliated to the TUC in 1937 (Ashton, 1971; Bain 1970). Similarly, in banking, the Bank Officers' Guild was, according to Lockwood, initially successful with 'the general depersonalisation of relations that followed the large-scale amalgamations... after the First World War'. By 1921, membership represented almost one-half of bank staffs in England and Wales (1958: 149).

However, companies responded to these developments by forming (internal) staff associations and it was not until the 1970s that unionization and employer recognition began to develop significantly again such that, by 1979, 55 per cent of finance employees were union members (Price and Bain, 1983: 54–5). There was considerable debate about the nature, causes and consequences of this development, particularly in terms of the specific character of white collar and, especially, finance unions and their members' class consciousness (Prandy and Blackburn, 1965; Blackburn, 1967; Crompton, 1979; Price and Bain, 1983; Hyman and Price 1983; Prandy *et al.*, 1983). In short, the process can be linked to the continued relative decline in terms, conditions and prospects with rationalization, bureaucratization and feminization. For example, it is important to emphasize that as early as 1955 'the average bank clerk of twenty-eight was getting a salary only a little higher than the average manual wage for men' (Lockwood, 1958: 51–2), and in the late 1960s salaries in insurance and banking fell below the non-manual male average (Crompton, 1979). In addition, the social legitimacy of unions in Britain at the time had increased. However, a 'no poaching' agreement between banking employers and limited comparable employment opportunities elsewhere encouraged employee dependence/'loyalty'. In addition, paternalistic benefits such as low-interest loans/mortgages, subsidized pensions (e.g. two-thirds of final salary after 40 years in banking) and often extensive sports and social facilities were commonplace even in smaller companies.

More generally, it was evident that finance unions and, even more so, staff associations remained particularly conservative if fiercely competitive (Storey, 1983; Heritage, 1980; Enderwick 1984). Similar debates have resurfaced today with increased union membership and industrial action and an apparent decline in 'internalism', if not in relative conservatism (Gall, 1997; Cressey and Scott, 1992). This has been linked to some more hostile and decentralized stances to collective employee representation and bargaining associated with the recent phase of organizational restructuring to which we now turn.

## THE END OF AN ERA?

> The era of the benevolent employer is past. Now we have hard nosed executives who are driven by sheer profit. Staff don't believe [their] loyalty is rewarded. The employers expect more and more for less and less. There has been a decline in trust and a feeling of no fairness and justice. (BIFU Deputy General Secretary, quoted in Gall, 1997: 230)

Such claims and feelings are commonplace. However, it is important to place changes in their context. There is, for example, nothing new about claims of the demise of paternalism in financial services (e.g. Blackburn, 1967; Crompton, 1979), nor of declining opportunities for promotion. The following quotation concerning the latter in large organizations including banks, is perhaps as relevant today as it was when it was made, 40 years ago:

> ...due to the general reduction in the ratio of managerial to lower office positions that accompanies rationalization, and to the policy of recruiting persons to these superior positions from outside the clerical grades. (Lockwood, 1958: 62)

This is not to downgrade the significance of the current changes, but to recognize that certain elements and their effects are less novel than is often assumed. In particular, rationalization and shifts in the form and location of employment, particularly with technological change, have occurred periodically.

**Job security and promotion**

The 1980s saw a massive increase in employment in financial services (e.g. 44 per cent between 1980 and 1990 in banking – Cressey and Scott, 1992) in response to growing and new markets – it even became fashionable to work in certain parts of the sector. Also, in banking many more managerial grades were created beyond the branch system for specialist (e.g. marketing) posts in head offices (Halford *et al.*, 1997). As a consequence of this employment growth, but particularly of the long history of relative job security in this non-manual group (Anderson, 1976) and the low-transferability of skills, the reshaping, relocation, containment and cutting of jobs, especially in banking, came as a shock and threat to many in the industry. In absolute terms, numbers declined in the major banks (see Cressey and Scott, 1992) from 445 000 to 370 000 between 1990–96, a process which has continued since and extended particularly into the building society sector (Storey *et al.*, 1997). For example, it was reported that NatWest had cut 23 000 jobs since 1989 with more to follow (Storey, 1995).

In general, the reductions were achieved through voluntary and compulsory redundancies and early retirement programmes for those over or approaching 50. As noted in the previous chapter, the latter practice allowed for the removal of those deemed to be too steeped in what was coming to be seen as an inappropriate (non-sales/service) culture (Burton, 1994; Halford *et al.*, 1997). The main targets were employees in branches as these were reorganized and reduced (clearing banks' branches fell from 12 315 in 1968 to 8912 in 1991, and have fallen further subsequently) (Storey, 1995) as part of the 'strategic' management of increasingly diverse distribution channels. Those within managerial levels were also targeted as hierarchical and grading structures were cut. Of particular significance was what a Cutting Edge TV programme in 1996 referred to be the 'death of the bank manager' (*Cutting Edge*, 1996) whereby it was claimed that in one bank, a whole generation was removed in less than six months. For many of those remaining, the cuts had the effect of reducing what promotion opportunities there were and, most significantly, undermining a sense of job/employment security that had been a central aspect of the sectoral culture (Herriot *et al.*, 1996).

**Careers, pay and measurement**

This situation was exacerbated by qualitative changes in employment. In particular, hierarchies were flattened. For example, in one bank 26 grades below branch manager were reduced to seven, while in another, 13 management grades were cut to five (Cressey and Scott, 1992). In addition, company, if not broader careers, have been curtailed by the increased recruitment of specialists from other (e.g. retail) sectors and financial service companies, even if the no-poaching arrangement largely persisted at branch level. Overall, employees are increasingly being weaned off the company career and encouraged to become more proactive and 'strategic' in marketing themselves (see du Gay, 1996) and pursuing 'personal development' in terms of horizontal moves, general (c.f. job or sector specific) skill-acquisition and changing employers. This is creating a new role and ethos for HRM and the training function (Antonacopoulou, 1998) as well as for the professional institutes (e.g. IOB and CII) which have long been at the centre of firms' employee development and credentialist policies.

As hierarchical careers are transformed, the expectation of financial progression is increasingly through individual and/or group (e.g. department, branch, team) performance (e.g. sales) and profit-related payments or other rewards. For example, Gall reports how in some cases annual cost-of-living increases have been removed (1997), and Burton's

(1994) study of a bank describes how non-managerial staff in the branches received prizes from a consumer goods catalogue for reaching branch-based targets. Individual performance-related pay (PRP) has been adopted cautiously; indeed, at the Midland Bank it was regarded as being incompatible with the emphasis on clerical team-working (Storey *et al.*, 1997). Nevertheless, more generally (apart from its long tradition in life assurance as sales commission), having been initially focused on managerial posts and call-centre staff, PRP is being increasingly applied to other service staff. Managers are being set or sometimes 'agreeing' personal objectives and targets against which they are assessed, rewarded and sometimes compared in league tables. In the branch environment, these were typically initially focused on sales or income-generating activities (e.g. insurance, loans, account charges, lead generation) and cost control (e.g. overtime). In one case, branch managers were set targets for 17 different services such that only one out of 22 managers in the area achieved them all (Burton, 1994). As we have seen in the previous chapter, attention shifted to a customer-relationship focus such that service measures and customer retention were also included. Also, at a broader level, managers' targets were increasingly linked to strategic objectives (e.g. market share) and therefore orientations as well as the development of particular skills or 'competences'. In this way, the concern within strategic discourses with measurement is extended to employees and their performance. Similarly, profit-related rewards have also been introduced as part of the broader cultural shift. This is illustrated in a quotation in Storey *et al.* (1997: 36) from a senior manager at the Co-operative bank where the notion of profit has somewhat distinctive connotations – 'unless we get [the staff's] minds linked with profit, we aren't going to get anywhere with the corporate plan'.

The changes in career patterns are not simply a consequence of job and grading level cuts. They also derive from related restructuring of tasks associated with the use of new technologies and the increasing range of services offered. This is illustrated in the changes to the situation of the bank branch manager who for a long time had control over all branch activities, except for some of the larger commercial accounts. In Halford *et al.*'s case study, these responsibilities have been largely distributed elsewhere in the structure. For example, the 'satelliting' of branches, whereby most are downgraded to retail service outlets, combined with the centralization of much corporate and SME business to specialist units at regional and/or national levels has reduced autonomy.

These developments compounded the earlier effects of credit-scoring systems in the case of personal lending, although failures ('laxed' lending) in this area restored some discretion (Halford *et al.*, 1997; Storey, 1995).

Overall, Cressey and Scott (1992) argue that current changes in banking have meant that recruitment and careers have become increasingly *segmented* into multiple tiers and four particular streams:

1. Mainly female/part-time/clerical for peak demand and routine processing;
2. The main, but declining, service/retail staff in the new branch environment;
3. Technical/Specialists in HO and computing;
4. Management 'high fliers'.

This might also be applied to areas of insurance, both within banking (bancassurance) and especially in direct (telephone-based) lines. The four streams certainly contrast with the previous dominance of full-timers and school-leaver (two-tier) entry into the branch networks. For example, the recruitment of school leavers fell from an average of 35 000 per annum in 1984 to 5500 in 1994 (Storey, 1995). As noted earlier, another important change is the willingness of companies to recruit specialists beyond computing, such as in marketing, from other industries. However, in the main the changes are largely quantitative in that graduate recruitment for 'high fliers' has been established since the early 1980s, although this has been cut back or even, in the case of the Co-operative bank, discontinued. Also, previously, there were few opportunities to move beyond the branch or regional system despite the growing number of managerial grades here. Similarly, data-processing centres have been used since the 1960s and filled with predominantly female recruits.

Halford *et al.* (1997) are critical of the view that branch banking careers have been 'dismembered' (Cressey and Scott, 1992: 84), arguing that changes are more complex. For example, they point to the perhaps short-term career gains derived from cuts in older workers. More significant are those opened up for full-timers with the demise of the branch manager and rise in part-timers who are mostly excluded from hierarchical progression (1997: 117). They claim that with the exception of cashiers (albeit the largest and mainly female category), secretaries and the former 'jumping off' post of Securities Clerk, 'no full-time clerical job within 'Sellbank' [a pseudonym] has been isolated from the promotion ladder' (1997: 120). They also note that within promotable job domains and regardless of A-level qualifications, a new gendered division is underway – 'women appear to have as much chance as men of moving rapidly through clerical grades, *as long as they do not have children*' (*ibid.*: 122, emphasis added). Finally, they suggest that with increased and individualized performance pressures being concentrated on management grades, senior clerical grades (which often attract similar salaries to achievable management posts) are considered as less risky and more secure to some staff at least (*ibid.*: 123).

**New technologies, jobs and conditions**

Although they argue that it has not been the dominant factor (compared, for example, to cost reduction *per se*), Cressey and Scott point out how the development and use of information and communication technology (ICT) has been an important element in structural changes. We have already seen in an earlier chapter how it became central to the emergence of strategic management. Also, most visibly, EFTPOS (Electronic Fund Transfer at the Point Of Sale, e.g. in supermarkets), extended ATMs (Automatic Teller machines) and telephone banking and insurance have effectively bypassed branch structures (see also Gandy and Chapman, 1996). At the same time, the automation of back-office functions (e.g. cheque clearing, account/policy data) has continued to develop since the first uses of mainframe computers, and is located in regional or national 'factory-like' (Storey, 1995) centres or even outsourced completely.

As intimated above, new jobs have also been created, albeit not as many as those lost, and new conditions introduced or expanded. In particular, the use of part time staff, principally women with children, increased steadily in the 1980s (8.5–12 per cent of bank employees in 1980–91 – Cressey and Scott, 1992) and accelerated subsequently. They tend to be employed at peak and non-traditional times in call and processing centres in banking and insurance and as cashiers in bank, building society and insurance branches/service centres (Kerfoot, 1993; Halford *et al.*, 1997; O'Reilly, 1992). These jobs and/or employees all lie largely outside of career ladders. By contrast, as we shall see in the following section, other service-based jobs in branches have been constructed and in some cases given a higher status than their clerical predecessors (Burton, 1994; Halford *et al.*, 1997).

**Individual performance**

Implicit in the above account of employment practices is a transformation of the *cultures* (e.g. occupational and organizational) of financial
services. Clearly, the loss of job security and changes in careers and
reward systems suggest or require shifts in work attitudes and values
such as organizational commitment and individual competitiveness.
These have been, to varying degrees, the object of management
through communication and staff development practices and strategies. In particular, for managers especially, where changes in rewards
and career have been most pronounced, a more competitive ethos is
emerging. For example, in one large composite insurer all middle
managers were recently required to re-apply for their jobs in a new
flattened grading structure. However, the transition is typically illustrated from banking by examining the situation of the bank manager in
earlier periods.

In bank branches, managers were seen, and saw themselves, as having a comfortable life, aloof, unhurried, cautious, reliable and trustworthy – customers came to them and, in most cases, were deferential.
Such an image of reliability was appropriate to the expansion of banking up to the end of the 1970s as more of the population opened
accounts. As banks competed more aggressively, sought to cut costs
and expanded their product ranges, it became less so. With changes in
employment practices and redundancies, combined with the recession
and bad debts of the early 1990s, it was soon unrecognizable. They
were told to go to the customer, they had performance targets imposed
from 'strategic' priorities and in some cases were motivated by fear.
This led to high levels of stress and absenteeism (*Cutting Edge*, 1996).
While such developments effectively undermined a form of male dominance in banking, they represented an emergent form of competitive
masculinity (Kerfoot and Knights, 1993; Halford *et al.*, 1997; c.f.
McDowell, 1998, who discusses changing forms of gendered identity
in the trading rooms of the City's financial institutions). As we noted
in the previous chapter, the contrast is also evident in the development
of bancassurance where banks, initially at least, sought to incorporate
the preexisting competitive (and masculine) ethos of life assurance
sales (Knights and Morgan, 1990). As we have described elsewhere,
this attempt to align market objectives and organizational structure
was plagued with implementation problems arising from the clash of
cultures.

At the risk of overstatement, we can summarize the differences as follows. Bankers [managers] are generally *risk averse*; they seek to develop a *long term relationship* with the client; they are rewarded on the *basis of seniority and qualifications*...*Insurance sellers* are concerned to *maximize their commission* based earnings; *turnover* amongst this group is very high and there is therefore traditionally very little loyalty to the company (and *little* expectation of 'career progression') or *expectation of a long term-relationship* with the client. (Morgan *et al.*, 1994: 182)

To a certain extent, the emerging performance culture was directed and/or filtered down to non-managerial staffs, particularly through an emphasis on sales, and a similar clash occurred – tellers to sellers (Burton, 1991). For example, it became clear through what was happening to managers that a more competitive orientation was increasingly valued. However, as we argued in the last chapter, a focus on sales alone increasingly came to be seen as neither sufficient nor effective. The orientation of all staff to the business environment, especially those at lower levels, was consciously redirected towards 'customer service'. This was, and continues to be sought through culture-change programmes and related initiatives. In addition to such initiatives, the promotion of customer service in organizations is being developed through the more or less unintended consequences of other structural and physical changes such as the redesign of branches (Burton, 1994; McGoldrick and Greenland, 1994) and the increasing proportion of staff who have regular customer contact. An emphasis on culture management and customer orientation is a core element of more general trends in UK business since the 1980s (see du Gay, 1996; Sturdy, 1998). However, here we are concerned with its particular forms and consequences in financial services. We explore this firstly through an ideal-typical account of customer-orientation practices drawn from our own and secondary research in banking (e.g. Smith and Lewis, 1989; Howcroft, 1993; Burton, 1994; Lewis, 1994; Leidner, 1993; Egan and Shipley, 1995), and secondly through a specific example of customer-service training to new recruits in a direct insurance company.

## CUSTOMER-SERVICE CULTURES

Customer orientation initiatives in financial services as elsewhere, vary in terms of the label attached to them (e.g. total quality management, human resource management) the scope of their objectives, and the sophistication and style with which they are implemented and maintained. For example, behavioural prescriptions for employees to adopt when in contact with customers (e.g. the number of telephone rings before answering) may be standardized, made explicit and monitored as part of existing control mechanisms. More commonly, the objectives are much deeper and the methods more varied – companies seek to engage or appropriate employees' values, attitudes and emotions in *new ways* and encourage particular, though diffuse, interpersonal skills. In short, the intention is for employees not just to smile at customers, but to 'smile and mean it' (Ogbonna and Wilkinson, 1990):

> Improvements in customer service must be ingrained into the culture of the organization, becoming an attitude of mind and normative behaviour ... [such as] friendliness, pleasantness, courteousness, warmth, spontaneity, reassurance and helpfulness. (Smith and Lewis, 1989: 20 and 16)

In contrast to the competitive qualities noted in the previous section, these are culturally linked to images of femininity and accessibility and are supported by the new open branch layouts where the counter, when present, no longer separates employees from the public so completely (Halford *et al.*, 1997). Indeed, in a study of building societies, Crompton and Sanderson show how ostensibly 'female qualities of friendliness, helpfulness, being non-threatening but efficient have been taken up and developed in the projection of the image of the services offered' (1990: 125). This introduces the possibility of a transforming basis for hierarchical polarization and gendered segregation and discrimination in financial services between feminine accessibility/dexterity (service staff and/or routine keyboard work) and competitive masculinity (managers) (Knights and Sturdy, 1987; Halford *et al.*, 1997). However, as we shall see, in practice not only is there a frequent confusion, overlap or oscillation between 'soft service' and 'hard sell' or performance, but at the margins sex segregation has become looser. Nevertheless, gender stereotyping is deployed in some of the practices aimed at developing a customer orientation in staff. An indication of the range of *possible* components of such culture change programmes is given below.

In theory, if companies are to be more responsive to customers' 'needs', then it is necessary to conduct market *research* regularly and, importantly, to incorporate its findings into both product/service development and employment practices. For example, along with regulatory requirements it would be used in the setting of service standards/ guarantees, developing training programmes and evaluating the progress of a customer-service initiative. As we saw in the last chapter, the use of research in this way rarely happens (Knights, Sturdy and Morgan, 1994; Egan and Shipley, 1995). However, research through market surveys and focus groups as well as monitoring customer complaints, using mystery shoppers, (internal and external) benchmarking and employee suggestion schemes have increased. Some of these are used to develop specific and general *service objectives* relating to response times, product knowledge and, in particular, employees' behaviour or orientation. These objectives may be *communicated* in a number of ways including 'events', workshops, company magazines and, as we shall see in the case below, *training*. The message is promoted to both management and staff with, perhaps, different emphases by imparting service *ideology* and *techniques*. The connection is made between the company's competitive success or survival, customer service and the role/importance of the individual employee. Indeed, the 'interests of the customer' have been used by management in seeking to justify or legitimate changes in working practices such as longer opening/working hours in branches and call-centres. Instruction is given in 'people skills' with subordinates as well as customers – 'the importance of behaviour in greeting, using the customer's name, eye contact, body language, dress etc... [and] to go out of their way to be helpful to the customer' (Smith and Lewis, 1989: 10).

These skills and orientations may be further encouraged by internal marketing initiatives and customer-service awards, and reinforced through monitoring and appraisal (Burton, 1994). The latter can involve the use of customer research information mentioned above. Performance *appraisal* is particularly important as service criteria have become incorporated and individuals may be set service objectives, sometimes against a formal performance check-list. Relatedly, *job descriptions*, which are increasingly being changed to more general, flexible and core-competence-based 'job profiles' (Storey *et al.*, 1997), may be altered to highlight customer contact. For example, in one bank, this was done to all jobs – they became 'part-time marketeers' with a hierarchy based more on communication than technical skills as previously (Burton, 1994: 55). Indeed, in some cases, given the newly-perceived importance of customer service to business success, 'front-stage' jobs with a high service or sales component have been ranked more highly (Burton, 1994) and may even offer a 'better, more speedy route to management', although such specialists are likely to have been streamed by gender and/or qualifications (Halford *et al.*, 1997: 119).

Relatedly, given the primacy of personal qualities such as interpersonal skills in improving service and their perceived relative paucity in financial services hitherto, attention is increasingly given to this in *recruiting* 'appropriate' staff (Burton, 1994). Here, as we have suggested, gender is important with women seen as ideally suited to customer contact as 'attractive' receptionists or 'a nice mumsy face' in branches for example (Kerfoot, 1993; Halford *et al.*, 1997; Crompton and Sanderson, 1990; Morgan and Knights, 1991). Finally, customer service may be sought through parallel or less explicitly focused initiatives such as 'empowerment' practices (e.g. quality circles, team-working and employee-satisfaction surveys). Indeed, a major insurance company recently (1998) commenced an organization-wide change programme which, according to senior management, is based on the 'employee–service–profit chain' principle (see Rucci *et al.*, 1998), whereby it is assumed that excellent customer service (and therefore, profit) will only emerge if employees are highly committed to working in the company by being 'looked after' and 'empowered'. In the following brief example, however, we describe more direct practices aimed at achieving customer-oriented practices and orientations in another company. We then go on to analyse employees responses more generally.

**An example: customer service training at Phoneco**

Much of the discussion so far in this chapter has been generalized and centred on transformations within the established branch-based structures of banking and insurance. By contrast, the following specific example serves to illustrate not only the way in which customer-service discourse can be introduced, through training, but new and '*strategy-based*' forms of working and distribution in financial services. Phoneco, a subsidiary of a large established composite insurer, sells and administers standard products such as car insurance. It is one of a number of 'direct' companies which have emerged since the 1980s offering customers the convenience of doing business by phone and implicit value through bypassing brokers. Combined with the backing of an established parent company, Phoneco thus matches customers' apparent preference for 'convenience and confidence' discussed in Chapter 6. It also conforms to the practices of selecting customer types (e.g. by accepting only relatively low risks) and 'personalizing' standard products. Operating in relatively competitive and price-sensitive areas of personal general insurance, Phoneco management seek to secure profits through cost control, commission from 'add-on' sales (e.g. car breakdown recovery) and customer service – it does not aim to offer the lowest prices.

The emphasis on customer service came with the arrival of a new chief executive (CEO) from a different service sector. A key element of this change was a new approach to service provided by an external training agency (which we have named Dent). The training, known informally as 'being dented' and originally developed in the USA, was given to all management and staff. The training course was conducted over two or three days. It comprised various exercises and information, ending in mock taped phone conversations with customers. The essence of 'making it easy [for the customer] to say "yes"' was to replace a largely fixed script and call 'structure' with a 'softer sell' approach which also gave employees more freedom over the words and phrases they used from a range of positive sounding, jargon-free or 'sexy' words. At the same time, certain words or phrases which had been used previously such as 'sorry', 'vehicle', 'premium' and, significantly, '*sales* training' were considered to have negative connotations for customers and were prohibited ('RIP words'). Finally, a new more flexible and 'customer-oriented' call structure was introduced with the aim of finding out more about the customer (e.g. their concerns) in order to sell the (standard) product accordingly. The new structure and phrases were designed to encourage affirmative responses from the customer and lead him/her through to an 'appropriate' sale. For example, 'true response questions' such as 'is that OK with you?' would be asked after stating the next set of information which was going to be requested (e.g. 'now I am going to ask you about the car'). Overall, a number of quite complex changes and new techniques were introduced and required of staff. However, this represented only part of the training.

In common with other, general, customer-service training we have observed in financial services and elsewhere, various rationales and rhetorical strategies were deployed in seeking to impart a customer orientation or ideology in staff. For example, in an implied threat, the importance of the sovereign consumer for company profitability and survival was emphasized:

> You all know how many new [direct] companies are coming in so we need to do more than stay still... could cause ourselves problems if we don't put it [service] right. (Trainer)

Less threateningly, the experience of being a consumer and of good and bad service generally was constantly referred to – 'OK, let's all go on a shopping trip together, say in Paris [trainees' response: ooh yes!]'. At the same time, trainers showed some recognition and anticipation of the trainees' possible scepticism and cynicism about the new approach – 'I can hear [imagine] some of you saying "ughh" to some of these "sexy words" . . .'.

Great emphasis was placed on the new language and trainees were even encouraged to adopt it out of office hours at home. More formally, the new words and style were incorporated into company and product literature as well as staff monitoring and rewards. Sales staff – renamed 'customer service staff' – were expected to reach a 'company standard' after three months in terms of language, call structure and the number of calls and conversions (to a sale) per day. Tempering managerial claims of 'empowerment', these requirements were monitored electronically and through supervisors randomly eavesdropping calls about twice a week. The bonus payment system was changed to include a 'quality' or service component related to the new approach alongside the existing measure for sales conversions.

Such changes illustrate well the shift from a sales to a broader marketing and customer-oriented approach we discussed in the previous chapter. Certainly, management saw them in this way. However, the transition might also be seen as somewhat marginal and as reflecting some of the tensions in the marketing concept we identified. Moreover, *in practice*, the discourse of selling retained a high profile such as the inclusion of increasing conversion rates and the value of each sale in training objectives. Also, trainers did not always follow the training course design. For example, one trainer introduced the session as '*sales* training' and '*sales* techniques'. Similarly, they were, perhaps understandably, reticent about encouraging trainees to adopt the new language at home.

Nevertheless, it was reported by management and trainers that staff had taken to the new approach although there had been problems in 'adjusting' to the required changes. New staff were, it was claimed, much better. Here, it was preferred that they should have 'no customer service experience so that we can shape them' (manager), but a 'strong customer orientation – attitude of putting the customer first' was 'essential' (job specification). However, again, this was not always possible partly because 'technical' (i.e. insurance) experience was sometimes required. Indeed and compounding the issue of conflicting discourses within a given field, in one office it was said that many different insurance companies' 'service traditions' were evident (manager). Moreover, in a session observed for new recruits, four of the seven clearly had customer-service experience – in tele-sales and the travel industry. Some indication of their and other Phoneco employees' initial responses to the training is provided in the following section which examines employee reactions to customer-service initiatives more generally.

### Employee responses: sources of ambivalence

We have seen that financial services employers have increasingly sought to transform the cultures of their organizations through numerous means whereby more competitive, performance and sales and/or service-oriented qualities are encouraged and valued. The outcomes of such developments are varied and often uncertain (Edwards *et al.*, 1998):

- Firstly, as we have seen in the case of Phoneco, initiatives may not always be implemented fully or exactly as intended (e.g. labour market constraints on recruitment). More generally, it is clear that changes, towards a marketing orientation for example, are ongoing and incomplete (e.g. Egan and Shipley, 1995; Storey *et al.*, 1997).
- Secondly, there will be more or less unintended consequences arising from the new regimes which are common to forms of control generally (e.g. Scott, 1994), but which also arise from tensions within the attendant managerial assumptions and practices. For example, the use of gender stereotyping to capture particular personal qualities is necessarily problematic, and we have already seen that there is a conflict between sales and service as well as the more familiar tension between rationalization (e.g. delayering and job cuts) and organizational loyalty.
- Thirdly, responses are likely to vary within the field depending on the particular situations of employee groups and individuals and the nature of changes and the form of their implementation within different organizations. For example, there are contrasting reports as to the responses of those employees with long-standing experience in pre-change cultures (Burton, 1994; c.f. Cressey and Scott, 1992).
- Fourthly, it is sometimes difficult to distinguish responses to particular developments from those to the experience of change generally.

Combined with the relative paucity of research on employee responses in financial services (Storey, 1995), there is not the scope to account for all these issues here. Rather, we outline some general patterns derived from the more substantial research on customer-service culture initiatives in other sectors (see Sturdy, 1998) and particular studies in financial services.

In keeping with the differential emergence of a marketing orientation we observed in the previous chapter, customer-orientation initiatives have been common in certain occupations for some time, especially in the USA. They have also been the focus of considerable research (e.g. Wright-Mills, 1951; Hochschild, 1983), particularly with their recent proliferation elsewhere with the growth of service sectors and strategic management discourses (e.g. TQM, HRM, BPR) in which the consumer is omnipresent (internal and external) and 'sovereign' (Keat *et al.*, 1994; du Gay and Salaman, 1992; Piercy, 1995; Mabey *et al.*, 1998). As in financial services, the *stated* managerial intention is typically to create a customer-oriented organizational culture. However, at the risk of oversimplification and generalization, far from creating a unitary culture of internalized values associated with care for the customer, various forms of ambivalence and, more commonly, behavioural compliance or cooperation are produced (c.f. Rosenthal *et al.*, 1997; Edwards *et al.*, 1998). Such ambivalence is often related to how much, if anything, of 'oneself' or 'oneselves' employees give to the required role or orientation (Hochschild, 1983; Kunda, 1991). It can be accounted for in different ways, both theoretically (e.g. du Gay, 1996 c.f. Ashforth and Humphrey, 1993) and empirically. Here, we draw attention to the latter and the importance of the employment relationship, opportunities to identify socially with new roles and, once again, tensions in the concept of marketing orientation.

*The employment relationship: smiling but not (always) meaning it*

At one level, particularly in conditions of blocked mobility, high work pressure and/or where required emotions and behaviour are more specifically prescribed, monitored and/or intensified, any cooperation is reported to be on the *surface only*. Such compliance can be seen as an, albeit defensive, form of resistance (Hochschild, 1983) although more overt forms may also occur – a 'smile strike' (Fuller and Smith, 1991: 12). Typically, this response involves cynicism and joking about initiatives with co-workers, particularly in 'backstage' areas (Van Maanen, 1991) and when superiors are equivocal (Scase and Goffee, 1989; Ogbonna and Wilkinson, 1990; Watson, 1994). In addition, employees may adopt a 'thick skin' to customer pressure ('depersonalization'), suppressing 'spontaneous' responses (Hochschild, 1983; Kunda, 1991; Rafaeli, 1989). In short, employees distance all but outward appearances, their thoughts and feelings, in an attempt to maintain or reassert their sense(s) of self and/or of control (Van Maanen, 1991; Wharton, 1993). However, some cooperation may be evident through the construction of workplace 'games' (Burawoy, 1979) out of the space available within (and sometimes beyond) managerial prescriptions. Here, employees 'escape into' the new requirements (Sturdy, 1992) as a way of coping with boredom or pressure (Whyte, 1948; Leidner, 1991; Edwards *et al.*, 1998).

Such 'low trust' conditions have become increasingly evident in areas of financial services. In particular, the perceived loss of job security and career opportunities in banking particularly have led to problems of commitment, and the more general imposition of performance targets have, as we noted earlier, created new stresses on managers especially. Similarly, the nature of the customer interaction has become increasingly prescribed, particularly in the new call centres (c.f. Kinnie *et al.*, 1998). Accordingly, we might expect considerable compliance and even some resistance to the changes. Certainly, studies report some low morale and friction among managers and clerks over career blockages and job cuts in bank branches (e.g. Cressey and Scott, 1992; Gall, 1997) and that this has undermined market orientation programmes (e.g. Burton, 1994).

Highly prescriptive management initiatives, then, can be self-defeating, or at least have contradictory consequences. Indeed, some managerial recognition of this is evident in the simultaneous deployment of, albeit token, empowerment programmes (e.g. quality circles, personal development plans) and the Phoneco example where increased autonomy in customer interaction was a theme of the training programme. More generally, studies of customer-orientation initiatives report that in conditions of greater job autonomy or more ambiguous behavioural prescription and higher work incentives, responses are more *ambivalent* (e.g. Hochschild, 1983; Sutton and Rafaeli, 1988; Wharton, 1993; Kunda, 1991). Here, rather than fixing employee orientations at one point on a continuum between compliance and internalization/commitment (see Etzioni, 1961; Mintzberg, 1983), there is simultaneous or alternate role embracement and distancing (Kunda, 1991).

The extent of attachment has been linked to the influence of job rewards/sanctions, peer pressure (*ibid.*) and/or to the difficulty in maintaining a 'phony' act ('emotive dissonance') which lead to an *adaptation* process – *'deep acting'* (Hochschild, 1983). This involves more or less consciously working on feelings, as is common in everyday life, so that an employee 'expresses spontaneously ... a *real* feeling that has been self-induced' – when they smile, *they mean it* (*ibid*.: 35 and 133, emphasis added). Similar processes are noted elsewhere (e.g. Wright-Mills, 1951: 185–6) and even prescribed in service training such as that at Phoneco – 'fake it 'til you make it!' Indeed, Ashforth and Humphrey argue that, over time, cultural control (i.e. value prescription) results in 'role playing becoming role taking' (1993: 102). However, 'full role embracement' has not been presented here as a third form of dominant orientation since, from the research reviewed, it seems to be a minority and precarious one – socially stigmatized and/or leading to 'burn-out' and emotional passivity (Van Maanen, 1991; Kunda, 1991). Even Ashforth and Humphrey (1993) note that role-taking coexists with the mental distancing and cynicism which we have associated with behavioural compliance (*ibid*.: 104–5).

Again, one would expect to find similar responses in areas of financial services. For example, initial cynicism towards emotional or cultural prescription was evident at Phoneco, although not among all trainees:

Trainee: 'This is naff: "always leave the customer with a warm feeling"'
Trainer and some trainees together: 'That's not naff!'

Moreover, where service qualities become established in organizations, adaptation processes are likely, including, as intimated in the above quotation, through peer pressure. Assuming a persistent emphasis on customer service, at least partial adoption should emerge, particularly for those with the most to gain (e.g. careers through service performance) or lose (e.g. job insecurity). More generally, where there is some perceived autonomy greater acceptance might be found (c.f. Edwards *et al.*, 1998). Burton, for example, noted how the majority of branch bank clerks in her study enjoyed and were confident in their new service roles, but saw them as an 'optional extra activity' in their job (1994: 57).

*Cultures as obstacles and bridges*

The above findings, whereby cultural control is typically achieved in a partial way at best, may well be unsurprising. As we saw in Chapter 1, there has been a sustained critique in much of the literature on the management of organizational cultures – their internally pluralistic and dynamic nature is denied and shared interests and/or managerial omnipotence presumed (e.g. see Smircich, 1983; Martin, 1992; Willmott, 1993). However, in relating responses to the employment relationship and its particular forms (e.g. high and low trust), the review has so far been largely abstracted from wider and interpenetrative social relations. We now continue to explore employee ambivalence, but as the product of an interplay between management control/business practices and other social structures and relations, such as occupation, culture, gender and consumerism. Here, particular social identities can be seen as obstacles and/or bridges in the diffusion of customer service discourses.

Cultural relations broadly defined are often seen in the literature as an impediment to culture initiatives and a basis of resistance to them and their imposition. For example, customer-service initiatives, such as at Phoneco, are often seen as distinctly North American and to conflict with (often somewhat stereotypical) *national* cultural norms – 'British people don't like to smile at people' (manager quoted in Ogbonna and Wilkinson, 1990: 14). Another key problem identified is the tensions presented with existing attachments to, and the norms and interests of, work groups and occupations – social identities (Ackroyd and Crowdy, 1990; Anthony, 1990). In the context of customer service, preexisting service ethics such as those in the medical professions may be challenged (Davies and Kirkpatrick, 1995; May, 1994). To the extent to which employees subscribe to such occupational orientations and practices, changes to them are likely to be resisted and/or resented. As we have noted, such a tension has been particularly evident in financial services in relation to bancassurance and the broader emergence of sales and marketing discourses. Similarly, Cressey and Scott reported 'considerable resistance' and 'friction', especially from experienced lower and middle managerial (bank branch) staffs to these changes (1992; see also Burton, 1991 and 1994):

> ...many personnel with a traditional administrative outlook...find it 'almost demeaning' to now be asked to go out and sell to customers with whom they may have built up long-established trust relationships. (Cressey and Scott, 1992: 90)

Such conflicts are likely in other sectors of financial services where alternative forms of service discourse date back to the original formation of building societies, mutual insurance companies and Friendly

Societies for example. Even in life assurance sales, a clash has emerged not with the emphasis on sales performance but with the increasing (regulatory and management) attention to addressing customer needs.

While considerable academic attention is given to emerging conflicts, there is always the possibility of other outcomes in the interaction between new and existing practices and norms (see Child and Rodrigues, 1996; Rosenthal *et al.*, 1997). Indeed, this is likely given the multiplicity and sometimes conflicting nature of prevailing social identities (Whittington, 1992; Parker, 1995) and the potential existential and material costs of resistance. A number of complementarities between prevailing cultures and service prescriptions have been cited as helping to account for the extent of role embracement or willing involvement by employees. For example, customer service can be seen as reinforcing, as well as conflicting with, certain national cultural norms of social interaction (e.g. politeness) (Ogbonna and Wilkinson, 1990: 14). Similarly, customer service and gender are frequently linked (James, 1989; Leidner, 1991; Duncombe and Marsden, 1993 and 1995) – giving 'good service' is 'doing gender' (Hall, 1993). Indeed, we have seen how management seek to exploit this, particularly in recruitment (Hochschild, 1983; O'Brien, 1994; Kerfoot, 1993). Also, service prescriptions can be seen as 'identity-enhancing' in terms of occupational norms (e.g., nurses feeling sympathetic) (Ashforth and Humphrey, 1993: 94). This may be particularly relevant in green/brownfield sites such as call centres and, to a lesser extent, with school leavers and new recruits to the sector. Here, new occupational definitions can be more easily established by management in accordance with the customer service (or sales) discourse and are less likely to be challenged by existing staff who may continue to identify with alternative service orientations. Indeed, the managerial preference for recruits without a service or finance background at Phoneco supports this view.

However, as we saw at Phoneco, realizing such aims from recruitment is far from straightforward. More generally, cultural practices such as gender and sexuality are unmanageable resources, subject to conflicting interpretations (Filby, 1992; McDowell, 1998). They thus provide an opportunity, through customer interaction for example, for workers to assert a sense of control and identity which may not always conform to management or customer expectations (Leidner, 1991). Indeed, customer interaction sometimes serves not only as a source of satisfaction (Mulkay and Howe, 1994), but as a conduit for cultural influences (Rafaeli, 1989), including consumerism (Sturdy, 1998).

*The contradictions of customer service*

Customer interaction may also be experienced as a source of frustration, pressure and anger (Wright-Mills, 1951; Blau, 1962), not least for customers' failure to deliver a sense of autonomy to employees. Thus, ambivalence over customer-service initiatives may not be purely attributed to managerial prescription, but also to customers' expectations and, perhaps, their increasing legitimacy. There are clear links between the two areas, but not simply in terms of customers substituting for management, for this equates management control and interests with addressing diverse customer 'needs'. As we discussed in the previous chapter, there is a tension between addressing the 'needs' of the customer and organizational profitability (e.g. cost reduction, sales, productivity) – a customer may want to talk for hours when buying a 'low margin' product, for example. This tension may further impede the diffusion of customer service or, at least, a sales emphasis and is illustrated in situations reported in financial services (Schneider, 1980; Howcroft, 1993; Burton, 1994) and elsewhere (Rosenthal *et al.*, 1997) where employees are *actually committed* to elements of a service orientation (e.g. to customers and quality), but are frustrated by, and critical of, management and its emphasis on efficiency *at the expense of the customer*. This is not simply a case of management failing to reconcile conflicting priorities (c.f. Weatherly and Tansik, 1993) and functional interests (e.g. between sales, operations and strategy managers) (c.f. Grafton-Small, 1987; Hooley and Mann, 1988; Whittington and Whipp, 1992; Burton, 1994). Rather, as we have seen in relation to selecting profitable consumers, for example, acting in the customers' interests is only part of marketing discourse. It is used as a rhetorical strategy more or less instrumentally to secure and obscure sales and profitability. Accordingly, the frequently observed employee cynicism may better reflect a scepticism based on the experience and recognition of the hypocrisy or instrumentality inherent in customer-service discourse than simply a form of cognitive or (national) cultural distancing (c.f. Kunda, 1991; Willmott, 1993). Once again, the trainees at Phoneco illustrate this:

> Trainee 1: '"Just sell, sell, sell!"' [stating own view of course aims]
> Group: laughter
> Trainee 2: '"To keep the customer happy"'
> Group: laughter
> Trainee 3: 'yeah right!' [ironic]

We were taught that if we were friendly with them [customers], then they'd find it difficult to say 'no'. (Trainee, new recruit)

Thus, rather than presenting an opportunity for companies to build a social bridge with preexisting or broader service ethics and orientations, customer-service initiatives in practice may emphasize sales and thereby undermine commitment to them.

## CONCLUSION

In this chapter we have sought to outline what the emerging strategic discourses in financial services mean for employees in terms of changing employment practices and experiences. In particular we have highlighted the areas of contrast between employment in the previous and emerging organizational fields. Here, notwithstanding the wide range, variety and depth of changes – in collective representation, careers, rewards, personal development and job cultures, holders and content – attention has been focused on the most historically distinctive and widespread development in financial service organizations. This is the move to transform administrative/technical cultures with relative job security and, for some, hierarchical careers to ones based more on the strategic marketing discourse of interpersonal customer-oriented skills linked to corporate and individual performance. This has also been connected to the emergence of HRM loosely defined; new forms of gender relations and segregation; structural and technological change; and shifts in the geographical and organizational location of employment.

Despite our focus, we are conscious of having presented a generalized account that has underplayed sectoral and organizational variations and peculiarities (see Egan and Shipley, 1995). Nevertheless, we have drawn on specific illustrations from our own and others' research, including the particular case of Phoneco which combines a number of the characteristics and tensions of emerging discourses and strategic organizational forms. Moreover, in keeping with our perspective in other chapters, we have sought to demonstrate that whatever the various rhetorics and managerial intentions, changes are contested and outcomes are often varied, contradictory and uncertain. This has been most visible in our account of patterns of employee responses to customer service culture initiatives. Here, employee ambivalence was linked to tensions and complementarities in terms of the employment relationship, prevailing cultures, customer interaction and the assumptions and practice of customer service. Relatedly, we pointed to the tension between masculine competitive performance cultures and the more feminine elements of customer service. Similarly, the more familiar 'tight–loose', 'control–engage' management tension is evident in the combination of rationalization and union growth with seeking employee commitment through 'empowerment', for example. To these may be added other dynamics such as individual versus team rewards.

Such tensions highlight the complex and problematic nature of the emergence and transformation of discourses and, therefore, of organizational change. They also show that for discourses to become *enacted* within organizations such as Phoneco, they need not be wholly accepted or internalized by all actors – the power of the labour market and job insecurity, for example, should not be underestimated. Indeed, through our discussion of employee ambivalence we have shown why only partial adoption is likely to be achieved. Nevertheless, the shift towards the establishment of these discourses cannot be simply accounted for by reference to market pressures, reactive managerial initiatives and employee responses. It is, as we have demonstrated in earlier chapters a condition and consequence of broader and longer-term transformations within the organizational field of financial services and beyond.

# Part IV

# The Emerging Organizational Field

# 8 Transformation and Change in Financial Services

## INTRODUCTION

As we have seen, during the 1980s and 1990s financial services organizations were being transformed from within and without. Inside these organizations, managers and employees came to learn a new way of conceiving of themselves, their roles and functions. As the language and practice of management shifted away from predominantly bureaucratic and traditional models towards strategy, marketing and the discourse of the sovereign consumer, patterns of work, organization and career were restructured. In this chapter, we show how these discourses produced a range of contradictory effects within the field of financial services as a whole.

In particular, the discourse of strategy began to reconstitute the organizational field as a 'free market' context in which sovereign and independent individual financial services organizations (freed from the restrictions placed on them by the formal and informal controls of the City, the Bank of England and associated bodies) met sovereign, independent actors (both individual consumers and collective economic actors such as firms). Money provided the medium through which this process could occur. Yet, as we saw in Chapter 3, money itself was changing form in this period. It was becoming more difficult to control for central banks, governments, financial institutions, individuals and companies as the forms and the ways in which it was distributed were becoming more complex. Financial services companies keen to demonstrate their 'strategic' acuity were encouraged to push the limits on the forms of money as far away from its materiality as they could as they strove to devise new sorts of products and services. In the process, they constructed new forms of what Leyshon and Thrift refer to as 'virtual money', 'a new system of fleeting *instants* ... based on quasi-private institutions and on the full range of instruments of fictitious capital. Money is accepted on the belief that whoever offered it will make it good *in the future*. Money is to that extent partly a fiction, "the stuff that dreams are made of" (Desai)' (Leyshon and Thrift, 1997: 20–1). Dodd links this to the idea of 'trust' when he states that 'in order to agree to hold money over time...the transactor must trust – or even hope, expect, be confident that, pray and so on – that the tokens received will do what they are supposed to do' (1994: 141). The more 'fictitious' and 'virtual' that money becomes, the more trust is needed and conversely the higher the degree of risk that something which was not 'supposed to' will actually happen.

This is most evident in the wholesale markets. With instantaneous information transfer across the globe facilitating 'time–space compression', major shifts in market sentiment or crises in particular institutions (e.g. against certain currencies or against particular borrowers) are not compartmentalized and controllable within national boundaries, but sweep across the key international financial centres within a matter of hours. These shifts work their way rapidly into a complex of interrelated products and services such as foreign exchange, options, futures and derivatives markets, the stock exchange and the provision of funds through bonds and other forms of loans (see Held *et al.*, 1999: 202–13, for a summary of the growth of these phenomena). Strange has referred to the result of these processes as 'mad':

> Why mad?...Because financial markets have been erratically manic at one moment, unreasonably depressive at others. The crises that have hit them have been unpredicted and, to most observers, surprising. Their behaviour has seriously damaged others. (1998: 1)

In this scenario, actors advance these processes by developing or buying new and more complex products and services which extend the forms of money and therefore enhance risk. Strategic discourse, with its emphasis on markets and competition, has been an integral part of those forces which have advanced the processes of what Strange (1998) calls 'mad money'. It provides the framework within which the managers of financial institutions can cast off the old controls and reveal themselves as sovereign independent market actors. It seeks to construct as 'truth' the idea that these extensions in the form of money are extensions of individual and corporate freedom. Actors are free to buy what they 'need' and companies are 'free' to supply those needs. Money can be 'trusted' to deliver this freedom.

The 'virtualization' of money clearly has implications on its distribution. Huge accumulations of money, wealth and power accrue in the hands of those organizations which manage and benefit from this process. The decisions made by multinational companies about where to invest or international financial institutions about which currencies to buy and sell result in complex effects which impact on patterns of wealth and power in particular countries. For example, the East Asian crisis has plunged millions of people into poverty as jobs have been lost and firms restructured. These same decisions impact on occupational structures and job opportunities in other countries. Arguments in the 1980s about the de-industrialization of the US and UK may have proved exaggerated but there is little doubt that there have been significant changes in the UK labour market arising from the loss of manufacturing jobs and the restructuring of existing firms to maintain competitiveness against overseas companies (see, for example, the discussions in Delbridge and Lowe, 1998; Felstead and Jewson, 1999; Gallie *et al.*, 1998; Goffee and Scase, 1995). As well as creating uncertainties and insecurities for many, these changes also establish wealth and income-enhancing opportunities for some of those in areas of high skill and professional expertise. In certain occupations, linking rewards to performance has led to huge annual bonuses for a small group, whilst others are left on standard salary packages (see e.g. McDowell's analysis of gender and inequality in the City, 1998).

Scott's work (1982, 1997) has shown how this leads towards a different notion of the rich in the contemporary era; rather than being a homogeneous group based on property or ownership, significant wealth can be achieved through a variety of means including entrepreneurship (Branson etc.), celebrityhood or management position (becoming chief executive of a major multinational). In the main, the existence of this category of wealth is dependent on the existence of 'virtual money' and the ability to deal in huge sums. Similarly, the existence of social exclusionary pressures is reinforced by the ability of firms to shift their resources around the globe (Bauman, 1998). Between these two categories, however, there exist a range of occupational positions, the dynamics of which are affected by sectoral conditions, skill and professional competences and forms of employment relationship. For this group, key elements of their fate are determined directly and indirectly by the operation of the financial institutions and multinational enterprises. However, their 'hold' on money, either in the present or the future, is uncertain not just because of this but also because of the investments which they themselves have in international financial markets (even if they do not realize it). Therefore, what we have described earlier as the 'service class' as well as other groups within the working class cannot assume any certainty in their present and future positions. 'Virtual money' and its power to flow across boundaries with limited conscious or overt control over its social consequences holds the whole of society in its grip, though the effects are differentially distributed.

The construction of the 'truth' of strategy (incomplete and partial as it may be) therefore has effects on actors and their powers which may be unpredictable and unexpected. As these effects reveal themselves, the language and practice of public policy and 'regulation' reemerges as a means of dealing with these uncertainties whilst retaining the sovereignty of strategic discourse and the 'free' market. However, this discourse itself carries a set of historical connotations and ambiguities which in turn have effects. In particular, the discourse of the market and the sovereign consumer was partially constructed in order to undermine the legitimacy of the notion of public policy and regulation as a form of paternalist 'protection' against the hazards of the market system. How is it possible to reconstruct the notion of public policy and regulation within (as opposed to against) the discourse of the free market? Even more crucially, how can the practice of public policy be aligned with the practices of the free market for, however this is done, it comes up against the power of multinationals and financial institutions to press for greater openness and less control. As was the case in earlier periods of change in financial services, these issues are about the distribution of power, wealth and income, and couching them as technical issues of transparency, control and accountability is merely a camouflage for the underlying conflicts.

In the realm of wholesale markets, these issues have become increasingly embedded in the interaction of national governments and central banks with international entities (such as the World Bank, the World Trade Organization and the IMF). In this arena of global financial decision-making, the major economic powers are involved in processes of coordination and conflict which try to shape and control the uncertainties that arise from the activities of companies seeking to survive and prosper in these markets. The interaction between these processes is unpredictable and uncertain. Rapid crises can engulf entire regions of the world as happened with the East Asian crisis in 1997 or specific countries such as Russia in 1998, bringing down governments and causing sudden shifts into poverty for huge numbers of people. At the global level, the concern is about creating a 'fire-wall' between these localized points of the crisis and the stability of the world financial system, primarily by ensuring that institutions within the main Western economies are given time and space to fill the holes in their balance sheets that have emerged from these collapses. Thus the tendencies of the system to create crises are reproduced and the regulators' aim is control the extent of the damage (or rather, to make sure that the damage is localized).

At the level of retail financial services, we can see similar and connected processes at work. As strategic discourse gradually colonized financial services during the 1980s and 1990s, senior managers increasingly perceived themselves as operating within a sphere of greater freedom and autonomy that would determine the performance of their companies (see Morgan and Quack, 2000, for a more detailed discussion of this process, comparing the British and German financial services sectors). In particular, the deregulation set under way by the Conservative government released the constraints set on certain types of companies about the sorts of business which they could enter. In theory, the old barriers between sectors (and firms) within financial services were dismantled. Organizations had the freedom to enter any sector so long as they conformed to certain rules mainly concerned with financial solvency. This neo-liberal discourse of market freedom meshed neatly with that of strategy. Managers of companies had the opportunity to shift their resources and efforts into a wide range of markets according to their preferred strategies. Their skills at using their own freedom and autonomy 'strategically' were seen as key to the success of their companies now they were no longer provided with the shelter of protection by formal or informal agreements. Companies evolved their own approaches to strategy, IT, marketing and customer service within the parameters outlined in the previous chapters. Success was seen to arise from achieving the appropriate mix of innovation and change.

The conditions under which these 'freedoms' could be exercised in retail financial services continued to differ according to past experience (reflected in existing market share and physical and human infrastructures devoted to particular patterns of business) and the capital resources of the organization. For those companies which were publicly quoted on the stock exchange, both the opportunities and the threats were largest. The capital markets were a useful source of funding for takeovers or new developments but they were also becoming increasingly intrusive and demanding. The performance of firms was closely scrutinized in terms of how it measured against others in either the same sector or in the market as a whole, and these benchmarks became the means for decisions on buying and selling stocks and bonds. Building societies and mutual insurance companies did not face quite the same challenges although their access to funds, both on the retail and the wholesale markets, was in part affected by their perceived performance. Even for them, therefore, managerial autonomy was exercised within an increasingly visible framework of performance indicators and comparisons which in turn had varying implications for the ability of the managers to maintain their autonomy. Strategies became the means whereby organizations not only framed their own actions but also legitimated these actions in the 'gaze' of the broader financial markets.

The range of forms of money was extended as companies expanded their products and services as part of their new strategic freedom. New forms of credit, investment, savings, insurance and money-transmission services have become available. The 'virtuality' and uncertainty characteristics of these products vary. Some, such as telephone or internet banking/insurance, 'virtualize' an existing product through technological innovations, thereby reducing costs and creating market uncertainties through changing competitive conditions. Other products, particularly those associated with long-term investments such as savings-based mortgages, pensions and collective investment schemes (life insurance savings, unit trusts, Personal Equity Plans) link the personal customer into the uncertainties of the 'virtual money' world more closely by their direct dependence on global financial markets as the medium of their activities in a way that savings products in the previous era did not (since they were often based on straightforward payments of nationally determined interest rates or investments in relatively stable stocks primarily located within the UK).

In the following section, we examine this particular sector of the retail financial services in more detail, showing how constructing the 'truth' of strategy has unexpected effects in this complex interrelated context. We argue in particular that ideas of 'freedom' – to compete, to develop strategy, to buy and to consume – produced effects that led back to the notion of restrictions on 'freedom' and the 'need for regulation'. In this arena, more than the wholesale markets, the national government is inevitably drawn in more visibly and publicly to this process primarily because the potential distributional effects of these processes have to become highly 'politicized'. Thus, what appeared as a self-evident truth in the early 1980s, based around the need to free up the market and allow companies to follow their own strategies in the marketplace, becomes by the 1990s a more complex structure of competing ideas and practices about how the market should be constructed and controlled. In the process, the actors themselves (both the firms operating in the sector and the consumers who buy the products and services) undergo processes of further transformation and change.

### Strategy and regulation: the case of savings and investment

The strategies of individual companies were complex and evolving constructions based on the perception of managers about their position within this wider context. As we have noted, particular strategy techniques, ranging from the Porter five-forces model through to the more recently popular, core-competences approach, were taken up at different times and in different ways. However, in the early phase of these changes during the early 1980s, for firms which were operating within the savings and investments products sector of retail financial services, the top strategic priority was articulated around the issue of shifting towards a selling culture. In particular, selling of products became increasingly a specialist activity. In both banking and life insurance, many organizations had previously mixed the task of 'selling' products with a broader range of administrative and service tasks which were performed for the customer. In the new environment, while cross-selling by counter staff was significantly stepped up, the creation of specialist sales forces for investment products became seen as a major strategic move either to sell more to existing customers or to 'prospect' more widely for new clients.

The shift towards selling, which we have described earlier, occurred within a particular context. This was in terms of, firstly, the broad perception which the industry had of its own 'rectitude' and 'moral standing' and, secondly, the conception of the customer which was held by the industry. With regard to the first point, the industry had generally had a reputation for trustworthiness based on the financial probity or, for some, longevity of the companies involved. This was built in to managers' conceptions of their status and role and went back to the nineteenth century origins of many banks and insurance companies in providing a means whereby middle-class professional and clerical families and the 'respectable' working class could secure their income and status (in life and death). As we have seen, being insured or having a bank account was a mark of respectability; it was not simply seen as the prerogative of the better-off (i.e. those who could afford to save), but as an indicator of moral worth. Savings constituted a sacrifice of present consumption for future happiness; deferred gratification for the individual, greater security and stability for the family. The companies traditionally bathed themselves in this aura of respectability and acted as the administrator of moral virtue through their control over loans and savings. Their stewardship of these savings was also seen as safe and respectable; they could be trusted to take care of the money which was invested with them. The customer was generally seen as neither very interested nor very competent in evaluating the actual products which the industry was offering.

However, because the industry portrayed itself as so 'respectable' and this was not typically challenged, the fundamental asymmetry of power between consumers and firms remained largely unquestioned (see Morgan and Knights, 1992). The relative absence of what were seen as collective cases of fraud or mismanagement in the sector also reinforced this perspective as did the relative stability of the investment process, which was primarily linked to UK stocks and government bonds. Individual dissatisfaction with investment performance or changes remained primarily at the individual level. Companies took no special measures to explain to customers, in language that could be understood, the nature and various charging systems for insurance and savings products; nor did they explain how the amount which they paid out to their customers, (which in the case of long-term savings contracts could be either the final redemption value with terminal bonuses or the value at early surrender) was affected by various factors (such as charging, investment returns and, possibly a life insurance component). Although some of this information was available, a customer had to be both persistent in order to get it and highly competent in the analysis of figures in order to make any sense of the resulting information. The industry as a whole was very reluctant to reexamine any of these presuppositions, not surprisingly since they underpinned the whole way in which profitability or organizational stability was achieved.

The process of becoming more selling-oriented operated at first within this context, and the expectation that in most other ways the company did not need to be changed. Companies were just going to be more aggressive in their selling techniques as they no longer had guaranteed markets. Therefore, they were going to graft on to or adapt their existing structure in ways which enabled them to sell more and/or to more clients. This approach was articulated as 'good for the company' (it would show their 'strategy' had been developed and was working) and 'good for the customer' (who would be persuaded of financial gains and/or made to realize their social responsibilities – and therefore buy a financial product).

As the companies became more 'strategic' and 'autonomous' in their decision-making, they remained bound by their view of how the industry worked. Key to this was their perception that they could operate what was effectively a 'cost-plus' pricing system even after the end of formal price fixing arrangements. Administrative, selling and investment costs (plus in the case of some products, a life insurance component) were built into the products and then overlaid with a profit margin in order to determine the final price. This process was more or less opaque to customers. It was almost impossible to compare between companies on these criteria as actual costs were carefully concealed. Companies also tried to ensure that their products were distinctive in some, often minor, way which further complicated the task of comparison. In theory, brokers were sometimes used as intermediaries in this process, in other words to explain to potential purchasers the differences between companies and products. However, in their case other factors came into play, most importantly the fact that it was the company rather than the client who paid the broker through a commission. Therefore, the broker's advice tended to be 'tainted' (whether or not it was in practice affected by the offer of different commission rates between companies).

The notion of building the price of the product on the basis of what the company perceived as necessary to cover its costs and margins was reinforced by the time framework for these products. Although there were variations in detail, broadly speaking, they were 'front-end loaded'. In other words, a high proportion of investors' savings in the first few years (often between 80–100 per cent of savings in the first two years) were not placed in actual savings funds, but were taken by the company to pay off their own front-end loaded expenses (i.e. the cost of paying a commission, setting up the product on the company's systems and providing initial insurance cover) as well as to contribute to profits (these issues were critically explored in detail in a series of reports produced by the Office of Fair Trading – OFT, 1992, 1993a, 1993b, 1994). This front-end loading on long-term products meant that the point at which investors could have expected their savings funds to actually match the amount of money they had put in was around 5–7 years. So long as savings were genuinely long-term, that is reaching fruition from year-10 onwards, this was not a particularly visible problem at least to the clients. However, it did imply that, in distributional terms, those who stayed longest benefited more than those who surrendered early (either because of personal circumstances or because a company sales person persuaded them to do so).

The opening up of new markets and the increasing emphasis on sales, therefore, meant that the same underlying structure of products (i.e. opaque pricing and front-end loading) was taken to a much wider set of customers. In particular, the extension of savings vehicles in the areas of mortgages and personal pensions meant that people were beginning to deal with new forms of money that were no longer immediately visible or redeemable (without loss) because they were increasingly locked into long-term investments. During the 1970s and 1980s, there was a switch away from straight repayment mortgages towards mortgages paid back through the medium of some sort of investment vehicle – at first life insurance endowments, but later unit-linked insurances, then PEPs and personal pension-related mortgages. Similarly, with the emergence of personal pension plans from 1988, these could be secured by a range of investment vehicles. People's futures were being increasingly tied in with how the money which they earned in the present was being converted into a set of complex relationships between themselves, the companies from which they had bought and the investments which those companies were making in uncertain and complex global economic environments. Consumers had to 'trust' the companies in a context which was increasingly distant from their own control and possession of money.

Furthermore, these customers were more varied in their circumstances than previously. For example, the 'freedom' to provide credit (for house purchase etc.) had led to competition between companies. Good customers (i.e. low credit risks) were most attractive to the companies, but these were in limited supply and therefore companies widened their risk criteria to groups which were previously considered poor risks (because of their low income or insecure employment prospects). These groups were encouraged to take on mortgages and associated products. Similarly, the emphasis on personal self-help, particularly in old age, led to the same groups taking on savings policies and in some cases personal pensions. Since the ability to sustain these long-term required stability of income and job circumstances, widening the net in order to increase sales also increased the possibility that this would result in policies being discontinued.

In the late 1980s, the shift towards a selling 'strategy' (encouraged by the government's wish to expand self-provision and self-help) led to a bonanza of selling in the retail financial services industry. It was achieved on the basis of the same basic and complementary assumptions about both products and the customers. The products were designed to secure the profitability of the company on the basis of its current structure. At the same time, customers were for the most part both 'ignorant' and 'incompetent'. While many might resist certain 'hard' forms of direct selling, for example, they were, as we have seen, unable and/or unwilling to exert market pressure on companies by shopping around which might challenge the assumptions and practices of product design (Knights *et al.*, 1993). However, this was not seen by 'trustworthy' companies as a recipe for exploitation, but a way of ensuring the customer's own welfare. They had a duty to sell to the customer because otherwise the customer would be unlikely to buy and would therefore be 'unprotected' from life's trials and tribulations. Thus, the practice of strategy and 'marketing' (selling) remained wrapped in an ideology of paternalism, whilst reinforcing existing practices at the level of product pricing.

So long as the economy was booming, wages and salaries were rising, house prices were increasing and unemployment falling, the risks of taking on a growing number and range of customers were contained. However, once each of these went into reverse, the risks became translated into defaults and discontinuances and associated publicity. By the late 1980s, the expansion of the housing market was beginning to slow and eventually receded drastically, leaving many people over-indebted and trapped in situations of negative equity with interest rates rising. Employment conditions were also changing for many people. Increasing unemployment was part of this, but so also was the shift into self-employment and temporary employment which became more common as firms, including those in financial services, slimmed down their workforces and contracted out certain services (Goffee and Scase, 1995: Gallie *et al.*, 1998). These changes meant that previously acceptable levels of debt and saving suddenly became untenable. However, as people tried to extricate themselves, they found that the warm paternalistic embrace of the financial services companies could not be easily shaken off. Further, they began to discover that the products which they had bought had certain consequences which they had not clearly understood. Thus, it was the interplay of the distributional consequences of changing employment structures allied with the impact on individuals' abilities to service their debts which raised the question of whether the system could be left to evolve in this direction. Primarily this was because its distributional consequences had clear political effects, particularly in growing numbers of homeowners having to sell their houses in order to pay off mortgage debts (and later, the sight of people who had paid into personal pensions realizing that they had potentially lost money). The system was working to distribute money in ways which were often counter to prevailing ideologies of self-help (i.e. it was the homeowner and the pensioner who were losing, those groups which the Conservative government claimed to want to help). Thus the political clamour for intervention arose as people sought to protect themselves from the impact of the uncertainties of this context.

The early 1990s saw these consequences revealed in two main areas. The first was in the crisis faced by home-owners. This manifested itself in a rising number of cases of foreclosure by building societies and mortgage lenders, together with increased negative equity locking borrowers into their existing properties because they had borrowed more than their houses were now worth. The fact that many borrowers had taken out loans based on investment products which were heavily front-end loaded led to the realization that the value of these policies was often lower than expected, particularly where people had purchased recently and therefore fund values had not built up. Since advisers generally encouraged house purchasers to switch out of one endowment mortgage to another when they moved house, the increasing rate of such removals in the late 1980s had led more people to be caught in this trap when the downturn came (OFT, 1995).

The second way in which these consequences were revealed was in the area of personal pensions. Sales forces had sold personal pensions to all sorts of people often without a detailed consideration of their financial circumstances. This became clearest in the case of encouraging people to opt out of existing occupational pension schemes and buy their own personal pensions. In the early 1990s, it became clear that very large numbers of people who had done this were in fact worse off as a result of the decision. Although the circumstances varied and the degree of disadvantage could only be calculated by getting detailed figures for each particular case, the overwhelming impression was that personal pensions had been sold without due regard for the interests of the customers (SIB, 1993).

In both these cases, the industry had sold a set of products which were probably no worse (if not better) than those they had been selling earlier. However, now they were selling them much more actively and to clients for whom the level of risk involved was higher than it had been in the past. This process was legitimized through the new language of strategy, competition and consumer choice. However, beneath the surface the industry was reproducing its old ways of working. In the new context this was having drastic unintended effects, not least on the distribution of wealth and income. Groups which perceived themselves as 'safe' because of their home ownership and their savings found that they were no longer insulated; on the contrary, they were increasingly tightly coupled to the dynamics of the world economy through its impact on interest rates, currency values and stockmarket positions.

## Selling, strategy and regulation

These unintended effects and the publicity they attracted became intricately linked with the development of the new regulatory system established under the Financial Services Act (FSA), 1986. In its early stages, this system was seen by companies and politicians as primarily about dealing with certain rogue elements within financial services. It was not expected to have much of an impact on the 'respectable' and often long-established companies which dominated the industry. This led the companies to complain about the imposition of rules under the FSA which required them to demonstrate in monitoring inspections that their sales were appropriate to the needs of the customer (usually this meant the development of a system of detailed recording of the client's financial circumstances in what was known as the 'fact-find' form). They railed against this as a bureaucratic imposition which drove up the costs to consumers whilst adding little in benefit (since, by implication, these companies could be trusted to act responsibly). The regulators appeared to vacillate in response to these concerns, trying to find ways to reduce the burden of bureaucracy whilst maintaining the principle of monitoring and its associated paperwork such as the fact-find (see Morgan and Soin, 1999, for an account of some of these debates).

While similar vacillations and conflicts over regulation have continued, this situation gradually changed as a clearer understanding of the consequences of the companies' responses to the bonanza of the 1980s began to emerge. One of the first stages in this was a growing recognition that the sellers of financial services products were often very poorly trained. In fact, this was endemic to the way in which many companies had added on sales forces to their existing operations. Sales forces were expanded on the basis of minimal training and, following life assurance traditions, employees were paid from front-end loaded charges according to the number of sales they made. Under this commission-driven system, an individual's failure to sell did not directly cost the company since there was little expenditure on training, administrative support or guaranteed salary. For the sales people, this made life particularly difficult, especially in the early months of their employment when they had few contacts. As a result, large numbers of the people recruited into sales forces lasted only a few months and high levels of sales force annual turnover (often reaching 100 per cent) were characteristic of the industry in the late 1980s and early 1990s (Knights and Morgan, 1990, 1991).

These characteristics of the sales forces conflicted with the notion that the industry could be trusted. A growing number of commentators argued that it was impossible to trust sales people who had very little training and an urgent need to sell in order to survive. These arguments were pulled together first by the McDonald report on training in the industry (McDonald, 1990) and then by the regulators themselves. Following instructions from the lead regulator, the Securities and Investment Board (SIB), the other regulators had to evolve a set of requirements for firms regarding the training, competence and development of their employees. In the case of LAUTRO (the main regulator for the retail investment sector), the Training and Competence scheme required companies to submit their proposed training framework for approval. In the main, these schemes led to a much higher level of enforced up-front expenditure on training. This meant that it became more difficult for firms to operate commission-only sales forces with high levels of turnover; they had to develop mechanisms for encouraging sales staff to stay longer. One way was to reduce the pressure to sell or increase the incentive to stay with the company, particularly in the early months, by offering some guaranteed salary. These changes transformed the overhead cost structure of sales forces. As will be argued later, this contributed to the exit decisions of a number of smaller firms whose strategy had been built on the commission-only/high-turnover model of sales force management.

The arguments about training were gradually becoming enmeshed in a much wider critique of the underlying assumptions of the industry. Key to this critique was the gradual emergence of a clearer understanding of the pricing structure of the industry described earlier. As discussed, the Office of Fair Trading took a major role in this process by commissioning a series of reports on aspects of savings and investments products (OFT, 1992, 1993a, 1993b, 1994, 1995). These reports revealed the full impact of the front-end loading procedures on early surrender values. They also showed how terminal bonuses were used to boost a company's position in performance league tables (essentially by holding back a substantial proportion of returns until the very last moment). They revealed the high number of surrenders which occurred in the first few years, demonstrating the low value of returns on these but also implying that this could be explained by people buying (under high pressure sales tactics) products which they did not need or could not afford. They showed the widely varying levels of commissions and expenses in the industry and how significantly this could affect the surrender and final value of products. Finally, they rejected the argument that the products were too complex to explain to customers in simple ways, demonstrating a variety of techniques through which issues of surrender values and charges could be displayed in a clear and graphic way to customers.

These arguments were supported and enlarged on by consumer groups and some sections of the press (including the tabloids as well as broadsheets and specialist publications). They gradually began to overwhelm the counter-arguments of both the regulators (who remained reluctant to act on this broader front) and the companies themselves. The pressure to develop a system of disclosure which revealed directly to consumers how much commission was being paid, to whom and when, how much was being taken out of the client's payments for expenses and how surrender values at various stages of the policy were being affected by these payments, became irresistible. The regulators were told by the government to stop procrastinating and come up with a workable system as quickly as possible. Following the publication of a Consultative Paper by the lead regulators (SIB, 1994) and the regulators for the sale of personal investment products (the Personal Investment Authority, successor to LAUTRO) (PIA, 1995), a system of disclosure was introduced with the aim of enabling customers and commentators to see more quickly and clearly how the pricing structure of products from different companies compared. This system was meant to ensure that customers could see the impact on their savings of all the constituent elements in a company's charging procedures in real terms (i.e. pounds sterling and not percentages and compound interest rates which were difficult to interpret). This included charges for the management of the funds, any commission paid to a broker or a salesperson and the cost of insurance cover.

Although generally believing in the importance of these changes, the regulators were cautious about the length of time it would take for them to have an impact. They therefore set in place certain monitoring procedures to provide annual benchmarks of changes in the industry which could be linked to the disclosure process. For example, the PIA established a Consumer Panel, which identified as one of its objectives the need to survey customers in order to track whether there were any changes in buying habits arising from the new system of disclosure (see PIA, 1997a). They also established their own tracking measures of 'objective' key performance indicators, such as rates of commission and persistency (i.e. numbers of early surrenders of investment products) which were perceived to be related to the issue of disclosure. It is clear that the *immediate* impact of these developments for consumers has, as the regulators expected, been limited. The issue of comparison remains very difficult, even for exports, as the qualifying statements which accompany product league tables in specialist magazines demonstrate. Moreover, it is doubtful how much even the more active middle-class consumers use this information – a large proportion of business continues to be sold through direct marketing such as newspaper advertising (*Guardian*, 6 March 1999) and customers continue to show remarkable 'loyalty' to the dominant companies rather than shop around (*Economist*, 17 April 1999). Finally, one can remain sceptical about the degree to which these changes actually impact on the fundamental disparity of power and knowledge which exists between companies, intermediaries and customers (see e.g. Clarke, 1999).

Nevertheless, these changes have impacted on the companies through forcing them to look more closely at the processes of selling and marketing products within this new framework. The regulatory changes have become more closely linked to the increased power of marketing and human resources as key aspects of shifting towards a customer-service driven strategy. The initial expectation that the expanding market could be met by the simple addition of products and new channels is no longer sustainable. To be strategic and market-focused in this context requires the reconsideration of how products are developed, priced, promoted and sold in the light of more sophisticated notions of how 'sovereign consumers' buy. Through changing the rules about selling and employing sales forces and about how products can be explained, the regulators have changed both the meaning of 'strategic' and the costs and consequences of being (or not being) strategic. The rules of the game in the industry have gradually changed. In broad terms, the changing nature of the rules have increased the costs of conformity with the regulatory process. Companies' varying abilities to absorb these changes in costs is more visible through the disclosure process, leading towards more 'open' (i.e. regulated) competition based on an increasing and more explicit differentiation of their performance.

These changes have been reinforced through the gradual emergence of new sorts of companies. The traditional financial services companies combined with those who emerged in the 1960s and 1970s (particularly in life assurance and investment products) had, as a group, undermined their own status and reputation with consumers through the processes described earlier. This, combined with the potential for high margins, left a gap into which companies without such a stigma could enter, following their own strategic logic of diversification and cross-selling. Such moves were made much easier by the use and development of technology which enabled potential customers to be approached in their home using targeted mailings or telephone calls. Large retailers with strong brand loyalty and regular customer contact together with well developed IT systems have found this a gap which they can fill, as have smaller companies establishing direct telephone selling on a much cheaper cost base than the traditional providers. Combining these advantages, they have been successful in gaining new business, particularly amongst those many customers who prefer simplicity and convenience. While their overall market share may have been limited, these entrants contributed to further heightening competitive pressures and changing the rules about customer expectations and work organization. As we saw in the case of the insurance subsidiary, Phoneco, in the previous chapter, traditional companies have responded by setting up or purchasing their own direct line facilities. Nevertheless, they found it difficult to wipe away the physical and financial legacy of their old ways of working and continue to struggle in this new market context.

In summary, then, taking on the mantle of 'strategy' led retail financial service companies to play the game of selling much harder than they had in the past. In doing so they increased both the risks which they were carrying and, more acutely, the risks amongst their customers. These effects were unintended and unexpected because the economic optimism of the mid to late 1980s condemned all pessimists as Cassandras. What was also unintended and unexpected was the way in which the impact of this downturn evolved into a more fundamental critique of the companies and their methods of working. The acquisition of 'strategy' had been meant to resolve the rules of the game, to create the competitive environment and the consumer choice which the market 'needed' in order to work properly. In the end, however, through pursuing 'strategy', companies had brought on themselves a higher degree of regulation and accountability. The freedom to develop new strategies, products and services which had been ushered in during the 1980s had had, by the 1990s, a number of unanticipated effects. Pushing new forms of money onto consumers led to new types of risk and uncertainty over key aspects of people's lives, particularly housing and pensions. As the distributional consequences of this for both those in employment (both stable and temporary) and those reliant on savings became more visible, the discourse of the free market was threatened. It began to be modified in practice and the notion of regulation reemerged.

This was part of a broader change in the political environment that had occurred in the 1990s. During the 1980s, the Thatcher project had clearly cemented an alliance between significant parts of the middle class and the working class (as well as obviously the financial institutions and multinational corporations) on the basis that freedom from regulation and constraint would bring them economic advantages. Whilst this project was partly predicated on Labour weakness and fragmentation, it had an ideological message about the nature of British society that sustained it in power. Even when the economy turned down in the early 1990s, the Conservatives were able to continue to win the general election. In the years between 1992 and 1997, however, the perceived incompetence and corruption of the government in a range of areas (not least in dealing with the economy and issues such as pensions) contributed to the revival of Labour. This revival was directed particularly at those in the middle class who had begun to feel economic uncertainty in the early 1990s. Labour sought to remove its reputation for redistribution through taxation and instead to appeal to just these groups by offering steady economic management and a form of regulation and consumer protection which would in theory avoid some of the scandals of the Conservatives' period in office.

With the advent of New Labour in 1997, the balance swung slightly more towards regulation. One of the Blair government's first acts was to rationalize the regulatory structure in the industry by the creation a single overarching body, the Financial Services Authority, charged to provide a more active disciplinary role in relation to the industry (as revealed particularly in its response to the delay in resolving the pension transfer scandal of the early 1990s) as well as becoming more involved in consumer education (FSA, 1998). It also instituted a series of enquiries into the issue of pension provision before producing its own proposals for 'Partnership in Pensions' in December 1998. It also established Individual Savings Accounts (ISAs); these were designed to replace PEPs, which were perceived as both more risky and more targeted at the wealthy sections of the population. ISA's also replaced the more conservative TESSAs (tax exempt savings accounts) which were accounts where regular savings were locked in for a minimum of five years in order to receive the benefit of tax exemption. In general, Labour's aim was to provide a more ordered and regulated (compared to self-regulated) framework to the industry whilst not undermining the dynamics of market competition. The effort was to ensure that consumers could choose from a range of savings vehicles and be safe in the knowledge that the products which they were being offered were appropriately monitored and regulated.

This still left two problems. Firstly, because there was such a range of products, how could there be a guarantee that each individual consumer bought the product that was right for him/her? Whilst the increased monitoring by the regulators has probably reduced this problem, it remains endemic in the system, though because it is a problem for the individual and not for collective groups of buyers, it has less impact on the political context. Secondly, the value of these products is still closely tied in with the dynamics the global financial system. As these still remain unpredictable and uncertain in the short and medium term, the system remains vulnerable to forces which it cannot control. However, the more obvious negative distributional consequences that arose out of the pensions scandal and through some forms of collective investment will ideally be policed out of the system. In these respects, financial services (at least at the retail end) can be seen as providing an arena in which the 'Third Way' (between the market and regulation) is being cautiously instigated. Whilst this may succeed in reducing obvious instances of fraud and malpractice, it does not break the link between global financial markets and the savings of individuals. The risks remain that the processes of these markets may lead to organizational or systemic failures with distributional and political consequences for people in the UK.

## CHANGING RULES, CHANGING ACTORS

Releasing companies to act as sovereign independent actors on the market has had an impact on profitability but, as might have been predicted, not in one direction only. There have been failures as well as successes at the company level (though these terms need to be considered as relative to the context in which market disciplines may operate on companies and according to varying types of performance criteria Meyer, 1994; Quack and Morgan, 2000). For example, one result of this process is a reduction of the numbers of companies operating in financial services. This is occurring partly through the exit of some companies from the market and partly through a process of merger and takeover. This process of concentration and centralization of capital is accompanied by a return within certain parts of the industry towards the situation of a limited number of companies with increasingly similar strategies and structures. In particular, there are a number of large diversified financial services conglomerates that are coming to dominate financial services in the UK.

In the wholesale markets, this process is reinforced by the need for companies to have large amounts of capital if they are going to compete in most of the business areas. Capital is needed in the high-risk areas where companies trade on their own account and seek to beat the market. The difficulties of controlling dealers in this area has been revealed not just by the Leeson example and the fall of Barings Bank in 1995, but also in the losses which Barclays took as a result of a particular trader in 1998. Other areas require substantial investments in technology and people in order to buy and sell shares, bonds and loans on a global basis. In some areas margins are increasingly narrowing, thus making profitability dependent on economies of scale, whilst in those areas with higher potential margins the need for supporting capital under various regulatory systems also reinforces the push towards size and economies of scale. In the UK, these factors have led to the withdrawal of both Barclays and NatWest banks from certain areas of their global operations as the costs of capital-adequacy requirements, risk-management systems, a global presence together with a supporting IT infrastructure and reduced margins have been emphasized by major losses incurred by a single individual. These aspects have also been reinforced by the swing in analysts' perceptions and favours away from the UK institutions becoming global financial companies towards a view that the safest and most efficient strategic use of shareholders' capital lies in the exploitation of the home market. This view particularly relies on the relative success of Lloyds Bank in withdrawing from significant international commitments in the early 1980s and instead concentrating on building a major presence in the UK market by acquisitions and mergers, most particularly with the Cheltenham and Gloucester Building Society and the TSB (*Economist*, 17 April 1999).

In the retail financial sector, also, the copying effect has been present as has the perceived need encouraged by business analysts, management consultants and investment managers to spread costs over a larger amount of business. In this sector, increased costs have emerged from the regulatory processes described earlier as well as the need to develop and maintain a complex infrastructure of physical space (often nationally spread out branches) and IT capacity. Thus, companies have struggled to recover higher and higher costs in a situation where competition is becoming more direct and visible and overall demand is growing only slowly. One possible solution is to continue to spread costs through bancassurance and cross-selling, thus achieving economies of scope and scale (Coopers and Lybrand, 1993). However, it became more and more difficult to grow market share organically in such a context. Therefore, and again combined with the encouragement of business analysts, management consultants and the example of other 'leading' firms in the sector and elsewhere, moves began to look for mergers, takeovers and amalgamations. This would, it was hoped, achieve the same result much more quickly than any internally generated process of growth. For example, back-office costs can be cut as some systems are closed down whilst others are worked more efficiently. Therefore, business and profits can be expanded through the cost-cutting effort.

In order to play in this game, however, companies have to become much more closely and visibly aligned to the financial markets. The ability to activate takeovers requires access to funds in the capital markets which are unlikely to be available to organizations that are not publicly owned. The largest building societies found it hard to resist the pressure to go public since failure to do so constrained their growth by making it difficult for them to take over other companies. Although for a time they were able to grow through agreed mergers with smaller societies within the sector, there was a limit to how far this could go. Beyond this limit, other ways to grow had to be found and these were likely to require access to wider funds and therefore a shift into private ownership. Although the largest mutual insurance societies were not so constrained because of their control over their own substantial reserves, they too began to feel similar pressures from the mid-1990s. In order to compete, they also perceived that they had to grow and this necessitated takeovers and mergers (*Guardian*, 3 October 1998). Therefore, this process is reducing the heterogeneous forms of ownership in the sector and pushing towards homogeneity around the public limited company model. Organizations of moderate size have been found offering themselves as takeover targets in recognition of the 'reality' that they can only survive as part of a larger, more cost-efficient financial conglomerate.

The result of these processes has been a series of phases of reconstruction in the actors participating in the industry. These phases of change have succeeded each other with increasing rapidity in the last 15 years. The initial phase during the 1980s was characterized by three main features. The first was a speeding up in what had been a long-term process in the mergers of building societies; the numbers of societies diminished rapidly over the decade as the difficulties of sustaining a competitive base for lending and deposits from a limited number of branch offices became increasingly obvious. This amalgamation movement created a group of societies which took the lion's share of business in the sector. Interestingly enough, however, most of these were 'friendly' mergers and the largest societies did not feel the need to seek funds from the capital markets to achieve their goals. Only the Abbey National decided in this period to move out of the building society sector and into being a publicly quoted company with a status as a bank. Larger size enabled the biggest societies to spread the costs of maintaining branch networks, IT investment and other overheads across a wider base.

The second feature derived from the expansion of the clearing banks into a range of investment banking and insurance activities from the mid-1980s. The processes of merger and takeover which occurred at this period created huge financial conglomerates with complex mechanisms of coordination, control and financial cross-subsidy between very different lines of business. Within these conglomerates, retail financial services in the UK market were seen as a steady and certain source of profitability, compared to international markets generally (where these banks generally made hesitant and ultimately unsuccessful forays) and the wholesale markets in particular (where high rewards were often counter-balanced by high risks and large losses). Thus, these banks sought to expand their market share and profitability in UK retail financial services to balance potential losses elsewhere. They particularly expanded this capacity into insurance, creating themselves as 'bancassurers' with integrated links amongst their bank branches and their insurance products. In seeking economies of scale and scope of this sort, they further threatened even the largest building societies with their expansionist plans. However, maintaining these conglomerates was not easy as was demonstrated by the gradual demise of the Midland Bank following various disastrous foreign adventures in the late 1970s and early 1980s and leading to its acquisition by the Hong Kong and Shanghai Bank. Barclays and NatWest were similarly weakened in the late 1990s by 'flawed' strategies at home and abroad. Whilst Barclays suffered boardroom conflicts as it sought to respond particularly to stock market pressures, NatWest found itself the target of an unfriendly takeover bid in September 1999.

The third feature was a gradual squeezing out of marginal operators as a result of the recession of the early 1990s. In the area of savings and investment, this was reinforced by the increasing expense of regulatory compliance. Thus, a number of foreign insurance companies, which had sought to establish direct sales forces based on commission, found they could no longer survive in the new context. Similarly, other foreign operators who had sought to establish market share in lending and mortgages were forced out as these markets crashed. By the early 1990s, therefore, there were a reduced number of actors in the retail financial services market. Those which remained were gradually becoming larger, mainly through swallowing up small units which were no longer viable given falling business levels, increasing compliance costs and heightened competition.

The second main phase of change began from the early 1990s. As the impact of regulation, new entrants and heightened competition increased, the drive to demonstrate 'strategy' became more powerful, particularly for those organizations which had remained outside the stock exchange. Their abilities to respond to the growing power of the bancassurers by themselves establishing a range of activities was limited by the rules under which they operated as building societies or mutual insurance companies. Thus, there began a gradual process of shift into private ownership, particularly amongst the largest building societies such as the Halifax but also amongst mutual insurance companies, such as the Norwich Union. These switches were associated with the almost simultaneous process of merger and takeover, for example in the case of the Halifax's takeover of the Leeds Permanent Building Society. The Halifax also went on to take over a major mutual insurance society, the Clerical and Medical. This push towards further concentration was reflected in the insurance sector where there were a number of major amalgamations such as those between the Royal and the Sun Alliance and General Accident and Commercial Union. Other companies in effect put themselves up for auction and were taken over and absorbed into a larger group, for example the takeover of Guardian Royal Exchange by the French insurer, Axa.

As more organizations shifted into being quoted on the stockmarket, the advantages of such a move in terms of opening up access to more capital had to be balanced against the fact that they were now more open to takeover. Furthermore, those organizations which retained building society status launched a vociferous campaign to convince their depositors that the lack of shareholders and a requirement to pay out dividends meant better value for customers. However, the numbers and market share of mutuals gradually dwindled as individuals launched campaigns to force them to take on plc status, culminating in 1999 with the surprise defeat of the board of the Bradford and Bingley Building Society (which had trumpeted its attachment to mutuality) by members preferring the option of immediate gains (through participating in the share launch) to the long-term drip-feed gains (available from lower borrowing rates and higher saving rates promised as the rewards of staying a mutual).

These changes increased the uncertainty within the industry since not only did they open up the prospect of merger and takeover within the UK itself, but they also raised the possibility of major new foreign entrants into the process. For example, Zurich Life which had previously operated in the UK on a fairly limited scale in niche markets, suddenly became a major actor due to the takeover by its Swiss parents of Eagle Star and Allied Dunbar which had previously been sheltered under the umbrella of the huge BAT company. Similarly, the French company Axa increased its size in the UK through its takeover of Guardian Royal Exchange. In the international capital markets themselves, foreign companies were becoming both more aggressively competitive against UK-based companies as well as exploiting the resulting weakness of the UK companies by buying out their failing international and wholesale-market operations.

By the end of the 1990s, then, the organizational actors who were trying to cope with the new rules of the game were themselves undergoing change. Many of the smaller actors had been squeezed out or had taken refuge in mergers and takeovers. The process of merger and takeover gradually increased throughout the decade as building societies and mutual insurers became both predators and victims. The industry shifted towards a greater degree of concentration based on large firms quoted on the stock exchange with a wide range of activities. The growing threat from so-called '*shopassurers*' such as Tesco, Marks and Spencer, Virgin and so on was also leading to a new group of actors within the organizational field. This group of actors had even less allegiance to the old ways of doing things and more willingness to accept the new rules of the game and extend their competitiveness by utilizing new technology with more mass-marketing techniques (based on brand consciousness and brand loyalty) to win customers. Another group that also lacked allegiance to the old rules was the foreign entrants into the UK which were increasingly (re-)appearing in both the retail and the wholesale sectors of the market.

What role did 'strategy discourse' play in this process? It became the accepted language through which senior managers articulated their decision-making processes and justified their outcomes. Searching for autonomy, certainty and freedom, managers also opened themselves up to scrutiny, insecurity and change (see also Chapter 5). Faced with the opportunities which the government was presenting them with in the 1980s, none of them could resist. However, as the rules of the new framework became clarified, survival became increasingly problematic even for large players. The population of organizational actors within the field was reconstituted leading to heightened levels of concentration with as yet uncertain consequences for consumers.

This process of concentration and centralization inevitably gives a new meaning to the discourse of strategy, competition and free markets. At the global level, it creates sites of power and influence within private institutions that can threaten the stability of national economic orders (what may be termed the 'George Soros' effect, after the rich financier whose currency dealings create fear and panic in central bankers and governments) and the stability of the global system (as their failure has knock-on effects on other interlinked institutions). Both processes lead in the direction of a further concentration of power as central bankers and governments in the major industrial economies seek forms of cooperation both to resist the consequences of speculation and to rescue firms from the consequences of speculation. Therefore, 'free markets' and processes of competition become subject to new forms of regulation within private institutions and multilateral governmental and quasi-governmental arenas (Strange, 1997; Sassen, 1996), none of which can be reduced to the level of a single nation-state. In the retail financial services, the concentration and centralization of financial institutions raises the further issue of the effects of this power on consumers and the state. In the following section, we explore this particularly by reference to the central role of these institutions in the management of welfare.

## THE POLITICS OF FINANCIAL SERVICES: CONSUMERISM, WELFARE AND THE ROLE OF THE COMPANIES

These changes have occurred within a context where the politicization of events within the sector was increasing all the time. The reasons which have already been discussed lay in the gradually emerging crisis of social welfare, perceptions of which were particularly shaped by the language and discourse of the Thatcher government. In these hands, the crisis was diagnosed as the creation of a state-dependent culture, leading to unrestrained public expenditure, high taxes and an increasing unwillingness to take on work at the market rate (Hall, 1998; Jessop *et al.*, 1988; Hay, 1996). This combination of factors was defined as leading to both social disorder (through the creation of an unemployed and alienated underclass) and economic decline (through a high taxation system which discouraged 'enterprise' and 'hard work'). As we have seen, the 'rescue' mechanisms were articulated as increased individual responsibility and savings encouraged by reducing taxation and public expenditure, making conditions more favourable for self-help and less favourable for dependence on the state. Central to achieving this shift was perceived to be the requirement for the financial institutions to make available products which could provide the individual saver with long-term security and good value for money. The 'bonanza' element for the retail financial services industry had a firm ideological foundation. It was not, however, delivered to the industry as of right but conditional on it being able to achieve these broad political goals of security and good value.

The Thatcher view of the '*crisis*' of social welfare was broadly accepted across the, albeit somewhat narrowed, political spectrum even when particular aspects of the 'solution' were rejected. In particular, the theme of 'choice' and 'individual autonomy' became embedded in the political discourse of all the main parties. Whilst this had a number of positive benefits for financial services companies, it was also crucial in setting a new context for their activities. From the point of view of the government (both Tory and Labour), state responsibility for the welfare of its citizens was becoming increasingly problematic. The UK state welfare system was generally built on a 'pay-as-you-go' basis; in other words, the benefits which were paid out at any one time had to be balanced by the revenues raised by the state (supported if necessary by borrowing). In theory, then, as the working population declined as a proportion of the whole population (due to people living longer, retiring earlier and entering the labour force later), taxes would have to rise in order to sustain the existing level of benefit (see Blackburn, 1999, for a review of this debate; also Budd and Campbell, 1999; Esping Andersen, 1996 provides a wider perspective on these debates). Governments accepted this analysis but sought to deal with it by shifting responsibility onto the individual. The state pension had anyway become an increasingly inadequate form of welfare, requiring a top-up from occupational pension schemes (Hannah, 1986; Esping Andersen, 1990; Knights, 1997).

Loading the responsibility entirely on occupational pension schemes was, however, equally impossible for a number of reasons. Firstly, there was growing concern that such schemes were also heading towards a financial crunch. This was because many occupational schemes had, in the past, been built on the basis of pension payments as a multiple of years in the scheme and final salary. Final salary schemes guaranteed the pensioner a certain level of benefit no matter what the value of the fund. Even though the funds were equity-based and therefore earning investment returns, there was a danger that if the numbers paying in shrank greatly whilst those receiving pensions grew, then there could be a stage when the fund could no longer meet its obligations. Since many occupational schemes were heading in this direction due to the drastic job losses of the 1980s, many companies began to shift their pension funds over to 'money purchase' schemes, whereby the amount of pension received is determined directly by the amount of money paid into the fund by the employee (and not by the level of the final salary).

Increasing job mobility was also making it difficult for individuals to keep track of their pension entitlements in company schemes. For women with intermittent patterns of labour-force participation (often in part-time or temporary employment where rights to membership of the company pension scheme were minimal), company schemes were particularly ineffective. Professional and managerial employees who moved between organizations frequently also found that firm-based occupational schemes were of less use to them than the previous generation for whom employment with a single employer was more likely to be the norm.

These pressures led to a coalition of interests in the construction of more flexible pension entitlements based on the individual's capacity and willingness to save. The state and occupational pension fund trustees were concerned to reduce their obligations in the future. Professional groups with mobile career patterns and variable levels of reward were also concerned to reduce what they perceived as ineffective expenditure to the state or occupational schemes and create their own personal pension funds as and when they could afford to save. Whilst this shift was articulated in terms of increased personal flexibility and individual choice, what was underplayed were two other aspects of the change. Firstly, the shift to personal pensions was inevitably a shift to money purchase schemes which were generally less generous on retirement than final salary schemes. This was also reinforced by the increased level of administration required for individual as opposed to collective pensions, thus increasing the level of charges and reducing the final value. Secondly, the shift to personal pensions reduced any redistributive effects which remained through the state welfare system. With individuals earning their own entitlements, those on low wages or in intermittent employment would earn less and thus in old age, inequalities would increase further as dependence on state benefits would be worth even less than in the past.

Shifting the system on to this new basis was a high priority with the Conservative governments. However, as has been described, it was partially thwarted by the failure of the financial services companies to adapt to these opportunities in a politically acceptable way. The Blair government has followed much of what the Conservatives were doing though it has made two broad changes in emphasis. The first is that as a new incoming government, it was able to announce its intention to rationalize the regulatory structure by creating a single over-arching regulator, the Financial Services Authority. It was also able to take a more aggressive stance towards the failures of the companies to rectify the mistakes which they made over the sales of personal pensions. It has therefore indicated to the industry that it will remain under pressure to improve its performance on selling. Secondly, the Labour government has continued to review the pension system. In particular, it has been more sensitive than the Tories to the charge that the shift towards personal responsibility will increase inequality. It has therefore looked to find ways of producing financial services products which can be sold to people on low incomes (e.g. ISAs). This has necessitated negotiating with the industry to agree on a particular design and cost structure for such products in order to ensure that they are not poor value. This has led to the announcement of what is termed the 'stakeholder pension' which, it is promised, will offer more flexibility and incentives to save for those with less income.

Apart from middle-class groups and those immediately or imminently effected (e.g. by pensions), such issues are not often an explicit concern.

However, within existing debates, the changes have some broad support. The middle class continue to wish to be able to secure their position and that of their children in the future on the basis of their own savings. Moreover and more generally, there appears to be little support for reconstructing the state welfare system exactly as before since this is perceived as having been ineffective and (for many female and male employees with high levels of job mobility and intermittent patterns of employment) inflexible. In addition, the redistributive effects of state welfare in the UK have long been dismissed as minimal and primarily redistributive across generations rather than classes (see for example the analyses of Esping Andersen, 1990, and Baldwin, 1990, which reveal the differences between European welfare states). Accordingly, in discussions such as those of Clarke and Newman (1995) and Blackburn (1999), which are broadly on the left of the political spectrum, there is a recognition of both the weaknesses of the previous system and also the depth of the changes achieved during the 1980s. The latter can be seen in terms of embedding notions of choice and freedom within a market rather than a social democratic framework (c.f. Castle *et al.*, 1996 who advocate an expansion of the state pension scheme).

However, this failure of the old welfare model in the British context did not mean that the state could opt out. On the contrary, as the effects of strategic discourse and competition worked themselves out, the contradictions between the notion of private provision of welfare and the competitive drive of the companies became more glaring. The credibility and reputation of the companies was severely undermined by the pensions scandal and the mortgage crisis of the early 1990s. Thus, there was a return to heightened state regulation which was, as we have seen, reinforced by the advent of the Labour government. The pattern of shake-out and concentration in the industry is useful to the government in so far as it reduces the range and variation of voices to which it must listen. As the larger companies take over more of the market, the government only has to deal with them and should therefore be able to reach agreement with the industry much more quickly than when there were hundreds of companies and thousands of independent brokers to deal with. There is, of course, a danger that this concentration of market power will lead back to the old informal arrangements such as price-fixing which the industry evolved earlier. In effect, strategy discourse which is part of the deregulation phenomenon induces the reemergence of both regulation and concentration, the antitheses of its supposed effects and its underlying justification.

CONCLUSIONS

In this chapter we have shown how the discourse of strategy partially transformed financial services companies. By constructing strategy as 'truth' and establishing a set of practices which pushed companies towards the extension of new forms of money, a series of unexpected effects were set in motion. Most crucial was the dialectical relationship between discourses of strategy, competition and 'free' markets with discourses based on regulation and protection. These dialectics emerged at various levels of the system. In the global contexts, their expression has increasingly come to be seen in the periodic crises which hit particular regions and countries, particularly through the foreign exchange markets. The 'truth' of the free market is reinforced through the statements, publications and actions of institutions such as the World Bank even when it is exactly the free market which has produced these crises (see for example the analyses of the East Asian crisis in authors such as Wade and Venesero, 1998; Henderson, 1998; Chang, 1998; Chang *et al.*, 1998; Jomo, 1998). For these authors it is the way in which political power is exercised through economic discourse that explains both the constitution and construction of the East Asian crises and its proposed solutions. The way in which the problem emerges and is defined and resolved has redistributive implications which technical analyses seek to conceal. In order for Western financial institutions to be propped up and supported, large parts of the population in countries such as Indonesia and South Korea are forced to accept insecurity and poverty. This emerges from the conditions which international institutions and markets make for helping these countries.

Similarly within retail financial services in the UK, the crises, problems and subsequent changes in the sector cannot be conceived of separately from their distributional effects. The process of concentration and centralization is not the working out of some inexorable law of economics, but rather the effect of the construction of a certain regime of truth which presses managers, consumers and governments to act in certain ways which have consequences. These consequences change the conditions under which the world of financial services is seen. The more this has become based on discourses of competitiveness, strategy and global markets, the more wealth and power has concentrated in the hands of the financial institutions operating these markets. Similarly the same process has introduced precariousness into the conditions of life for large populations around the globe. Becoming more 'strategic' has had 'power'-ful effects in terms of bringing uncertainty and risk to individuals and organizations.

Governments have tried to respond to this for fear that radical disruption of the existing system of distribution could undermine social order. State involvement has changed some of the 'rules of the game' and has had some distributional consequences in that some companies have been pushed out of existence or have begun to change the basis of their costing structure. This has, in turn, led to a consolidation of the industry through mergers, takeovers and the shift away from collective forms of ownership towards stockmarket flotation with a consequent loss of permanent jobs (and their replacement by temporary ones) as rationalization has proceeded. As the industry consolidated around an ever-decreasing number of huge conglomerates, the focus of these companies shifted increasingly towards economies of scale. The larger the market, the cheaper the products and the more competitive the large companies would be. To be large required access to capital resources beyond the mutuals and pushed more of them into the arms of the capital markets or each other.

In this way, strategy discourse was reasserted – as a means of legitimating the power of top managers in these companies to shape the destiny of their organization. It placed more organizations into the context of global financial markets and, with them, their employers and those people who through pension schemes, insurances and others savings instruments indirectly owned shares in them. Whilst certain aspects of their operation were constrained by a tightened national regulatory system, others remained uncertain and risky, dependent on the relatively uncontrolled flows of capital dictated through markets. The organizational field for financial services which has come into existence by the turn of the millennium is therefore in many ways fundamentally different from that of just 20 years ago. The organizations have been transformed; the role of the state has been transformed; the nature of consumers has been transformed. Central to this has been the discourse of strategy and the way in which it has reshaped companies, employees and customers in both intended and, importantly, unintended and contradictory ways.

# 9 Conclusion

## INTRODUCTION

In the preceding chapters we have explored the conditions, processes and outcomes of change in the field of UK financial services with a particular focus on emerging management discourses such as strategy and marketing. In doing so, we have sought to develop a distinctive contribution to understanding organizational change more generally which incorporates and connects different levels and types of analysis – historical, institutional, structural, sectoral, organizational and existential – and might be applied and developed in other contexts. At the same time, we hope to have offered a range of insights into the process of change that has occurred over the last 20 years in UK retail financial services. As we have emphasized, there are no clear cut-off points to change and the processes which we have described are ongoing with the combination of existing and newly-emerging conditions, contradictions and discourses.

In this conclusion, we wish to summarize our key arguments. Firstly, we review the relationship between structures, discourses and organizational change. We emphasize the need for a coherent approach to these concepts, which enables the development of a critical understanding of change processes. Secondly, we review the development of our argument with respect to an understanding of change in UK financial services. Our purpose is to emphasize the need to stand outside managerialist accounts of these processes and examine their embeddedness in fundamental changes in the nature of money and power. The discourse of strategy has been an essential part of constructing an account of these changes and in the process has had 'truth effects' on this structure of power and inequality. We insist upon the idea that 'strategy' is not a neutral term in a technical vocabulary of management; rather it is part of a discourse which constructs the world in specific ways and has distinctive 'truth' effects that impact on how people secure their well-being and identity. In the third part of the chapter, this leads us to speculate on 'post-strategic' discourse – what might this be and what would be the 'truth effects' which might stem from post-strategic discourse. In the final part, we sum up our view of the directions in which critical studies of the management of change should proceed in the future.

## STRUCTURES, DISCOURSES AND THE MANAGEMENT OF CHANGE

Our starting point was the limitations of the dominant managerial and political approaches to change in the literature. In the former case especially, the manageability of change and/or human subjectivity is exaggerated while the context and ideological nature of managing and management knowledge are ignored. With political approaches, context, process and pluralistic conflict are more central. But, there is still a tendency towards prescription and promoting the *control* of change by managers. In addition, both approaches tend to rely upon and reproduce, rather than problematize, the way in which managers in organizations perceive the problems and solutions of change. They do not examine management thought and practice critically in terms of its social and historical constitution and outcomes. By contrast, we have focused on existing and emerging managerial discourses asking how and why they developed in particular ways and what may be the implications for organizational change. Our starting point was therefore to construct an approach to change, which treated managerial discourses as socially produced. The language within which managers problematized the change process was itself part of the issue to be analysed. We rejected the notion that as researchers we could stand within that discourse and use it as a resource for our own understandings. Instead, we sought to place ourselves within another set of discourses which could provide us with the concepts and frameworks that could problematize the management view.

We emphasized the need to develop our position from what we termed a 'social' perspective in which discourses are seen in terms of the processes which construct them as 'acceptable understandings of the world'. We found that a disparate set of literature, which is rarely considered within the management of change literature, could offer us a range of insights into how discourses of strategy and change are constructed. These perspectives ranged from the macro-level approaches of Marxism and institutionalist sociology, to ethnographic and psychodynamic studies of managers in action. We also found that recent literature within the Foucauldian genealogical approach provided a means of understanding discourses and practices as interconnected phenomena that have distinctive power effects. The Foucauldian approach also links subjectivity and identity issues in a way which is very relevant to the management of change.

In considering these frameworks, however, we faced the issue of the status of the forms and categories of knowledge that were being constructed. Most challenging of all was the Foucauldian post-structuralist view that 'there is nothing beyond discourse'; in other words, that we needed to focus no further than discourses of change and strategy and how these constructed and developed specific 'truth effects'. Whilst our research reinforced arguments about the *potentially* constitutive power of discourse and those rejecting an essentialist and determinist view of the human subject, we also felt it important to reassert the idea of a social structure that provides the framework within which social actors with specific powers and potentialities are constituted. Otherwise, it appears that discourses are driven along by their own logic into 'capturing' and encapsulating social space. Our research, led us to the view that we could not understand fundamental transitions in discourse without a conception of a changing underlying structure.

This need to reinstate structure to a role also reinforced our concern that Foucauldian analysis did not help us deal with what in our view remains an absolutely vital element of any social approach to change or organizations which calls itself 'critical'. By this, we are referring to our underlying conviction that structures are about inequality of power and wealth. Therefore it was necessary not just to connect discourses with structures but to connect both of these with issue of inequality. We sought to highlight that discourses had effects on the distribution of power and inequality which in turn were emergent from underlying structures. Therefore, processes of change in organizations have to be examined through three distinct but interrelated lenses – changing structures, changing discourses and the effect of both these processes on power and inequality. We have sought to hold in balance the role of social structure and the role of the mediating human subject. Social structures empower and constrain groups in different ways. Thus, social structure does not entrap actors in a static monolith but opens up possibilities and potentials in specific ways. Out of this structure of possibilities, human reflexivity can mould new discourses which ultimately (though not necessarily) can become the basis of new structures through their effects on power and inequality. Therefore at any particular time, one needs to identify the specific combinations of structures, discourses and relationships, which exist.

Furthermore, this combination cannot be conceived of as a smooth unified social system but rather as one in which there are potential mismatches between the levels. It is within these mismatches that we see power, tensions and resistance. Any approach to the management of change which does not see power and resistance from a structural point of view and instead reduces it to features of intra-organizational politics, makes in our view two fundamental errors. First, it cannot account for the power of actors adequately as these are ultimately based on structural locations. Secondly, it trivializes the significance of organizational contexts and neglects the fundamental role which organizations play in wider, including global, structures of power and inequality. This may be perfectly acceptable if one retains a managerialist perspective where one's implicit goal is to collude in the 'management of change' (using management to mean control, surveillance and repression). If one wishes to develop a critical social approach to the management of change, these blinkers must be discarded.

In our approach then the concern is to reveal the interaction between discourses, structures and patterns of inequality. For example, the discourse of customer service only became significant as the structure of relationships between financial service organizations, the state and consumers began to change. Elaborating 'customer service' meant that it became a 'truth' which transformed the practices and sense of identity of employees inside and consumers outside the organization. It was, however, a precarious 'truth'. One can write and talk about customer service without necessarily 'doing it'. Employees and consumers can resist this truth because it involves them having to think about themselves in a different way. Understanding the conditions under which discourses become transformed into and through practices (or resisted) and thereby gain a wider meaning as the 'truth' of how actors and organizations should behave in particular contexts is, in our view, central to moving beyond the managerialist and political accounts of change, without at the same time getting trapped in an approach based purely on text and language. It is necessary to understand the changing structural conditions which give rise to the possibility that actors can use their differential powers to construct (and resist) new discourses.

This aspect of our framework derives from taking seriously the social embeddedness of economic action as discussed within Marxism and institutionalist theories, though here again we are concerned to ensure that limitations of certain variants of this approach are not reproduced in our analysis. In particular, scope for human (and therefore organizational) agency is important to establish, not in the form of voluntarism or as a humanist project of individual freedom, but to account for variation, socially enabled choice and, crucially, change. Social structures are not simply reproduced through practices, but may also be transformed. For example, we have seen how managerial actions were partly shaped by an emerging class structure and associated consumption patterns, but also that they were conditions of such changes. Here, the multiplicity and interaction of social structures and related discourses and tensions within and between them were also shown to be important. In customer service and marketing, for instance, gender and employment relations combined with contradictions within competitive capitalism were shown to inform the ways in which the discourses were experienced, transformed and resisted. This also marks a distinction with much institutional theory in giving emphasis to the material and ideological basis of capitalist social relations. Practices can become established in organizations and sectors through the material power relations in employment without being fully institutionalized at the level of legitimacy/ meaning. Even where discourses appear to be internalized and/or identified with, a necessarily political process is involved such as that in consultancy interactions and the use of customer service and marketing rhetoric to secure increased productivity or instil organizational loyalty and a strategic orientation for profit.

The final dimension to our analysis was derived from ethnographic and psychodynamic literature with its focus on social identity and/or related ontological insecurities. This element is not just concerned with the subjective experience of change and new discourses, but is central to an understanding of the mediating role of the human subject and agency in change processes viewed from wider levels of social structures. New management ideas may be internalized, complied with and/ or resisted and transformed on the basis of a preoccupation with maintaining a sense of control and (e.g. gender, managerial, occupational) identity in particular socially and historically constituted situations. For example, we have seen how the emergence of strategic discourses and its particular forms and transformations can be linked to the nature of, and changes in, the organizational field which themselves are conditions and consequences of self-defeating concerns to secure a sense of certainty and control over identity, career and environment. This was demonstrated most explicitly in our study of IT strategy consultancy and the paradox of a continued demand for solutions.

In conclusion, our agenda is based on breaking the bounds of understanding which actors construct for themselves and instead treating those constructions (or discourses) as themselves deriving from a set of social factors. In general, we would argue that the 'management of change' is an area, which has been dominated by managerialist accounts of more or less obvious kinds. There have been few critical studies which have sought to show what an alternative approach needs to consider and how this can be achieved. In our view, we have set up one possible answer to this. Firstly, a critical approach to the management of change must uncover the underlying discourses which shape how actors perceive their role. It must treat this discourse as an object of analysis, not as a free resource which can be drawn on to explain the change process. Secondly, the discourses have to be understood in terms of the potentialities and constraints which arise from structures. Discourses are responses to these changes but they are not a mechanical predetermined response. They have to be articulated, developed and put into practice. As they become practices, they have, as the Foucauldians insist, 'truth effects'; they start to change the world in ways which were unpredictable initially and, indeed, in ways which eventually may change the very structure out of which they developed. Thirdly, we cannot understand structures and discourses without understanding them as phenomena of inequality and power. Their 'truth effects' are effects on the distribution of inequality. Any analysis of the 'management of change' which ignores this or treats it as a side issue is, in our view, simply colluding in the attempt to neutralize and conceal underlying conflict.

## FINANCIAL SERVICES AND CHANGE

We began our analysis by setting out the broad and *specific* context of UK financial services and changes therein through the concept of an organizational field. Here, we identified four key categories of actors – the financial institutions themselves, the state, business organizations in general and consumers. We went beyond conventional accounts of an external context which organizations respond to and/or act upon. Emphasis was placed upon the way in which the *interacting* elements of the field (e.g. class differences; state regulation etc.) are actually part of organizations (shaping their structures, practices and behaviours). In UK financial services, this context emerged over the course of the eighteenth and nineteenth centuries and was sustained as a dynamic system and structure of power, interest and tension into the 1960s. These organizations were embedded in, *rather than enveloped or determined by*, these social contexts. We emphasized the obvious but frequently neglected point (at least in conventional approaches), that financial services are about money. Few things are more obviously about power and inequality than money. Therefore, we discussed both sociological accounts of money and what these had to say about power and inequality. Structures of inequality in the nineteenth and twentieth centuries were about access to forms of money. Financial services organizations constituted the conduits for that access. Their shape and structure cannot be understood outside of this interaction between social groups struggling over issues of money and inequality. Therefore the structure which emerged and the discourses which acted as a way of understanding, explaining and legitimating that structure arose out of the peculiar distribution of money and power in British society. We sought to reveal the differentiation between types of financial organizations, how these related to the state (which in turn had a peculiarly 'British' structure owing to its emergence out of an eighteenth-century commercial and liberal – but not democratic – society) and the role which these organizations played in the reproduction of inequalities, and status distinctions between social groups.

It is impossible to fully understand changes within organizations without seeing the ways in which previous ways of working and understanding were being challenged and/or dismantled, and the spaces opened up were being and continue to be colonized by the new, competing and possibly fragile discourses being carried into and generated by organizations. In Chapter 3 we saw how the tensions and conflicts which had been accumulating in the British context and the global capitalist economy reached such a point that underlying continuities began to be broken up. Again, we traced this to the changing nature of money and the shift away from national monetary systems to a more complex and unpredictable global monetary order. In particular, the network of specialist institutions dominated and structured by the preexistence of the City of London as a financial and social (e.g. class and gender) network was no longer fully sustainable. The participants within the sector began to look at new ways of organizing and recreating a sense of order and stability. In this process, new ways of thinking, new specialisms, new market mechanisms, new organizational structures and new regulatory structures emerged.

In Part III, our attention shifted to some of the particular discourses to arise as part of the transforming field of financial services. Our focus was on how they emerged and developed *within* organizations; how they were introduced, experienced, contested and transformed; and the new structures and practices associated with them. In exploring strategy, IT and the role of management consultants, marketing and HRM discourses were shown to be socially and historically specific and to take particular forms founded on internal contradictions and interactions with other existing and emerging discourses. For example, their emergence and form in the financial services sector did not coincide exactly with similar processes in other business sectors. Rather, they were also a condition and consequence of the broader change processes identified in the earlier chapters.

Emphasis was placed on strategy discourse, not because current organizational changes can be reduced to its emergence (which they cannot), but because of its overarching and integrative claims and practices as well as its explicit connection to understanding and controlling organizational contexts. In Chapter 4, the distinctive characteristics of strategy discourse were introduced. Strategy in organizations is neither natural nor inevitable, but has been socially produced or naturalized and contested since the 1960s as a particular way of looking at the organization in the world. Crucial to this was the link which strategy established to the discourse of the market and the idea that markets work through the creation of a set of autonomous firms with managers exercising their discretion to determine particular forms of action. The dis-embedding of companies from their more obvious links both with each other and the state was articulated as deregulation and the 'freeing' of companies and managers from constraints. The burden of freedom was that one's fate was in one's own hands. For organizations this became part of the idea of the sovereignty of the consumer, but also the increased importance of management and managerial skills. Strategy became the highest of those skills, the central determining factors in success and failure. Companies were to be held accountable for their exercise in freedom by financial markets, which in turn would evaluate strategies and their outcomes as key indicators of managerial responsibility.

Strategy therefore emerged as a high-status corporate activity with an ever-increasing body of knowledge, theories and techniques through which companies could demonstrate their responsibility. Strategy was seen as distinct from the other organizational functions and actors which it sought to manage, integrate and measure. As it began to assume a dominance in organizational hierarchies, these 'operational' groups reinforced and responded to its legitimacy by becoming more 'strategic'. In doing so, conflict shifted to its nature or contents – the 'best strategy' – rather than strategy *per se*. This is not, however, to discount the contested and sometimes 'messy' nature of its continuing emergence in practice. This was illustrated in Chapter 5 which examined the specific situation of financial services and the key role of strategy and related IT consultants. Here, we examined some of the precise ways in which consultants and managers sought to promote, deploy and transform strategy. This account highlighted the interactive and often conflictual nature of the process. Also, by developing some of the themes of psychodynamics from Chapter 1, it drew a further connection in our analysis of change by linking field instability and discourses with individual actors and their existential and material anxieties. Moreover, it showed how not only the sales practices of consultants, but strategy itself combined the prospect of reassurance and control (over the organizational environment for example) with exposure to uncertainty and change.

In Chapter 6, we explored the emergence of marketing discourse. This both extended and fed into strategic practices of knowing and controlling the organizational environment. However, our main concerns were to highlight the conflicts and contradictions associated with its emergence and the conditions and consequences in terms of the different elements of the field of financial services such as the state and consumers. This revealed that there were certain 'truth' effects, which emerged from the growing dominance of strategy. In particular, the emergence of marketing was explored in terms of its competition and contradistinction with a 'production' view of the world both generally and in financial services where it took the form of a sales orientation. The drive towards selling which was sponsored and reinforced within this emerging strategic discourse had powerful consequences. It drew large numbers of individuals into purchasing financial products. As economic conditions changed, the value of these products and people's ability to keep paying for them became a greater issue. In a range of debates in the press and Parliament, it became clear that in a number of areas but particularly housing finance and pension, the results were highly unfavourable to the consumers. Out of this emerged stronger regulation and within the companies a sense that the selling impulse had to be curbed, primarily by increasing the role of marketing with its emphasis on (constructing) customer needs. Marketing, which resonated with both strategic and broader consumer discourses, started to become embedded in financial services companies.

This is not to argue, as much of the marketing literature does, simply that increasing competitive pressures forced companies to address better the needs of consumers. Attention was drawn to some of the tensions within marketing. Aside from inherent faults within the marketing concept (e.g. the sovereign consumer as an undersocialized actor), competitive pressures on profitability combined with consumer inertia shift corporate attention towards particular products and customer segments. This sets in train a more or less explicit mechanism which selects out the poorest groups in society who, as we saw in earlier chapters, have long been marginalized within financial services. Relatedly, companies had to be forced by regulators to address consumer interests such as in the case of the disclosure of commission charges in investments. At the same time and paradoxically, marketing rhetoric, both within the sector and elsewhere, combined with these regulatory concerns to raise consumer expectations/'activity' and, therefore, to reconstitute many consumers. In doing so, like strategy it contributed to the conditions of its own emergence and, possibly, fragility. This raises two important additional themes in terms of our analysis of change. Firstly, it highlights the mutually constitutive nature of elements within the field rather than adopting a form of environmental determinism whereby, say, growing consumer activity leads to increased marketing. Secondly, it highlights the importance of the albeit specific form of wider structures – capitalist social relations – and of associated tensions within discourses.

These issues and the complementarity and competition between discourses reemerged in Chapter 7 which explored changes in work and employment as a condition and consequence of strategic and marketing discourses. For example, we saw how the shift away from sales and traditional discourses and the contradictions within marketing discourse were reflected in employment practices and responses to them. Employees concerned about consumers' interests would resent firms' concomitant emphasis on profitability issues and see through service rhetoric. However, we also saw how, despite a tendency towards ambivalent employee responses where, at best, they would engage only partially with the emerging discourse, widespread changes have occurred in the sector. The breakdown of the organizational field can be linked to what many see as the 'end of an era' in financial services employment. There have always been periodic and gradual changes in the nature of jobs, the workforce and careers, such as those associated with expansion, rationalization, new technologies and social change. However, in setting out the contrasting nature of employment in current and previous periods, we focused on the decline of administrative/technical cultures characterized by job security and, for some, company careers to ones based more on customer-oriented skills and orientations which are increasingly linked to corporate and individual performance. Such developments are typically linked by commentators to the general emergence of a more or, typically, less coherent HRM discourse with its attendant contradictions and its connection to strategy (see Legge, 1995). Our concern was to highlight not only strategic links, but also those with marketing and the discourse of the sovereign consumer outlined in Chapter 6. Employees are becoming constituted as strategic marketeers in their relations with customers, colleagues ('internal customers') and even in terms of their own 'personal development'.

Our account of employees' responses to changes in work and employment directed at eliciting customer oriented practices and values can also be compared to the discussion in Chapter 5 of strategy consultancy and how managers received it. In both cases, the new discourses competed with others and were contested. However, in the case of strategy, we saw how managers might adopt and promote discourses in order to defend or further their material and career interests. Similar processes are evident with service staff, particularly as service criteria become incorporated into recruitment and reward systems and hierarchies and as employment security becomes more fragile. But the *positive* incentives are usually less pronounced for employees at lower and often segregated hierarchical levels. Indeed, we saw how constraints to a widespread diffusion of customer service at the level of orientation, if not also practice, are conditioned not only by competing discourses and their associated social identifications (e.g. other service discourses) and internal contradictions, but by the nature of the employment relationship. Generic patterns of response – degrees of ambivalence – were linked to issues such as trust levels, job autonomy and work intensification. Moreover we saw how values such as customer service were used instrumentally by employers to legitimate power relations – increased work effort and sales.

However, and as our analysis shows more generally, focusing on capitalist employment and market relations provides only a limited explanatory framework. Other social structures and related practices such as class, occupation, culture and gender interact in complex and unpredictable ways providing resonances as well as tensions with new discourses. For example, as Halford *et al.* (1997) demonstrate in banking, the changes mark a shift in the gendered nature of organizational practices, deploying notions of femininity and a transformed, more competitive, masculinity. Drawing such connections with the emerging orientations and practices of employees highlights once again how organizational change cannot be adequately understood without a social and historical perspective, whether this is general and societal in nature (e.g. Casey, 1995; Jacques, 1996) or specific to a particular field.

In Chapter 8, we returned to a specific focus on the organizational field of financial services – firms, consumers, the state and City – linking it to emerging organizational and socio-political structures. In particular, we continued the analysis of Part II by charting the developments to occur *following* the breakdown of the established system of largely tacit agreements between institutional actors. We saw how the adoption in organizations of marketing and strategic discourses gradually began to have wider structural and sometimes unintended and contradictory effects. Through the language of the sovereign consumer and of 'free' competition, 'boom' turned to 'bust'. This was in turn related to the changing nature of money in global financial markets. Flows of money across borders increased through the use of instantaneous computer-based transfers. The instability of markets, prices, currencies, stocks and so on that grew out of this changed the way in which money worked for states, organizations and individuals. At the level of the state, these changes were part of the general loosening of power which states had over their national economic and social policies. At the level of financial organizations, they opened up a range of new risks and opportunities which reinforced the sense that companies had of their own destinies. Strategies that could find ways to make money in these environments became the goal of every company, but risks and uncertainties had grown immeasurably. The result was a growing group of global corporations through which flowed huge amounts of capital. The concentration of power and wealth in these hands meant that the fates of whole regions could be determined in a matter of a few minutes through large deals on the international markets. In all parts of the world, though in different ways, this integration had an effect on individuals. In the UK, that effect was felt particularly through the increasing importance of forms of investment to house purchase, pensions and savings generally.

The 1980s and 1990s saw a number of phases of reconstruction of the actors in UK financial services as organizations sought to respond to these changes. The emergence of some new players and increased diversification (e.g. bancassurance) coincided with a process of concentration overall with mergers and 'strategic' and technological alliances. The survivability of certain (e.g. small, mutual and/or 'under-capitalized') organizations and practices (e.g. branch distribution) came to be questioned under the increasing gaze of financial markets and/or potential predators from the UK and overseas. At the same time and as part of this process, the field became more openly politicized in terms of the symbolic and financial costs to firms of protective consumer regulation and a related reorganization of welfare. Somewhat paradoxically given the discourse of competition and marketing, addressing consumer 'interests' was largely forced onto corporate agendas. Doing so, it was hoped, would support a broader transition whereby the responsibility for welfare would shift away from the state towards the individual and, therefore, financial services companies.

The uncertainties and ambiguities in these processes led firms to undertake certain 'strategic' ventures that had unexpected effects. Some firms, which sought to establish a global presence, found that they could not maintain themselves successfully in this sector and withdrew. Other organizations such as building societies and mutual insurance companies found that in order to pursue their 'strategies' they needed more 'freedom' and therefore opted to launch themselves on the stockmarket. Still others voluntarily gave themselves up to a bigger company in the belief that they were too small to survive. Adapting to the increasing size of operations in financial services consequent on the globalization of markets and the increased costs of conducting business (as a result of regulation) led to a gradual restructuring of the industry and in particular a further concentration and centralization of capital. Thus the discourse of strategy which had opened up with the possibility of multiple deregulated companies pursuing their own business ended with a decreasing number of companies and an increasing amount of regulation.

Central to these processes were the responses of various actors to the impact which these activities were having on the distribution of wealth and income. Middle-class groups losing out as a result of poor selling of mortgages and pensions were becoming increasingly articulate about the need for regulation. Governments aiming to restructure the welfare state sought to create an environment in which the private sector could take on more of a role, but this was threatened by the uncertain distributional consequences of the strategic actions of the firms. Whilst the Blair government sought to limit the potential disruptive consequences of this by tighter regulation over processes and products, the uncertainties in the global markets remained. Whilst the distributional consequences of these uncertainties are made to fall most heavily on people in East Asia, Latin America, Africa and Russia, there can be no guarantee that eventually these uncertainties will not also impact drastically on standards of living in countries like the UK where the integration of organizations and individuals into the global context is high.

In summary, the processes of change which have occurred in financial services cannot be understood outside these contexts. A particular structure of organizations, related in very specific ways to the state and the various groups in British society, had emerged in the nineteenth century. This structure relied on a particular approach to money and power which was based on a peculiar interrelationship between the City of London and government. As money itself changed due to its increasing internationalization and virtualization, this structure could no longer be sustained and new discourses emerged to explain what was occurring and to direct action in particular ways. Through the discourse of strategy reinforcing the 'free market' and consumer sovereignty debates of the 1970s and 1980s, a new set of effects emerged. These led to changes in the structure of organizations and the distribution of money and power. A centralization and concentration of capital at the global level was reflected with a similar process in Britain. At the global level this was largely unregulated, but at the local level the distributional consequences of these processes necessarily led to increased politicization and control. In our account, therefore, the management of change in financial services can only be understood by holding in balance all of these levels – the changes in discourse, the changes in the underlying structure deriving from the changing nature of money, and the impact of this on the structure of power and inequality in British society.

## POST-STRATEGIC DISCOURSES: CONTRADICTION AND UNCERTAINTY

We have focused our analysis on how new ways of acting and understanding the world in organizations, such as through strategy and marketing, emerge and move *towards* dominance. However, we have emphasized how such discourses are not natural, inevitable nor even necessarily effective, but subject to processes of 'naturalization' (e.g. through consultancy and isomorphism). Arising from and feeding into particular combinations of historical and contemporary structural patterns, meanings and actions come to assume specific forms within organizational fields. Moreover, they are enacted and worked on *continuously* in order to be reproduced and transformed. We have also seen how they do not become dominant within particular organizations without conflict and interaction with prevailing, alternative and other emerging discourses. Accordingly, even if particular discourses become dominant, *they cannot be assumed to remain so*. Indeed, while much conflict may begin to assume an apparently conservative form – framed *within* a particular dominant discourse – we have also pointed to tensions, contradictions and unintended consequences. These constitute another, *internal*, source of fragility or instability in discourses which may contribute to the conditions of their demise and to the emergence of new discourses.

The case of strategy is especially important given its centrality to our analysis. We have shown how, at its heart, strategy is a form of knowing and controlling internal and external organizational 'environments'. As it assumes dominance, other emerging discourses such as marketing and HRM begin to take 'strategic' forms such as through new objects of measurement. Strategy offers existential, symbolic and material rewards through the prospect of greater certainty – knowing, controlling and integrating. This was illustrated in our discussion of the selling of strategy through consultancy. However, we also pointed to two paradoxes in this process. Firstly, by drawing attention to the nature and significance of organizational environments, uncertainty is made more visible through strategy, particularly when preexisting conditions and relations are breaking down – new 'problems' are exposed. Indeed, and secondly, strategy emerged at a time when uncertainty and change were seen (and promoted) as endemic in dynamic and globalizing markets.

This latter paradox and the practical difficulties it poses – knowing and controlling – is recognized by many practitioners who may then pursue an intermediate and compromise path between planning and fire-fighting (Burnes, 1996; Eden and Ackermann, 1998; Ilinitch *et al.*, 1998). It is also receiving increasing attention in mainstream as well as more critical management texts and education. In short, new 'post-strategic' discourses can be seen as emerging. For example, Weick's (1987) notion that 'any old map [strategy] will do' emphasizes the role of strategy as a *process* that provides a '*sense*' of order and reassurance rather than objective knowledge and control. Apparently more radical is Peters' celebration of contemporary chaos in calling for doing 'crazy' things in organizations for our 'crazy times' (1989, 1993; see also Stacey, 1992). Such prescriptions are sometimes linked to broader debates in social theory which point out that even in apparently stable contexts, the future, the environment and other actors are inevitably unpredictable and therefore that control 'solutions' are bound to be partial and self-defeating. Here, strategy, like management generally, can be seen as reflecting a *modernist* and masculine preoccupation with securing knowledge and control (Kerfoot and Knights, 1993; Jacques, 1996).

> Management in modernist discourse works on the basis of control – the progressive rationalization and colonization of nature and people whether workers, potential consumers or society as a whole. But there are structural limits to control – the costs of integration and control systems often exceed the value added by management within the corporation. (Alvesson and Deetz, 1996: 192)

The idea of 'post-strategic discourse' therefore has an appeal both to managerialist proponents of 'flexibility' and to social theorists endorsing the notion of a shift towards post-modernism. In our view, however, the case for this has yet to be clearly made. There are specific social and broader existential and material conditions associated with a preoccupation with seeking control. Thus, as attention to the changing and uncertain nature of the world increases, so too do associated anxieties and attempts to resolve them. As we have seen, management consultants' offerings continue to find buyers in financial services as sectoral transformations continue, even if strategy consultancy may have peaked. Moreover, new approaches can, as we have seen, be absorbed into strategy discourse. Similarly, there are material and structural considerations which favour control, whether 'strategic' or not. For example, management gurus such as Peters may appear to decry bureaucracy and celebrate disorder and chaos, but only so long as basic structures of capitalism (e.g. ownership, profit) remain unchallenged (Willmott, 1992; Boje, 1996). Indeed, Jacques talks of a 'Procrustean' tendency in management thought of reshaping any potentially new ideas to conform to modernist thinking despite its increasing inappropriateness in the contemporary era (1996). If, as we have argued, strategic discourse is deeply embedded and implicated in the reproduction of a particular structure of power and inequality, then notions of 'post-strategic discourse' must also contain notions of what this means at the levels of structure and power and inequality.

On the other hand, despite the continuing broad conditions favouring discourses of control, we have seen here how tensions *within* strategy discourse and the associated emergence of competing discourses may lead to debates on 'post-strategic' ways of organizing. It can be argued that the conditions associated with the emergence of strategy (e.g. environmental change and complexity) are also those of its possible decline. Indeed, commentators are increasingly pointing to the inherent failings of strategy both generally and in terms of practices such as the integration of management functions. This is unsurprising for, as we have shown, discourses are historically and socially constituted and therefore transient. However, it is already clear that strategy discourse is more than a passing fad as it has become embedded in diverse organizational fields, including that of financial services.

## ORGANIZATIONAL CHANGE AND BEYOND

In the introductory chapter, we expressed a hope that by the end of the book the reader will have been challenged to think about organizational change in new ways. Through an historical and critical perspective, discourses, institutions and identities in a particular sector were explored integratively. In doing so we sought to go beyond conventional accounts of organizational change, but there remains considerable scope for further 'social' research on change (see Collins, 1998; Reed, 1997) not least because orthodox (i.e. managerial, political) views continue to emerge and remain dominant (e.g. Senior, 1998). Social research on change would embody the two key aspects of our analysis. Firstly, such research would pay detailed attention to the construction of firms within particular sectors and the ways in which the structure, practices and behaviour of these firms are embedded within specific social, political and economic structures of power and inequality. Secondly, such research would shift from the unproblematic focus on individual agency and rationality and instead examine how discourses of rationality are constructed and how they constitute certain, often contradictory, truths and practices. Bringing these two together avoids the failings of managerial and political approaches to change and leads to the potential for constructing a critical and socially informed understanding of change practices.

As well as hoping that others will follow this model in order to produce a new understanding of change processes, our analysis suggests a number of other possible avenues to follow. Firstly and most importantly, while we have explored change through emerging 'strategic' discourses, it is clear from our introductory review that a *change discourse* has emerged and developed. Indeed, in a modest way we are contributing to this discourse here. More generally, within work organizations managers are coming to adopt 'change' as an imperative; a choice between radical and incremental approaches; a value ('change is good'); and an account of their own and others' behaviour for example. This discourse has yet to be subject to the critical scrutiny applied to other managerial knowledges and practices such as BPR, quality, enterprise and strategy. How, for instance, was change perceived prior to the contemporary discourses informed by organizational development and systems theories? Under what conditions did they emerge and transform? Such analysis would complement our own in seeking to make sense of change practices, consequences and experiences.

Secondly, the inevitable selectivity of our account means that there are certain dimensions and approaches which remain inadequately addressed, both in relation to change and financial services. Some of these have already been discussed here and, to a certain extent, explored elsewhere, such as cross-national comparisons (Morgan and Knights, 1997; Morgan and Engwall, 1999). We have also examined some of the gendered characteristics and outcomes of change and discourses, but this remains an underdeveloped area along with related structures of inequality such as ethnicity and class. Similarly, in developing the concept of an organizational field, we have sought to be sensitive to its internal complexity, variety and dynamism. However, some of this has been lost such as the differences and commonalities between the different financial service sectors and organizations and changes therein. Further research on managerial discourses and change might explore fields and companies more intensively. For example, the emergence of strategic discourse in specific companies in different sub-sectors might be compared, albeit with due sensitivity to the limitations of change research which takes the organization as the prime unit of analysis. In addition, while we have made constant references to managerial discourses being imported to, and exported from, financial services (through consultancy and recruitment for example), a 'social' analysis of change which compares different or overlapping fields might yield further insights. For example, the emergence of strategic discourse in health care and retailing could reveal the importance of other dynamics or structures.

Despite these limitations or opportunities, our aim has been to develop and provide a critical framework for exploring change which can be applied to other organizational fields. In doing so, we also faced theoretical challenges. We combined, developed and applied a range of sometimes seemingly incompatible 'social' approaches. In particular, we sought to extend and transform discourse analysis and some of the insights it brings towards a critical realist approach and non-determinist institutional theory. This may be seen as being over-ambitious such that supporters of particular perspectives will be frustrated or dismissive rather than inspired. Indeed, there remains some scope for further research, which serves to break up intellectual encampments. In pursuing theoretical development and criticality, it is essential to challenge and develop frameworks continuously without losing coherence and consistency.

# Bibliography

Abercrombie, N. (1994) 'Authority in Consumer Society', in Keat, R. *et al.* (eds), *op cit.*

Abrahamson, E. (1996) 'Management Fashion', *Academy of Management Review*, 21(1), 254–85.

Ackrill, M. (1993) 'Marketing in British Banking, 1945–80', in Tedlow, R. S. and Jones, G. (eds), *The Rise and Fall of Mass Marketing*, London: Routledge.

Ackroyd, S. and Crowdy, P. A. (1990) 'Can Culture be Managed?', *Personnel Review*, 19(5), 3–13.

Aldridge, A. (1994) 'The Construction of Rational Consumption in *Which?* Magazine: The More Blobs the Better?', *Sociology*, 28(4), 899–912.

Aldridge, A. (1997) 'Engaging with Promotional Culture: Organised Consumerism and the Personal Financial Services Industry', *Sociology*, 31(3), 389–408.

Allen, J. and Du Gay, P. (1994) 'Industry and the Rest: the Economic Identity of Services', *Work Employment and Society*, 8(2), 255–71.

Alvesson, M. (1993), 'Organisations as Rhetoric: Knowledge Intensive Firms and the Struggle with Ambiguity', *Journal of Management Studies*, 30(6), 997–1019.

Alvesson, M. (1994) 'Talking in Organizations: Managing, Identity and Impressions in an Advertising Agency', *Organization Studies*, 15(4), 535–63.

Alvesson, M. and Deetz, S. (1996) 'Critical Theory and Postmodernism Approaches to Organizational Studies', in Clegg, S. R., Hardy, C. and Nord, W. R. (eds), *Handbook of Organizations Studies*, London: Sage.

Alvesson, M. and Willmott, H. (eds) (1992) *Critical Management Studies*, London: Sage.

Alvesson, M. and Willmott, H. (1996) *Making Sense of Management*, London: Sage.

Anderson, G. L. (1976) *Victorian Clerks*, Manchester: Manchester University Press.

Anthony, P. D. (1977) *The Ideology of Work*, London: Tavistock.

Anthony, P. D. (1994) *Managing Culture*, Buckingham: Open University Press.

Anthony, P. D. (1990) 'The Paradox of the Management of Culture or "He Who Leads is Lost"', *Personnel Review*, 19(4), 3–8.

Antonacopoulou, E. (1998) 'Individual Development v Organizational Development in the Context of Change – A Process of Joint Negotiation?', Occasional Paper No. 296, Warwick Business School.

Archer, M. S. (1995) *Realist Social Theory: The Morphogenetic Approach*, Cambridge: Cambridge University Press.

Archer, M. S. (1996) 'Social Integration and System Integration: Developing the Distinction', *Sociology*, 30(4), 679–700.

Argyris, C. (1961) 'Explorations in Consulting – Client Relationships', *Human Organization*, 20, 121–33.

Armstrong, P. (1986) 'Management Control Strategies and Inter-professional Competition', in Knights, D. and Willmott, H. (eds), *Managing the Labour Process*, Aldershot: Gower.

Armstrong, P. (1989) 'Management Labour Process and Agency', *Work Employment and Society*, 3(3), 307–22.

Armstrong, P. (1991) 'Contradiction and Social Dynamics in the Capitalist Agency Relationship', *Accounting Organizations and Society*, 16(1), 1–25.

Armstrong, P., Glyn, A. and Harrison, J. (1984) *Capitalism since World War II*, London: Fontana.

Ashforth, B. E. and Humphrey, R. H. (1993) 'Emotional Labor in Service Roles: The Influence of Identity', *Academy of Management Review*, 18(1), 88–115.

Ashton, F. (1971) *A History of the Guild of Insurance Officials*, London: ASTMS.

Bain, G. S. (1970) *The Growth of White Collar Unionism*, Oxford: OUP.

Baldwin, P. (1990) *The Politics of Social Solidarity: Class Bases of the European Welfare State 1875–1975*, Cambridge: Cambridge University Press.

Baritz, L. (1960) *The Servants of Power*, New York: Wiley.

Barley, S. R. and Kunda, G. (1992) 'Design and Devotion: Surges of Rational and Normative Ideologies of Control in Managerial Discourse', *Administrative Science Quarterly*, 37, 363–99.

Barney, J. B. (1986) 'Organizational Culture: Can it be a Source of Sustained Advantage', *Academy of Management Review*, 11(3), 656–65.

Barsoux, J-L. (1993) *Funny Business: Humour Management and Business Culture*, London: Cassell.

Bate, P. (1984) 'The Impact of Organizational Culture on Approaches to Organizational Problem-Solving', *Organization Studies*, 5(1), 43–66.

Bate, P. (1990) 'Using the Culture Concept in an Organization Development Setting', *Journal of Applied Behavioural Science*, 26(1), 83–106.

Bate, P. (1994) *Strategies for Cultural Change*, Oxford: Butterworth.

Bauman, Z. (1987) *Legislators and Interpreters*, Cambridge: Polity Press.

Bauman, Z. (1988) *Freedom*, Milton Keynes: Open University Press.

Bauman, Z. (1989) *Modernity and the Molocaust,* Cambridge: Polity Press.

Bauman, Z. (1993) *Postmodern Ethics*, Oxford: Blackwell.

Bauman, Z. (1998) *Globalization – The Human Consequences*, Cambridge: Polity Press.

Bauman, Z. (1998b) *Work, Consumerism and the New Poor*, Milton Keynes: Open University Press.

Baxter, B. (1996) 'Consultancy Expertise: A Post-Modern Perspective', in Scarborought, H. (ed.), *The Management of Expertise*, London: Macmillan.

Beane, J. P. and Ennis, D. M. (1987) 'Market Segmentation: A Review', *European Journal of Marketing*, 21(5), 20–42.

Beck, U. (1992) *The Risk Society – Towards a New Modernity*, London: Sage.

Becker, E. (1973) *The Denial of Death*, New York: Free Press.

Beckhard, R. and Harris, R. (1987) *Organizational Transitions*, 2nd edn, New York: Addison Wesley.

Beer, M., Eisenstat, R. A. and Spector, B. (1990) *The Critical Path to Corporate Renewal*, Harvard: Harvard Business School Press.

Bennett, R. (1990) *Choosing and Using Management Consultants*, London: Kogan Page.

Berger, P. L. and Luckman, T. (1971) *The Social Construction of Reality*, Harmondsworth: Penguin.

Berry, L. L. (1981) 'The Employee as Customer', *Journal of Retail Banking*, 3(1), 33–40.

Bertrand, O. and Noyelle, T. (1988) *Human Resources and Corporate Strategy: Technological Change in Banks and Insurance Companies*, Paris: OECD.

Bierstecker, T. J. (1995) 'The "Triumph" of Liberal Economic Ideas in the Developing World', in Stallings, B. (ed.), *Global Change, Regional Response*, Cambridge: Cambridge University Press.

Blackburn, R. (1999) 'The New Collectivism: Pension Reform, Grey Capitalism and Complex Socialism', *New Left Review*, 233, 3–65.

Blackburn, R. M. (1967) *Union Character and Social Class*, London: Batsford.

Blau, P. M. (1962) *The Dynamics of Bureaucracy*, 2nd edn, Chicago: University of Chicago Press.

Block, F. (1977) *The Origins of International Economic Disorder*, Berkeley: University of California Press.

Bloomfield, B. P. and Danieli, A. (1995) 'The Role of Management Consultants in the Development of IT', *Journal of Management Studies*, 32(1), 23–46.

Bloomfield, B. and Best, A. (1992) 'Management Consultants: Systems Development, Power and the Translation of Problems', *Sociological Review*, 40(3), 533–60.

Boje, D. (1996) 'Lessons from Premodern and Modern for Postmodern Management', in Clegg, S. R. and Palmer, G. (eds), *Constituting Management: Markets, Meanings and Identities*, Berlin: De Gruyter.

Boxall, P. (1996) 'The Strategic HRM Debate and the Resource-based View of the Firm', *Human Resource Management Journal*, 6(3), 59–75.

Booth, C. (1889–1902) *The Life and Labour of the People of London*, London: Macmillan.

Braverman, H. (1974) *Labour and Monopoly Capital*, New York: Monthly Review Press.

Broadbent, J. and Guthrie, J. (1992) 'Changes in the Public Sector: A Review of Recent "Alternative" Accounting Research', *Accounting, Auditing and Accountability Journal*, 5(2), 3–31.

Brearley, R. A. and Kaplanis, E. (1994) *The Growth and Structure of International Banking*, London: London Business School City Research Project.

Brownlie, D. and Saren, M. (1992) 'The Four Ps of the Marketing Concept – Prescriptive, Polemical, Permanent and Problematical', *European Journal of Marketing*, 26(4), 34–47.

Buchanan, D. and Boddy, D. (1992) *The Expertise of the Change Agent*, London: Prentice Hall.

Budd, A. and Campbell, N. (1999) 'The Roles of the Public and Private Sectors in the UK Pension System' (available at hhtp://www.hm-treasury.gov.uk/pub/html/docs/misc/pensions.html).

Bulmer, M. (1982) *The Uses of Social Research*, London: Allen & Unwin.

Burawoy, M. (1979) *Manufacturing Consent*, London: University of Chicago Press.

Burrell, G. (1996) 'Hard Times for the Salariat?' in Scarborough, H. (ed.), *The Management of Expertise*, London: Macmillan.

Burnes, B. (1996) *Managing Change – A Strategic Approach to Organizational Dynamics*, London: Pitman.

Burton, D. (1991) 'Tellers into Sellers?' *International Journal of Bank Marketing*, 9(6), 25–9.

Burton, D. (1994) *Financial Services and the Consumer*, London: Routledge.

Byrne, J. A. (1986) 'Business Fads: What's In and What's Out', *Business Week*, 20, 40–7.

Cain, P. J. and Hopkins, A. G. (1993) *British Imperialism: Innovation and Expansion 1688–1914*, London: Longman.

Cain, P. J. and Hopkins, A. G. (1993) *British Imperialism: Crisis and Deconstruction 1914–1990*, London: Longman.

Campbell Keegan (1984) *Consumer Finance Today* (market research report).

Canny, N. (ed.) (1998) *The Origins of Empire*, Oxford: Oxford University Press.

Carrier, J. G. and Miller, D. (1998) *Virtualism: A New Political Economy*, Oxford: Berg.

Carter, R. L., Chiplin, B. and Lewis, M. K. (1986) *Personal Financial Markets*, Oxford: Philip Allan.

Casey, C. (1995) *Work, Self and Society – After Industrialism*, London: Routledge.

Cash, W. B. and Minter, R. L. (1979), 'Consulting Approaches – Two Basic Styles', *Training and Development Journal*, 26–28 September.

Cassis, Y. (1985) 'Management and Strategy in the English Joint Stock Banks 1890–1914', *Business History*, 27, 301–15.

Cassis, Y. (1994) *City Bankers, 1890–1914*, Cambridge: Cambridge University Press.

Castle, B., Davies, B., Land, H., Townsend, P., Lynes, T. and McIntyre, K. (1998) *Fair Shares for Pensioners*, London: Security in Retirement for Everyone.

Chamberlain, E. H. (1933) *Theory of Monopolistic Competition*, Cambridge, Mass.: Harvard University Press.

Chandler, A. D. (1962) *Strategy and Structure*, Cambridge, Mass.: MIT Press.

Chang, H. J. (1998) 'Korea: The Misunderstood Crisis' *World Development*, 26(8), 1555–61.

Chang, H. J., Park, H. J. and Yoo, C. G. (1998) 'Interpreting the Korean Crisis: Financial Liberalisation, Industrial Policy and Corporate Governance', *Cambridge Journal of Economics*, 22(6), 735–46.

Channon, D. F. (1988) *Global Banking Strategy*, New York: Wiley.

Cheadle, N. (1994) 'The History and Growth of the Profession' in *IMC, 1995, op.cit.*

Child, J. (1984) *Organization*, London: Harper & Row.

Child, J. and Rodrigues, S. (1996) 'The Role of Social Identity in the International Transfer of Knowledge through Joint Ventures', in Clegg, S. R. and Palmer, G. (eds), *The Politics of Management Knowledge*, London: Sage.

Clark, J., McLoughlin, I., Rose, H. and King, R. (1988) *The Process of Technological Change*, Cambridge: CUP.

Clark, L. H. (ed.) (1955) *Consumer Behaviour – Volume II: The Life Cycle*, New York: New York University Press.

Clark, P. and Mueller, F. (1996) 'Organisations and Nations: From Universalism to Institutionalisation?', *British Journal of Management*, 7(2), 125–39.

Clark, T. (1995) *Managing Consultants – Consultancy as the Management of Impressions*, Buckingham: Open University Press.

Clarke, M. (1986) *Regulating the City*, Milton Keynes: Open University Press.

Clarke, M. (1999) 'The Regulation of Retail Financial Services in Britain: An Analysis of a Crisis' in Morgan and Engwall (eds), *op. cit.*, 213–31.

Clarke, J. and Newman, J. (1997) *The Managerial State*, London: Sage.

Clarke, P. D., Edward, P. M., Gardener, E. F., Feeney, P. and Molyneux, P. (1988) 'The Genesis of Strategic Marketing Control in British Retail Banking', *International Journal of Bank Marketing*, 6(2), 5–19.

Clegg, S. R., Hardy, C. and Nord, W. (eds) (1996) *Handbook of Organization Studies*, London: Sage.

Cleverley, G. (1971) *Managers and Magic*, London: Longman.

Coates, D. (1994) *The Question of UK Decline*, Brighton: Harvester.

Cockburn, C. (1985) *Machinery of Dominance*, London: Pluto.

Cohen, P. S. (1968) *Modern Social Theory*, London: Heinemann.

Cohen, S. and Taylor, L. (1976 and 1992), *Escape Attempts: The Theory and Practice of Resistance to Everyday Life*, London: Allen Lane (1st edn) and Routledge (2nd edn).

Coleman, W. D. and Porter, T. (1994) 'Regulating International Banking and Securities: Emerging Cooperation among National Authorities', in Stubbs and Underhill, *op. cit.*, 190–203.

Colley, L. (1992) *Britons: Forging the Nation 1707–1837*, London: Harvill.

Collins, D. (1998) *Organizational Change – Sociological Perspectives*, London: Routledge.

Collins, M. (1990) 'English Bank Lending and the Financial Crisis of the 1870s', *Business History*, 198–224.

Coopers and Lybrand (1993) *Making Bancassurance Work*, London: Coopers and Lybrand.

Colville, I., Dalton, K. and Tomkins, C. (1993) 'Understanding Cultural Change in HM Customs and Excise', *Public Administration*, 71, Winter, 549–66.

Corbridge, S., Martin, R. and Thrift, N. (eds) (1994) *Money, Power and Space*, Oxford: Blackwell.

Craib, I. (1995) 'Some Comments on the Sociology of Emotions', *Sociology*, 29(1), 151–8.

Cressey, P. and Scott, P. (1992) 'Employment, Technology and Industrial Relations in the UK Clearing Banks – Is the Honeymoon Over?', *New Technology, Work and Employment*, 7(2), 83–96.

Crompton, R. (1979) 'Trade Unionism and the Insurance Clerk', *Sociology*, 13(3), 403–26.

Crompton, R. and Jones, G. (1984) *White Collar Proletariat: Deskilling and Gender in Clerical Work*, London: Macmillan.

Crompton, R. and Sanderson, K. (1986) 'Credentials and Careers – Some Implications of the Increase in Professional Qualifications Amongst Women', *Sociology*, 20(1), 25–42.

Crompton, R. and Sanderson, K. (1990) *Gendered Jobs and Social Change*, London: Unwin Hyman.

Crouch, C. (1993) *Industrial Relations and European State Traditions*, Oxford: Clarendon Press.

Currie, W. L. (1989) 'The Art of Justifying New Technology to Top Management', *Omega*, 17(5), 409–18.

Curtis, T. (1988) 'The Information Society – A Computer Generated Caste System?', in Mosco, V. and Wasko, J. (eds) *The Political Economy of Information*, Wisconsin: University of Wisconsin Press.

*Cutting Edge* (1996) 'The Death of the Bank Manager', Channel 4 TV.

Daft, R. (1998) *Organization Theory and Design*, 6th edn, Cincinnati, Ohio: South Western College Publishing.

Davidoff, L. and Hall, C. (1987) *Family Fortunes: Men and Women of the English Middle Class 1780–1850*, London: Hutchinson.

Davies, A. and Kirkpatrick, I. (1995) 'Performance Indicators, Bureaucratic Control and the Decline of Professional Autonomy', in Kirkpatrick, I. and Martinez, M. (eds), *The Politics of Quality*, London: Routledge.

Davison, H., Watkins, T. and Wright, M. (1989) 'Developing New Personal Financial Products – Some Evidence of the Role of Market Research', *International Journal of Bank Marketing*, 7(1), 8–15.

Dawson, P. (1994) *Organizational Change – A Processual Approach*, London: Paul Chapman.

Delbridge, R. and Lowe, J. (eds) (1998) *Manufacturing in Transition*, London: Routledge.

Derrida, J. (1978) *Writing and Difference*, London: Routledge.

DiMaggio, P. and Powell, W. W. (1983) 'The Iron Cage Revisited: Institutional Isomorphism and Collective Rationality in Organizational Fields', *American Sociological Review*, 35, 147–60.

DiMaggio, P. and Powell, W. W. (1991) 'Introduction', in Powell, W. W. and DiMaggio, P. (eds), *The New Institutionalism in Organisational Analysis*, London: University of Chicago Press.

Dixon, D. F. (1992) 'Consumer Sovereignty, Democracy and the Marketing Concept', *Canadian Journal of Administrative Science*, 9(2), 116–25.

Djelic, M-L. (1998) *Exporting the American Model – The Postwar Transformation of European Business*, Oxford: Oxford University Press.

DTI (1991) *Evaluation of the Consultancy Initiatives, Stages 1–3*, London: HMSO.

Dodd, N. (1994) *The Sociology of Money*, Cambridge: Polity Press.

Donaldson, L. (1996) 'The Normal Science of Structural Contingency Theory' in Clegg *et al.* (eds), 57–76.

Doorewaard, H. and Van Bijsterveld, M. (1998) 'The Integrated Approach of IT – Rise and Fall', EGOS conference paper, July, Maastricht.

du Gay, P. (1993) 'Markets and Souls: Re-imagining Organizational Life', paper presented at Re-thinking Marketing conference, Warwick Business School.

du Gay, P. (1996) *Consumption and Identity at Work*, London: Sage.

du Gay, P. (1997) *Production of Culture/Cultures of Production*, Milton Keynes: Open University Press.

du Gay, P. and Salaman, G. (1992) 'The Cult (ure) of the Customer', *Journal of Management Studies*, 29(5), 615–33.

Duncombe, J. and Marsden, D. (1993) 'Love and Intimacy: The Gender Division of Emotion and "Emotion Work"', *Sociology*, 27(2), 221–41.

Duncombe, J. and Marsden, D. (1995) '"Workaholics" and "Whingeing Women" – Theorising Intimacy and Emotion Work – The Last Frontier of Gender Inequality?', *Sociological Review*, 43(2), 150–69.

Dunphy, D. C. and Stace, D. A. (1988) 'Transformational and Coercive Strategies for Planned Organizational Change: Beyond the OD Model', *Organizational Studies*, 9(3), 317–34.

Dyer, N. and Watkins, T. (eds) (1988) *Marketing Insurance – A Practical Guide*, London: Kluwer.

Eaglesham, J. (1992) 'Product Tie-Ins and Property Loans', *Consumer Policy Review*, 2(4), 233–7.

Easterby-Smith, M. (1997) 'Disciplines of Organizational Learning – Contributions and Critiques', *Human Relations*, 50(9), 1084–113.

*Economist* (1988) 'Survey of Management Consultancy', 13 February.

*Economist* (1991) 'Solution Peddlars Lose Their Charm', 9 February, 81–2.

*Economist* (1993) 'Usury: The Lenders' Long Lament', 25 December, 107–9.

*Economist* (1994) 'Good Guru Guide', 7 January, 21–4.

*Economist* (1997) 'Survey of Management Consultancy', 22 March.

*Economist* (1999) 'Survey of International Banking', 17 April.

Eden, C. and Ackermann, F. (1998) *Making Strategy – The Journey of Strategic Management*, London: Sage.

Edwards, P., Collinson, M. and Rees, C. (1998) 'The Determinants of Employee Responses to TQM: Six Cases Studies', *Organization Studies*, 19(3), 449–75.

Edwards, R. (1979) *Contested Terrain*, New York: Basic Books.

Egan, C. and Shipley, D. (1995) 'Dimensions of Customer Orientation – An Empirical Investigation of the UK Financial Services Sector', *Journal of Marketing Management*, 11, 807–16.

Elden, M. (1986) 'Socio-Technical System Ideas as Public Policy in Norway', *Journal of Applied Behavioural Science*, 22(3), 239–55.

Enderwick, P. (1984) 'Patterns of Industrial Conflict in Private Sector Service Industries – Evidence From British Survey Data', *Service Industries Journal*, 4(1), 30–47.

Engel, J. F., Fiorillo, H. F. and Cayley, M. A. (eds) (1972) *Market Segmentation: Concepts and Applications*, New York: Holt, Rinehart & Winston.

Engwall, L. and Morgan, G. (1999) 'Regulatory Regimes', in Morgan and Engwall (eds), *op. cit.*, 84–107.

Engwall, L., Furusten, S. and Wallerstedt, E. (1993) 'Bridge Over Troubled Water – Professors in Management Consulting', EGOS Conference Paper.

Ennew, C. T. (1990) 'Marketing Strategy and Planning', in Ennew, C. *et al.* (eds), *op. cit.*, 60–79.

Ennew, C. T. (1992) 'Consumer Attitudes to Independent Financial Advice', *International Journal of Bank Marketing*, 10(5), 13–18.

Ennew, C. T., Watkins, T. and Wright, M. (eds) (1990) *Marketing Financial Services*, Oxford: Heinemann.

Esping-Andersen, G. (1990) *The Three Worlds of Welfare Capitalism*, Oxford: Polity Press.

Esping-Andersen, G. (ed) (1996) *Welfare States in Transition*, London: Sage.

Etzioni, A. (1961) *Complex Organizations*, New York: Free Press.

Evans, P. and Gumby, J. (1992) 'Going For Broke?', *Post Magazine*, 28 May, 9–12.

Featherstone, M. (1991) *Consumer Culture and Post-Modernism*, London: Sage.

Felstead, A. and Jewson, N. (eds) (1999) *Global Trends in Flexible Labour*, London: Macmillan.

Filby, M. P. (1992) 'The Figures, The Personality and The Bums: Service Work and Sexuality', *Work Employment and Society*, 6(1), 23–42.

File, K. M., Cermark, D. S. P. and Prince, R. A. (1994) 'Word of Mouth Effects in Professional Services Buyer Behaviour', *Service Industries Journal*, 14(3), 301–14.

Financial Services Authority (1999) *Promoting Public Understanding of Financial Services: A Strategy for Consumer Education*, London: Financial Services Authority.

Fincham, R. and Roslender, R. (1995) 'IT and the Strategy Process: The UK Financial Services Industry', *Critical Perspectives on Accounting*, 6, 7–26.

Fineman, S. (ed.) (1991) 'Change in Organizations', in Smith, M. (ed.), *Analysing Organizational Behaviour*, London: Macmillan.

Fineman, S. (ed.) (1993) *Emotion in Organizations*, London: Sage.

Fineman, S. (1993a) 'An Emotion Agenda', in Fineman, S. (ed.), *op. cit.*

Fiol, M. (1991) 'Managing Culture as a Competitive Resource', *Journal of Management*, 17(1), 291–311.

Flam, H. (1993) 'Fear, Loyalty and Greedy Organizations', in Fineman, S. (ed.), *Emotion in Organizations*, London: Sage.

Fligstein, N. (1996) 'Markets as Politics', *American Sociological Review*, 656–73.

Fligstein, N. and Mara-Drita, I. (1996) 'How to Make a Market', *American Journal of Sociology*, 102(1), 1–33.

Ford, J. (1992) *The Indebted Society*, London: Routledge.

Ford, J. D. and Ford, L. W. (1994) 'Logics of Identity, Contradiction and Attraction in Change', *Academy of Management Review*, 19(4), 756–85.

Foucault, M. (1972) *The Discourse on Language*, New York: Pantheon.

Foucault, M. (1977) *Discipline and Punish*, Harmondsworth: Penguin.

Fox, A. (1966) *Industrial Sociology and Industrial Relations*, Research Paper No. 3, Royal Commission on Trade Unions and Employers' Associations, London: HMSO.

Fox, A. (1974) *Beyond Contract – Work, Power and Trust Relations*, London: Faber & Faber.

Friedland, R. and Alford, R. R. (1987) 'Bringing Society Back In – Symbols, Structures and Institutional Contradiction', Institutional Change Conference Paper, Stanford, CA.

Friedman, A. L. and Cornford, D. S. (1989) *Computer Systems Development: History, Organization and Implementation*, London: Wiley.

Fromm, E. (1980) *The Fear of Freedom*, London: Routledge & Kegan Paul.

Frost, P. J. *et al.* (1991) *Reframing Organizational Culture*, London: Sage.

Fuller, L. and Smith, V. (1991) 'Consumers' Reports: Management by Customers in a Changing Economy', *Work Employment and Society*, 5(1), 1–16.

Gabriel, Y. (1996) 'The Hubris of Management', Working Paper, School of Management, University of Bath.

Gabriel, Y. and Lang, T. (1995) *The Unmanageable Consumer – Contemporary Consumption and its Fragmentations*, London: Sage.

Gall, G. (1997) 'Developments in Trade Unionism in the Financial Sector in Britain', *Work, Employment and Society*, 11(2), 219–35.

Gallie, D. and White, M. (1993) *Employee Commitment and the Skills Revolution*, London: Policy Studies Institute.

Gallie, D., White, M., Cheng, Y. and Tomlinson, M. (1998) *Restructuring the Employment Relationship*, Oxford: Oxford University Press.

Gandy, A. and Chapman, C. (1996) *The Electronic Bank*, Canterbury: Chartered Institute of Bankers.

Garratt, R. (1981) 'From Expertise to Contingency: Changes in the Nature of Consulting', *Management Education and Development*, 12(2), 95–101.

George, S. (1988) *A Fate Worse than Debt*, London: Penguin.

George, W. R. (1990) 'Internal Marketing and Organizational Behavior', *Journal of Business Research*, 20, 63–70.

Gergen, K. J. (1991) *The Saturated Self – Dilemmas of Identity in Contemporary Life*, New York: Basic Books.

Gerlach, N. (1996) 'The Business Restructuring Genre – Some Questions for Critical Organization Analysis', *Organization*, 3, 425–38.

Giddens, A. (1984) *The Constitution of Society*, Cambridge: Polity Press.

Giddens, A. (1990) *The Consequences of Modernity*, Cambridge: Polity Press.

Giddens, A. (1991) *Modernity and Social Identity*, Cambridge: Polity Press.

Giddens, A. and Mackenzie, G. (eds) (1982) *Social Class and the Division of Labour*, Cambridge: Cambridge University Press.

Gill, J. and Whittle, S. (1993) 'Management By Panacea: Accounting for Transience', *Journal of Management Studies*, 30(2), 281–95.

Gleick, J. (1987) *Chaos*, Harmondsworth: Penguin.

Goffee, R. and Scase, R. (1995) *Corporate Realities*, London: Routledge.

Goffman, E. (1974) *Frame Analysis: An Essay on the Organization of Experience*, New York: Harper & Row.

Goldman, R. (1992) *Reading Ads Socially*, London: Macmillan.

Goldthorpe, J. (1982) 'On the Service Class: Its Formation and Future', in Giddens and Mackenzie, *op. cit.*

Goodman, J. B. and Pauly, L. W. (1993) 'The Obsolescence of Capital Controls? Economic Management in an Age of Global Markets' *World Politics*, 46 (October), 50–82.

Gosden, P. (1973) *Self-help: Voluntary Associations in Nineteenth-century Britain*, London: Batsford.

Grafton-Small, R. (1987) 'Marketing or the Anthropology of Consumption', *European Journal of Marketing*, 21(9), 66–71.

Gramsci, A. (1971) *Selections from the Prison Notebooks*, London: Lawrence & Wishart.

Granovetter, M. (1985) 'Economic Action and Social Structure: The Problem of Embeddedness', *American Journal of Sociology*, 91(3), 481–510.

Grant, D., Keenoy, T. and Oswick, C. (eds) (1998) *Discourse and Organization*, London: Sage.

Greenwood, R. and Hinings, C. (1993) 'Understanding Strategic Change: The Contribution of Archetypes', *Academy of Management Journal*.

Grint, K. (1994) 'Reengineering History: Social Resonances and BPR', *Organization*, 1(1), 179–201.

Grint, K. and Case, P. (1998) 'The Violent Rhetoric of Reengineering – Management Consultancy on the Offensive', *Journal of Management Studies*, 35(5), 557–77.

Gronroos, C. (1981) 'Internal Marketing', in Donnelly, J. H. and George, W. R. (eds), *Marketing of Services*, Chicago: American Marketing Association.

Grosvenor, J. (ed.) (1988) *Management Consultants 1989*, Oxford: Ivanohoe/ IMC.

*Guardian*, 'The Masters of Illusion', 6 March 1999.

*Guardian*, '£2000 bonus for NPI Policyholders', 3 October 1998.

Guillen, M. F. (1994) *Models of Management*, London: University of Chicago Press.

Hacking, I. (1991) 'How Should We Do the History of Statistics?', in Burchell, G., Gordon, C. and Miller, P. (eds), *The Foucault Effect*, London: Harvester.

Halford, S., Savage, M. and Witz, A. (1997) *Gender, Careers and Organizations*, London: Macmillan.

Hall, E. J. (1993) 'Smiling, Deferring and Flirting: Doing Gender by Giving "Good Service"', *Work and Occupations*, 20(4), 452–71.

Hall, S. (ed.) (1988) *The Hard Road to Renewal*, London: Lawrence & Wishart.

Hamel, G. and Prahalad, C. K. (1989) *Competing for the Future*, Boston, Mass.: Harvard Business School Press.

Hamilton, A. (1986) *The Financial Revolution*, London: Penguin.

Hammer, M. and Champy, J. (1993) *Reengineering the Corporation*, London: Nicholas Brealey Publishing.

Hamnett, C., Harmer, M. and Williams, P. (1991) *Safe as Houses: Housing Inheritance in Britain*, London: Paul Chapman.

Handy, C. (1989) *The Age of Unreason*, London: Random House.

Handy, C. (1993) 'Balancing Corporate Power: A New Federalist Paper', *The McKinsey Quarterly*, 3, 159–79.

Hannah, L. (1986) *Inventing Retirement*, Cambridge: Cambridge University Press.

Harris, H. J. (1982) *The Right to Manage – Industrial Relations Policies of American Business in the 1940s*, Madison: University of Wisconsin Press.

Harris, J. (1993) *Private Lives, Public Spirit: Britain 1870–1914*, London: Penguin.

Hassard, J. (1994) 'Postmodern Organizational Analysis: Towards a Conceptual Framework', *Journal of Management Studies*, 31(3), 301–24.

Hassard, J. and Sharifi, S. (1989) 'Corporate Culture and Strategic Change', *Journal of General Management*, 15(2), 4–19.

Hatch, M. J. (1997) *Organization Theory*, Oxford: Oxford University Press.

Hay, C. (1996) *Re-Stating Social and Political Change*, Buckingham: Open University Press.

Held, D. and McGrew, A., Goldblatt, D. and Perraton, J. (1999) *Global Transformations*, Cambridge: Polity Press.

Helleiner, E. (1994) 'From Bretton Woods to Global Finance: A World Turned Upside Down', in Stubbs and Underhill, *op. cit.*, 163–75.

Henderson, J. (1998) 'Uneven Crises: Institutional Foundations of East Asian Economic Turmoil', Transnational Communities Working Paper, WPTC-98-13, Faculty of Anthropology and Geography, University of Oxford.

Heritage, J. (1980) 'Class Situation, White Collar Unionization and the "Double Proletarianization" Thesis – A Comment', *Sociology*, 14, 283–94.

Herriot, P., Pemberton, C. and Hawtin, E. (1996) 'The Career Attitudes and Intentions of Managers in the Finance Sector', *The British Journal of Management*, 7(2), 181–90.

Hinings, C. R. and Greenwood, R. (1988) *The Dynamics of Strategic Change*, Oxford: Blackwell.

Hochschild, A. R. (1983) *The Managed Heart: Commercialization of Human Feeling*, London: University of California Press.

Holland, J. F. (1999) 'The Regulation of Price Sensitive Information', in Morgan and Engwall, *op. cit.*, 125–46.

Hollway, W. (1991) *Work Psychology and Organizational Behaviour*, London: Sage.

Hooley, G. J. and Mann, S. J. (1988) 'The Adoption of Marketing by Financial Institutions in the UK', *Service Industries Journal*, 8(4), 488–500.

Hooley, G. J. Lynch, J. E. and Shepherd, J. (1990) 'The Marketing Concept – Putting the Theory into Practice', *European Journal of Marketing*, 24(9), 7–24.

Hopkins, E. (1995) *Working Class Self-Help in Nineteenth-Century England*, London: University College, London Press.

Houston, F. S. (1986) 'The Marketing Concept – What it is and What it is Not', *Journal of Marketing*, 50, April, 81–7.

Howcroft, B. (1993) 'Staff Perceptions of Service Quality in a UK Clearing Bank', *International Journal of Service Industry Management*, 4(4), 5–24.

Huczynski, A. A. (1987) *Encyclopedia of Organizational Change Methods*, Aldershot: Gower.

Huczynski, A. A. (1993) *Management Gurus*, London: Routledge.

Huczynski, A. A. (1993a) 'Explaining the Succession of Management Fads', *International Journal of HRM*, 4(2), 443–63.

Hyman, R. and Price, R. (eds) (1983) *The New Working Class? White Collar Workers and their Organizations*, London: Macmillan.

Ilinitch, A. Y., Lewin, A. Y. and D'Aveni, R. (eds) (1998) *Managing in Times of Disorder – Hypercompetitive Organizational Responses*, London: Sage.

IMC (1986) *IMC Yearbook 1987*, London: Institute of Management Consultants.

IMC (1995) *Guide to Choosing and Using Professional Management Consultants Effectively*, London: Institute of Management Consultants.

*In Business* (1994) 'McKinsey', BBC Radio 4, 9 October.

Ingham, G. (1984) *Capitalism Divided? The City and Industry in British Social Development*, Cambridge: Polity Press.

Jackall, R. (1988) *Moral Mazes – The World of Corporate Managers*, Oxford: Oxford University Press.

Jacques, R. (1996) *Manufacturing the Employee*, London: Sage.

James, N. (1989) 'Emotional Labour: Skill and Work in the Social Regulation of Feelings', *Sociological Review*, 37(1), 5–42.

Jameson, F. (1991) *Postmodernism: the Cultural Logic of Late Capitalism*, London: Verso.

Jayasinghe, S. and Yorke, D. A. (1992) 'A Technique to Evaluate Secondary Data on Personal Financial Services to Identify Potential Customer Segments', Occasional Paper, Manchester School of Management, UMIST.

Jensen, M. C. and Meckling, W. H. (1976) 'Theory of the Firm: Managerial Behaviour, Agency Costs and Ownership Structure', *Journal of Financial Economics*, 3, 305–60 (cited in Armstrong, 1989, *op. cit.*).

Jessop, B., Bonnett, K., Bromley, S. and Ling, T. (1988) *Thatcherism: A Tale of Two Nations*, Cambridge: Polity Press.

Johnson, G. and Scholes, K. (1993) *Exploring Corporate Strategy*, 3rd edn, London: Prentice Hall.

Johnson, P. (1985) *Saving and Spending*, Oxford: Oxford University Press.

Johnson, P. and Falkingham, J. (1993) *Ageing and Economic Welfare*, London: Sage.

Jomo, K. S. (1998) *Tigers in Trouble: Financial Governance, Liberalization and Crises in East Asia*, London: Zed Books.

Joseph, L. and Yorke, D. A. (1989) 'Know Your Game Plan: Market Segmentation in the Personal Financial Services Sector', *Quarterly Review of Marketing*, 15(1), 8–13.

Kanter, R. M. (1985) *The Change Masters*, London: Unwin.

Kanter, R. M. (1989) *When Giants Learn to Dance*, London: Unwin.

Kanter, R. M. (1995) *World Class: Thriving Locally in the Global Economy*, New York: Simon & Schuster.

Kanter, R. M., Stein, B. A. and Jick, T. D. (1992) *The Challenge of Organizational Change*, New York: Free Press.

Kapstein, E. (1994) *Governing the Global Economy*, Cambridge, Mass.: Harvard University Press.

Kay, J. (1993) *Foundations of Corporate Success*, Oxford: Oxford University Press.

Keat, R. (1994) 'Scepticism, Authority and the Market', in Keat, R. *et al.* (eds) *op. cit.*

Keat, R. and Abercrombie, N. (1991) *Enterprise Culture*, London: Routledge.

Keat, R., Abercrombie, N. and Whiteley, N. (1994) *The Authority of the Consumer*, London: Routledge.

Keenoy, T. (1990) 'HRM: A Case of Wolf in Sheep's Clothing?', *Personnel Review*, 19(2), 3–9.

Keenoy, T. (1998) 'HRM as Hologram: A Polemic', paper presented at HRM conference, Cardiff Business School, January.

Keith, R. J. (1960) 'The Marketing Revolution', *Journal of Marketing*, 24, January, 35–8.

Kerfoot, D. (1993) 'Responding to Demography', FSRC Report, Manchester School of Management, UMIST.

Kerfoot, D. and Knights, D. (1993) 'Masculinity, Management and Manipulation', *Journal of Management Studies*, 30(4), 659–79.

Kirkpatrick, I. and Lucio, M. M. (eds) (1995) *The Politics of Quality*, London: Routledge.

Kinnie, N., Hutchinson, S. and Purcell, J. (1998) 'Fun and Surveillance – The Paradox of High Commitment Management in Call Centres', WERC Research Paper, University of Bath.

Kipping, M. (1996) 'The US Influence on the Evolution of Management Consultancies in Britain, France and Germany Since 1945', *Business and Economic History*, 39, 67–83.

Kipping, M. and Bjarnar, O. (1998) *The Americanization of European Business*, London: Routledge.

Klingender, F. D. (1935) *The Condition of Clerical Labour in Britain*, London: Martin Lawrence.

Knights, D. (1997) 'Governmentality and Financial Services: Welfare Crises and the Financially Self-Disciplined Subject', in Morgan and Knights, *op. cit.*, 216–36.

Knights, D. (1997) 'Organization Theory in the Age of Deconstruction: Dualism, Gender and Postmodernism Revisited', *Organization Studies*, 18(1), 1–19.

Knights, D. and McCabe, D. (1997) 'How Would You Measure Something Like That? Quality in a Retail Bank', *Journal of Management Studies*, 34, 371–88.

Knights, D. and Morgan, G. (1990) 'Management Control in Sales Forces: A Case Study from the Labour Process of Life Assurance', *Work, Employment and Society*, 4(3), 369–89.

Knights, D. and Morgan, G. (1990) 'The Concept of Strategy in Sociology', *Sociology*, 24(3), 475–83.

Knights, D. and Morgan, G. (1991) 'Corporate Strategy, Organizations and Subjectivity', *Organization Studies*, 12(2), 251–74.

Knights, D. and Morgan, G. (1992) 'Leadership and Corporate Strategy: Toward a Critical Analysis', *Leadership Quarterly*, 3(1), 171–90.

Knights, D. and Morgan, G. (1993) 'Organization Theory and Consumption in a Post-Modern Era', *Organization Studies*, 14(2), 211–34.

Knights, D. and Morgan, G. (1995) 'Strategy Under the Microscope', *Journal of Management Studies*, 32(2), 192–214.

Knights, D. and Murray, F. (1994) *Managers Divided – Organization Politics and IT Management*, Chichester: Wiley.

Knights, D. and Sturdy, A. J. (1987) 'Women's Work in Insurance – I.T. and the Reproduction of Gendered Segregation', in Davidson, M. J. and Cooper, C. L. (eds), *Women and Information Technology*, London: Wiley.

Knights, D. and Sturdy, A. J. (1990) 'New Technology and the Self-Disciplined Worker in Insurance', in Varcoe, I. *et al.* (eds), *Deciphering Science and Technology*, London: Macmillan.

Knights, D. and Vurdubakis, T. (1994) 'Foucault, Power, Resistance and All That', in Jermier, J., Knights, D. and Nord, W. (eds), *Resistance and Power in Organizations*, London: Routledge.

Knights, D. and Willmott, H. (1985) 'Power and Identity in Theory and Practice', *Sociological Review*, 33(1), 22–46.

Knights, D., Morgan, G. and Murray, F. (1991) 'Strategic Management, Financial Services and IT', EGOS Conference Paper.

Knights, D., Morgan, G. and Sturdy, A. J. (1993) 'Bancassurance and Consumer Protection in the UK: Problems and Prospects', School of Management Occasional Paper, Manchester: UMIST.

Knights, D., Sturdy, A. J. and Morgan, G. (1993) 'Quality for the Consumer in Bancassurance?', *Consumer Policy Review*, 3(4), 232–40.

Knights, D., Sturdy, A. J. and Morgan, G. (1994) 'The Consumer Rules? The Rhetoric and Reality of Marketing', *European Journal of Marketing*, 28(3), 42–54.

Kondo, D. K. (1990) *Crafting Selves: Power Gender and Discourses of Identity in a Japanese Workplace*, London: University of Chicago Press.

Kotler, P. (1988) *Marketing Management*, 6th edn, New York: Prentice Hall.

Kotter, J. P. (1990) 'What Leaders Really Do', *Harvard Business Review*, May–June, 103–11.

Kotter, J. P. and Heskett, J. L. (1992) *Corporate Culture and Performance*, New York: Free Press.

Kunda, G. (1991) *Engineering Culture: Control and Commitment in a Hi-Tech Corporation*, Philadelphia: Temple University Press.

Kynaston, D. (1994) *The City of London: Vol. 1: A World of its Own 1815–1890*, London: Chatto.

Kynaston, D. (1995) *The City of London: Vol. 2: The Golden Years 1890–1914*, London: Pimlico.

Labour Research Department (1988) *Management Consultants: Who Are They and How to Deal with Them?*, London: Labour Research Department.

Lazonick, W. and O'Sullivan, M. (1995) 'Organization, Finance and International Competition', *Industrial and Corporate Change*, 1–49.

Leidner, R. (1991) 'Gender, Work and Identity in Interactive Service Jobs', *Gender and Society*, 5(2), 154–77.

Leidner, R. (1993) *Fast Food Fast Talk: Service Work and the Routinization of Everyday Life*, London: University of California, Los Angeles Press.

Legge, K. (1995) *HRM – Rhetorics and Realities*, London: Macmillan.

Levitt, T. (1960) 'Marketing Myopia', *Harvard Business Review*, 38(4), 45–56.

Levitt, T. (1983) 'The Globalization of Markets', *Harvard Business Review*, 61(3), 92–102.

Levy, A. (1986) 'Second-Order Planned Change', *Organizational Dynamics*, Summer, 5–20.

Lewin, K. (1951) *Field Theory in Social Science*, New York: Harper & Row.

Lewis, B. R. (1984) 'Marketing Bank Services', *Service Industries Journal*, 4(3).

Lewis, B. R. (1989) 'Customer Care in the Service Sector: The Employees Perspective', Manchester School of Management paper, UMIST.

Lewis, B. R. (1989) 'Customer Care in Service Organizations', *Marketing Intelligence and Planning*, 7(6), 18–22.

Lewis, B. R. (1990) 'Bank Marketing', in Ennew *et al.* (eds) *op. cit.*, 157–77.

Lewis, B. R. (1994) 'Customer Service and Quality', in McGoldrick, P. J. and Greenland, S. J. (eds), *Retailing of Financial Services*, London: McGraw Hill.

Leyshon, A. and Thrift, N. (1997) *Money Space: Geographies of Monetary Transformation*, London: Routledge.

Littler, C. R. (1982) *The Development of the Labour Process in Capitalist Societies*, London: Heinemann.

Locke, R. L. (1996) *The Collapse of the American Management Mystique*, Oxford: Oxford University Press.

Lockwood, D. (1958) *The Blackcoated Worker – A Study in Class Consciousness*, London: Allen & Unwin.

Lorenz, C. (1986) 'Europe Warms to Business Punditry', *Financial Times*, 2 July, 18.

Lury, A. (1994) 'Advertising: Moving Beyond the Stereotypes' in Keat, R. *et al.* (eds), *op. cit.*

Mabey, C. and Mayon-White, B. (eds) (1993) *Managing Change*, London: Paul Chapman.

Mabey, C. and Mayon-White, B. (eds) (1993) *Understanding and Managing Organizational Change*, London: OUP/Paul Chapman.

Mabey, C., Salaman, G. and Storey, J. (eds) (1998) *Strategic HRM – A Reader*, Milton Keynes: Open University Press.

MacDonald, O. (1990) *Report on Training and Competence in the Financial Services Industry,* London: Securities and Investments Board.

Mackay, L. (1987) 'The Future with Consultants', *Personnel Review*, 16(4), 7–10.

Macnicol, J. (1998) *The Politics of Retirement in Britain, 1878–1948*, Cambridge: Cambridge University Press.

*Management Consultancy* (1992a) 'Anchors Up and Plain Sailing Ahead in the Financial Sector', May, 29–30.

*Management Consultancy* (1992b) 'Andersen Tops Shuffled League', June, 32–40.

*Management Consultancy* (1992c) 'Strategists Have No Great Expectations', October, 28–30.

*Management Consultancy* (1993) 'Financial Dealings Dip but Income Increases', October, 15–17.

*Management Consultancy* (1997a) 'Financial Sector Pays Healthy Dividends', June, 21–2.

*Management Consultancy* (1997b) 'Top 100 Firms See Steady Rise in Fee Income', July–August, 22–33.

Mann, M. (1993) *The Sources of Social Power Vol. II: The Rise of Classes and Nation-States 1760–1914*, Cambridge: Cambridge University Press.

March, J. G. (1981) 'Footnotes to Organizational Change', *Administrative Science Quarterly*, 563–77.

Marglin, S. A. (1976) 'What Do Bosses Do? The Origins and Functions of Hierarchy in Capitalist Production', in Gorz, A. (ed.), *The Division of Labour*, Brighton: Harvester.

Marglin, S. A. (1979) 'Catching Flies With Honey: An Inquiry into Management Initiatives to Humanise Work', *Economic Analysis and Workers Management*, 13, 473–85.

Markham, C. (1997) 'Consultancy: A Fashion Industry?', *Management Accounting*, April, 50.

Marshall, C. E. (1985) 'Can We Be Consumer Oriented in a Changing Financial Service World?', *Journal of Consumer Marketing*, 2(4), 37–43.

Marshall, P. J. (ed.) (1998) *The Eighteenth Century*, Oxford: Oxford University Press.

Marshall, T. H. (1948) *Sociology at the Crossroads*, London: Heinemann.

Martin, J. (1992) *Cultures in Three Organizations – Three Perspectives*, Oxford: Oxford University Press.

Matthews, H. L. and Slocum, J. W. (1969) 'Social Class and Commercial Bank Credit Card Usage', *Journal of Marketing*, 33(1), 71–8.

May, T. (1994) 'Transformative Power: A Study in a Human Service (Probation) Organization', *Sociological Review*, 42(4), 618–38.

McDowell, L. (1998) *Capital Culture: Gender at Work in the City*, Oxford: Blackwell.

McGivern, C. (1983) 'Some Facets of the Relationship Between Consultants and Clients in Organizations', *Journal of Management Studies*, 20(3), 367–86.

McGoldrick, P. J. and Greenland, S. J. (1992) 'Competition Between Banks and Building Societies in the Retailing of Financial Services', *British Journal of Management*, 3, 169–79.

McGoldrick, P. J. and Greenland, S. J. (eds) (1994) *Retailing of Financial Services*, London: McGraw Hill.

McKechnie, S. (1992) 'Consumer Buying Behaviour in Financial Services – An Overview', *International Journal of Bank Marketing*, 10(5), 4–12.

Meek, V. L. (1988) 'Organizational Culture: Origins and Weaknesses', *Organization Studies*, 9(4), 453–73.

Mendras, H. and Cole, A. (1991) *Social Change in Modern France: Towards a Cultural Anthropology of the Fifth Republic*, Cambridge: Cambridge University Press.

Meyer, A. D., Tsui, A. S., Hinings, C. R. (1993) 'Configurational Approaches to Organizational Analysis', *Academy of Management Journal*, 1175–95.

Meyer, J. W. and Rowan, B. (1977) 'Institutionalized Organizations – Formal Structure as Myth and Ceremony', *American Journal of Sociology*, 83(2), 340–63.

Meyer, M. W. (1994) 'Measuring Performance in Economic Organizations', in Smelser, N. and Swedberg, R. (eds), *Handbook of Economic Sociology*, Princeton: Princeton University Press, 556–78.

Meyer, M. W. and Zucker, L. G. (1989) *Permanently Failing Organizations*, London: Sage.

Michie, R. (1992) *The City*, London: Heinemann.

Miller, D. and Friesen, P. (1984) *Organizations: A Quantum View*, Englewood Cliffs, NJ: Prentice Hall.

Miller, D. (1987) *Material Culture and Mass Consumption*, Oxford: Blackwell.

Mills, C. Wright (1951) *White Collar: The American Middle Classes*, London: Oxford University Press.

Mintzberg, H. (1978) 'Patterns in Strategy Formation', *Management Science*, xxiv (9), 934–48.

Mintzberg, H. (1983) *Power in and Around Organizations*, Englewood Cliffs: Prentice Hall.

Mintzberg, H. (1987) 'Crafting Strategy', *Harvard Business Review*, July/August, 66–75.

Mintzberg, H. (1990) 'The Design School: Reconsidering the Basic Premises of Strategic Management', *Strategic Management Journal*, XI, 171–95.

Mintzberg, H. (1994) *The Rise and Fall of Strategic Planning*, New York: Prentice Hall.

Mitchell, J. and Weisner, H. (1992) 'Savings and Investments – Consumer Issues', Occasional Paper of OFT, London: Office of Fair Trading.

Mitchell, V. W. (1994) 'Problems and Risks in the Purchasing of Consultancy Services', *Services Industries Journal*, 14(3), 315–39.

Moran, M. (1986) *The Politics of Banking*, 2nd edn, London: Macmillan.

Morgan, Gareth (1986) *Images of Organization*, London: Sage.

Morgan, G. (1990) *Organizations in Society*, London: Macmillan.

Morgan, G. (1994) 'Problems of Integration and Differentiation in the Management of Bancassurance', *Service Industries Journal*, 14(2), 153–69.

Morgan, G. (1997) 'The Global Context of Financial Services: National Systems and the International Political Economy', in Morgan and Knights, *op. cit.*, 14–41.

Morgan, G. and Engwall, L. (eds) (1999) *Regulation and Organizations*, London: Routledge.

Morgan, G. and Knights, D. (1990) 'The Concept of Strategy in Sociology', *Sociology*, 24(3), 475–83.

Morgan, G. and Knights, D. (1991) 'Gendering Jobs: Corporate Strategy, Managerial Control and the Dynamics of Job Segregation', *Work, Employment and Society*, 5(2), 181–200.

Morgan, G. and Knights, D. (1991) 'Constructing Consumers and Consumer Protection: The Case of the Life Insurance Industry in the UK', in R. Burrows and C. Marsh (eds), *Consumption and Class*, London: Macmillan, 32–51.

Morgan, G. and Knights, D. (eds) (1997) *Regulation and Deregulation in European Financial Services*, London: Macmillan.

Morgan, G. and Quack, S. (2000) 'Confidence and Confidentiality: The Social Construction of Performance Standards in Banking', in Quack *et al.* (eds) *op. cit.*, 129–56.

Morgan, G. and Soin, K. (1999) 'Regulatory Compliance' in Morgan and Engwall (eds), *op. cit.*, 166–90.

Morgan, G., Sturdy, A. J., Daniel, J-P. and Knights, D. (1994) 'Bancassurance in Britain and France', *Geneva Papers on Risk and Insurance*, 71, April, 178–95.

Morgan, N. (1990) 'Financial Services – Introduction', in Teare, R. *et al.* (eds), *Managing and Marketing Services in the 1990s*, London: Cassel.

Morgan, N. and Piercy, N. (1988) 'Marketing Organization in the Financial Services Sector', *International Journal of Bank Marketing*, 6 (4).

Morgan, N. and Piercy, N. (1990) 'Marketing in Financial Services Organizations: Policy and Practice', in Teare, R. *et al.* (eds), *Managing and Marketing Services in the 1990s*, London: Cassel.

Morrison, L. (ed.) (1998) *Management Consultancy*, London: Key Note.

Moser, C. A. (1958) *Survey Methods in Social Investigation*, London: Heinemann.

Mulkay, M. and Howe, G. (1994) 'Laughter For Sale', *Sociological Review*, 42(3), 481–500.

Nadler, D. and Tushman, M. (1990) 'Beyond the Charismatic Leader: Leadership and Organizational Change', *California Management Review*, 32(10), 77–87.

Newman, K. (1984) *Financial Marketing and Communications*, Eastbourne: Holt, Rinehart & Winston.

Nonaka, I. and Takeuichi, H. (1995) *The Knowledge Creating Company*, Oxford: Oxford University Press.

O'Brien, M. (1994) 'The Managed Heart Revisited: Health and Social Control', *Sociological Review*, 42(3), 393–413.

Oberbeck, H. and D'Alessio, N. (1997) 'The End of the German Model? Developmental Tendencies in the German Banking Industry', in Morgan, G. and Knights, D. *op. cit.*, 86–104.

O'Connor, J. (1973) *The Fiscal Crisis of the State*, London: St James' Press.

Office of Fair Trading (1992) *Savings and Investments: Consumer Issues*, London: OFT.

Office of Fair Trading (1993a) *Fair Trading and Life Insurance Savings Products*, London: OFT.

Office of Fair Trading (1993b) *Financial Services Act: The Marketing and Sale of Investment-Linked Insurance Products*, London: OFT.

Office of Fair Trading (1994) *Surrender Values of Life Insurance Policies*, London: OFT.

Office of Fair Trading (1995) *Mortgage Repayment Methods*, London: OFT.

Ogbonna, E. (1992) 'Organizational Culture and HRM: Dilemmas and Contradictions', in Blyton, P. and Turnbull, P. (eds), *Reassessing HRM*, London: Sage.

Ogbonna, E. and Wilkinson, B. (1990) 'Corporate Strategy and Corporate Culture: The View from the Checkout', *Personnel Review*, 19(4), 9–15.

Oliver, C. (1992) 'The Antecedents of Deinstitutionalization', *Organization Studies*, 13(4), 563–88.

O'Reilly, J. (1992) 'The Societal Construction of Labour Flexibility – Employment Strategies in Retail Banking in Britain and France', in Whitley, R. (ed.), *European Business Systems*, London: Sage.

O'Shea, J. and Madigan, C. (1997) *Dangerous Company – The Consulting Powerhouses and the Businesses they Save and Ruin*, London: Nicholas Brearley.

Ott, J. S. (1989) *The Organizational Culture Perspective*, Chicago: Dorsey Press.

Packard, V. (1956) *The Hidden Persuaders*, Harmondsworth: Penguin.

Parker, M. (1992) 'Post-modern Organizations or Postmodern Organization Theory?', *Organization Studies*, 13(1), 1–17.

Parker, M. (1995) 'Working Together, Working Apart: Management Culture in a Manufacturing Firm', *Sociological Review*, 43(3), 518–47.

Parker, M. (1995b) 'Critique in the Name of What? Postmodernism and Crit-
    ical Aproaches to Organization', *Organization Studies*, 16(4), 553–64.
Parker, M. (ed.) (1998) *Ethics and Organizations*, London: Sage.
Pascale, R. (1990) *Managing on the Edge*, London: Penguin.
Penn, R. (1995) 'The Role of Consulting Knowledge in the Transformation of
    Work', EMOT Workshop paper, IESE, Barcelona.
Perkins, H. (1989) *The Rise of Professional Society: England since 1880*, London:
    Routledge.
Personal Investment Authority (1995) *Consumer Panel Report 1995*, London: PIA.
Personal Investment Authority (1996) *Consumer Panel Report 1996*, London: PIA.
Personal Investment Authority (1996) *Life Assurance Disclosure: One Year on,
    January 1996*, London: PIA.
Personal Investment Authority (1997) *Consumer Panel Report 1997*, London: PIA.
*Personnel Review* (1994) 'Quality and the Individual' special issue, 23(2).
Peters, T. (1989) *Thriving on Chaos*, London: Pan.
Peters, T. (1993) *Liberation Management: Necessary Disorganization for the
    Nanosecond Nineties*, London: Pan.
Peters, T. and Austin, N. (1985) *A Passion for Excellence*, London: Collins.
Peters, T. J. and Waterman, R. H. (1982) *In Search of Excellence*, New York:
    Harper & Row.
Pettigrew, A. M. (1985) *The Awakening Giant*, Oxford: Basil Blackwell.
Pettigrew, A. M. (1987) 'Context and Action in the Transformation of the
    Firm', *Journal of Management Studies*, 24(6), 649–69.
Pettigrew A. M. (1990) 'Is Corporate Culture Manageable?', in Wilson and
    Rosenfeld, *op. cit.*
Pettigrew, A. M. and Whipp, R. (1991) *Managing Change for Competitive Suc-
    cess*, Oxford: Basil Blackwell.
Pettigrew, A. M., Ferlie, E. and McKee, L. (1993) *Shaping Strategic Change*,
    London: Sage.
Philippe, M-A. (1992) 'La Saga de la Distribution', *Directions* (Paris: CAPA)
    19, 46–51.
Phills, J. A. (1996) 'Tensions in the Client–Consultant Relationship', Academy
    of Management Conference paper.
Piercy, N. F. (1995) 'Customer Satisfaction and the Internal Market', *Journal of
    Marketing Practice*, 1(1), 22–44.
Plummer, J. T. (1971) 'Lifestyle Patterns and Commercial Bank Credit Card
    Usage', *Journal of Marketing*, 35(2), 35–41.
Podolny, J. (1993) 'A Status-based Model of Market Competition', *American
    Journal of Sociology*, 98(4), 829–72.
Porter, M. (1980) *Competitive Strategy*, London: Free Press.
Porter, M. (1985) *Competitive Advantage*, London: Free Press.
Porter, M. (1996) 'What is Strategy', *Harvard Business Review*.
Povall, M. (1986) *The Finance Sector – Equal Opportunity Developments*,
    London: City University Business School.

Power, M. (1990) 'Modernism, Postmodernism and Organization', in Hassard, J. and Pym, D. (eds), *The Theory and Philosophy of Organizations*, London: Routledge.

Power, M. (1997) *The Audit Society – Rituals of Verification*, Oxford: Oxford University Press.

Prandy, K. and Blackburn, R. M. (1965) 'White Collar Unionisation', quoted in Carter, R. (1979), 'Conservative Militants – The Case of the ASTMS', in Hyman and Price (eds), *op. cit.*

Prandy, K. *et al.* (1983) *White Collar Unions*, London: Macmillan.

Price, R. and Bain, G. S. (1983) 'Union Growth in Britain – Retropsect and Prospect', *British Journal of Industrial Relations*, 21, 46–68.

Purcell, J. (1995) 'Corporate Strategy and its link with HRM Strategy', in Storey, J. (ed.), *HRM – A Critical Text*, London: Routledge.

Quack, S. and Morgan, G. (2000) 'Institutions, Sector Specialisation and Economic Performance Outcomes', in Quack, Morgan and Whitley, *op. cit.*

Quack, S., Morgan, G. and Whitley, R. (eds) (2000) *National Capitalisms, Global Competition and Economic Performance*, Amsterdam: John Benjamin Publishing.

Rafaeli, A. (1989) 'When Cashiers Meet Customers: An Analysis of the Role of Supermarket Cashiers', *Academy of Management Journal*, 32(2), 245–73.

Rajan, A. (1984) *New Technology and Employment in Insurance, Banking and Building Societies*, Aldershot: Gower.

Ramsay, H. E. (1977) 'Cycles of Control', *Sociology*, 11(3), 481–506.

Ramsay, H. E. (1996) 'Managing Sceptically', in Clegg, S. R. and Palmer, G. (eds), *The Politics of Management Knowledge*, London: Sage.

Rassam, C. and Oates D. (1991) *Management Consultancy – The Inside Story*, London: Mercury.

Ray, C. A. (1986) 'Corporate Culture: The Last Frontier of Control?', *Journal of Management Studies*, 23(3), 287–97.

Reed, M. (1994) 'Expert Power and Organization in High Modernity', paper presented at the ESRC Professions Seminar Series, Cardiff, May.

Reed, M. (1996) 'Organizational Theorising: An Historically Contested Terrain', in Clegg *et al.* (eds) *op. cit.*

Reed, M. (1997) 'In Praise of Duality and Dualism: Rethinking Agency and Structure in Organizational Analysis', *Organization Studies*, 18(1), 21–42.

Reed, M. (1998) 'Organizational Analysis as Discourse Analysis – A Critique', in Grant, D. *et al.* (eds) *op. cit.*

Roberts, J. (1995) *$1000 Billion A Day*, London: HarperCollins.

Rose, M. (1975) *Industrial Behaviour*, 2nd edn, Harmondsworth: Penguin.

Rose, N. (1989) *Governing the Soul: The Shaping of the Private Self*, London: Routledge.

Rosenthal, P., Hill, S. and Peccei, R. (1997) 'Checking Out Service: Evaluating Excellence, HRM and TQM in Retailing', *Work, Employment and Society*, 11(3), 481–503.

Rothman, J. (1989) 'Geodemographics' [Editorial], *Journal of Market Research*, 31(1).

Rowntree, B. S. (1901) *Poverty: A Study of Town Life*, London: Macmillan.

Rucci, A., Kirn, S. P. and Quinn, R. T. (1998) 'The Employee–Customer–Profit Chain at Sears', *Harvard Business Review*, January, 83–98.

Ruggie, J. (1982) 'International Regimes, Transactions and Change: Embedded Liberalism in the Postwar Economic Order', *International Organization*, 36(2), 379–415.

Runciman, W. G. (1993) 'Has British Capitalism Changed since the First World War?', *British Journal of Sociology*, 44(1), 53–67.

Runciman, W. G. (1997) *A Treatise on Social Theory Vol. III: Applied Social Theory*, Cambridge: Cambridge University Press.

Salaman, G. (ed.) (1992) *Human Resource Strategies*, London: Sage.

Salancik, G. R. and Pfeffer, J. (1978) *The External Control of Organizations: A Resource Dependence Perspective*, New York: Harper & Row.

Saunders P. (1990) *A Nation of Homeowners*, London: Allen & Unwin.

Savage, M., Barlow, J., Dickens, P. and Fielding, T. (1992) *Property, Bureaucracy and Culture: Middle Class Formation in Contemporary Britain*, London: Routledge.

Scarborough, H. (ed.) (1992) *The IT Challenge – IT Strategy in Financial Services*, London: Macmillan.

Scarborough, H. (ed.) (1996), *The Management of Expertise*, London: Macmillan.

Scarborough, H. and Burrell, G. (1996) 'The Axeman Cometh – The Changing Roles and Knowledges of Middle Managers', in Clegg, S. R. and Palmer, G. (eds), *The Politics of Management Knowledge*, London: Sage.

Scarborough, H. and Corbett, J. M. (1992) *Technology and Organization*, London: Routledge.

Scase, R. and Goffee, R. (1989) *Reluctant Managers – Their Work and Lifestyles*, London: Unwin Hyman.

Schaffer, R. H. and Thomson, H. A. (1992) 'Successful Change Programs Begin with Results', *Harvard Business Review*, January–February, 80–9.

Schendel, D. and Cool, K. (1988) 'Development of the Strategic Management Field' in Grant, J. (ed.) *Strategic Management Frontiers,* Greenwich, CT; JAI Press.

Schein, E. H. (1992) 'Coming to a New Awareness of Organizational Culture', in Salaman, G. (ed.) *op. cit.*

Schein, E. H. (1969) *Process Consultation*, Reading, Mass: Addison-Wesley.

Schmidt, V. (1996) *From State to Market? The Transformation of French Business and Government*, Cambridge: Cambridge University Press.

Schneider, B. (1980) 'The Service Organization – Climate is Crucial', *Organizational Dynamics*, 9(2), 52–65 (quoted in Ashforth and Humphrey, 1993, *op. cit.*).

Scott, A. (1994) *Willing Slaves? British Workers Under HRM*, Cambridge: Cambridge University Press.

Scott, J. (1982) *The Upper Classes: Property and Privilege in Britain*, London: Macmillan.

Scott, J. (1997) *Corporate Business and Capitalist Classes*, Oxford: Oxford University Press.

Scott, W. R. (1987) 'The Adolescence of Institutional Theory', *Administrative Science Quarterly*, 32, 493–511.

Scott, W. R. (1992) *Organizations: Rational, Natural and Open Systems*, 3rd edn, Englewood Cliffs, NJ: Prentice Hall.

Scott, W. R. and Meyer, J. W. (1991) 'The Organization of Societal Sectors: Propositions and Early Evidence' in Powell, W. W. and Dimaggio, P. *The New Institutionalism in Organizational Analysis*, London: University of Chicago Press.

Seccombe, W. (1993) *Weathering the Storm: Working Class Families from the Industrial Revolution to the Fertility Decline*, London: Verso.

Securities and Investments Board (1993) *Pension Transfers: Report to SIB by KPMG Peat Marwick*, London: SIB.

Securities and Investment Board (1994) *Life Assurance: Disclosure of Commission and Other Matters: Consultative Paper 77*, London: SIB.

Senior, B. (1998) *Organizational Change*, London: Pitman.

Shapiro, E. C., Eccles, R. G. and Soske, T. L. (1993) 'Consulting: Has the Solution Become Part of the Problem?', *Sloan Management Review*, Summer, 89–95.

Shelton, D. (1991) 'Impact of Financial Services Act on Investment Products', *International Journal of Bank Marketing*, 8(2), 12–16.

Smircich, L. (1983) 'Concepts of Culture and Organizational Analysis', *Administrative Science Quarterly*, 28, September, 339–58.

Smith, A. M. and Lewis, B. R. (1989) 'Customer Care in Financial Service Organizations', *International Journal of Bank Marketing*, 7(5), 4–12.

Smith, C. and Meiksins, P. (1995) 'System, Society and Dominance Effects in Cross-National Organizational Analysis', *Work, Employment and Society*, 9(2), 241–67.

Smith, N. C. (1987) 'Consumer Boycotts and Consumer Sovereignty', *European Journal of Marketing*, 21(5), 7–19.

Smith, W. R. (1956) 'Product Differentiation and Market Segmentation as Alternative Strategies', *Journal of Marketing*, July, 3–8. Reprinted in Ennis, B. M. and Cox, K. K. (eds) (1988) *Marketing Classics*, 6th edn, London: Allyn & Bacon.

Speed, R. and Smith, G. (1992) 'Retail Financial Services Segmentation', *Service Industries Journal*, 12(3), 368–83.

Speed, R. and Smith, G. (1993) 'Customers, Strategy and Performance', *International Journal of Bank Marketing*, 11(5), 3–11.

Spero, J. E. and Hart, J. A. (1997) *The Politics of International Economic Relations*, 5th edn, London: Routledge.

Stacey, R. D. (1992) *Managing Chaos*, London: Kogan Page.

Stanley, T. J., Moschis, G. P. and Danko, W. D. (1987) 'Financial Service Segments – The Seven Faces of the Affluent Market', *Journal of Advertising Research*, 27(4), 52–67.

Starkey, K., Wright, M. and Thompson, S. (1991) 'Flexibility, Hierarchy, Markets', *British Journal of Management*, 2, 165–76.

Stevens, M. (1981) *The Big Eight*, New York: Macmillan.

Storey, J. (1983) *Managerial Prerogative and the Question of Control*, London: Routledge & Kegan Paul.

Storey, J. (1995) 'Employment Policies and Practices in UK Clearing Banks: An Overview', *HRM Journal*, 5(4), 24–43.

Storey, J., Cressey, P., Morris, T. and Wilkinson, A. (1997) 'Changing Employment Practices in UK Banking: Case Studies', *Personnel Review*, 25(1/2), 24–42.

Strange, S. (1998) *Mad Money*, Manchester: Manchester University Press.

Stubbs, R. and Underhill, G. (eds) (1994) *Political Economy and the Changing Global Order*, London: Macmillan.

Sturdy, A. J. (ed.) (1989) *Managing IT in Insurance*, Harlow: Longman.

Sturdy, A. J. (1990) 'Clerical Consent – An Analysis of Social Relations in Insurance Work', PhD thesis, UMIST.

Sturdy, A. J. (1992a) 'Clerical Consent', in Sturdy, A. J., Knights, D. and Willmott, H. (eds), *Skill and Consent*, London: Routledge.

Sturdy, A. J. (1992b) 'Banks A Lot (Banks, General Insurance and the Consumer)', *Post Magazine*, 4 December.

Sturdy, A. J. (1997a) 'The Consultancy Process', *Journal of Management Studies*, 34(3), 389–413.

Sturdy, A. J. (1997b) 'The Dialectics of Consultancy', *Critical Perspectives on Accounting*, 8(5), 511–35.

Sturdy, A. J. (1998) 'Customer Care in a Consumer Society', *Organization*, 5(1), 27–53.

Sturdy, A. J. and Knights, D. (1996) 'The Segmentation of Subjectivity', in Clegg, S. R. and Palmer, G. (eds), *Constituting Management: Markets, Meanings and Identities*, Berlin: De Gruyter.

Sturdy, A. J. and Morgan, G. (1993) 'Review of Marketing Trends in French Retail Banking', *International Journal of Bank Marketing*, 11(7), 11–19.

Sturdy, A. J., Ackers, P., Jones, I., Nicholls, P. and Newman, I. (1991) 'Clients, Management Consultants and IT in the UK Financial Services Sector', Final Report, Bristol Business School.

Sturdy, A. J., Knights, D. and Willmott, H. (eds) (1992) *Skill and Consent*, London: Routledge.

Sturdy, A. J., Morgan, G. and Daniel, J-P. (1997) 'National Management Styles – The Strategy of Bancassurance in Britain and France', in Morgan, G. and Knights, D. (eds), *op. cit.*, 154–77.

Sturdy, A. J., Nicholls, P. and Newman, I. (1990) 'Management Expertise, Agency and Practice: A Case of Management Consultants', Labour Process Conference Paper, Aston.

Sturdy, A. J., Nicholls, P. and Wetherley, P. (1989) 'Management Consultants and the Politics of IT Strategy', EGOS Conference Paper, Berlin.

Supple, B. (1970) *The Royal Exchange Assurance – A History of British Insurance, 1720–1970*, Cambridge: Cambridge University Press.

Sutton, R. I. and Rafaeli, A. (1988) 'Untangling the Relationship Between Displayed Emotion and Organizational Sales', *Academy of Management Journal*, 31(3), 461–87.

Sykes, J. (1926) *The Amalgamation Movement in English Banking, 1825–1924*, London: P. S. King & Son Ltd.

Tayeb, M. H. (1996) *The Management of a Multi-cultural Workforce*, Chichester: Wiley.

Teulings, A. (1986) 'Managerial Labour Processes in Organized Capitalism', in Knights, D. and Willmott, H. (eds), *Managing the Labour Process*, Aldershot: Gower.

Therborn, G. (1995) *European Modernity and Beyond*, London: Sage.

Thomas, A. B. (1993) *Controversies in Management*, London: Routledge.

Thomas, A. B. (1993a) 'Sacred Cows and Other Animals', *Times Higher Education Supplement*, 26 November.

Thompson, E. P. (1967) 'Time, Work Discipline and Industrial Capitalism', *Past and Present*, 38, 56–97.

Thompson, P. and Ackroyd, S. (1995) 'All Quiet on the Workplace Front?', *Sociology*, 29(4), 615–33.

Thrift, N. (1998) 'Virtual Capitalism: The Globalization of Reflexive Business Knowledge', in Carrier and Miller, *op. cit.*

Thwaites, D. and Lynch, J. E. (1992) 'Adoption of the Marketing Concept by UK Building Societies', *Service Industries Journal*, 12(4), 437–62.

Tienari, J. (1999) *Through the Ranks Slowly – Studies on Organizational Reforms and Gender in Banking*, PhD thesis, Helsinki School of Economics and Business Administration.

Tiratsoo, N. and Tomlinson, J. (1998) *The Conservatives and Industrial Efficiency 1951–64*, London: Routledge.

Tisdall, P. (1982) *Agents of Change – The Development and Practice of Management Consultancy*, London: Heinemann.

Tolbert, P. S. and Zucker, L. G. (1996) 'The Institutionalization of Institutional Theory', in Clegg, S. R. *et al.* (eds), *Handbook of Organization Studies*, London: Sage.

Trungpa, C. (1976) *The Myth of Freedom and the Way of Meditation*, London: Shambhala.

Tuckman, A. (1994) 'The Yellow Brick Road: TQM and the Restructuring of Organizational Culture', *Organization Studies*, 15(5), 727–51.

Van de Ven, A. H. and Poole, M. S. (1995) 'Explaining Development and Change in Organizations', *Academy of Management Review*, 20(3), 510–40.

Van Maanen, J. (1991) 'The Smile Factory: Work at Disneyland', in Frost, P. J. *et al.* (eds), *Reframing Organizational Culture*, London: Sage.

Wade, R. (1990) *Governing the Market*, Princeton, N. J.: Princeton University Press.

Wade, R. (1996) 'Japan, the World Bank and the Art of Paradigm Maintenance', *New Left Review*, 21(7), 3–37.

Wade, R. and Veneroso, F. (1998) 'The Asian Crisis: The High Debt Model versus the Wall Street–Treasury–IMF Complex', *New Left Review*, 228, 3–24.

Waire, B. (1992) 'The Ideology and Practice of Personal Pensions', *Economy and Society*, 21(1), 27–44.

Walker, D. S. and Child, J. (1979) 'The Development of Professionalism as an Issue in British Marketing', *European Journal of Marketing*, 13(1), 27–54.

Warde, A. (1994) 'Consumers, Identity and Belonging: Reflections on Some Theses of Zygmunt Bauman', in Keat, R. *et al*. (eds) *op. cit*.

Watkins, J. (1989) 'Linking IT Strategy to the Business', in Sturdy, A. J. (ed.), *Managing IT in Insurance*, Harlow: Longman.

Watkins, T. (1990) 'The Demand for Financial Services', in Ennew, C. *et al*. (eds), *op. cit*.

Watkins, T. and Wright, M. (1986) *Marketing Financial Services*, London: Butterworth.

Watson, I. (1982) 'The Adoption of Marketing by the English Clearing Banks', *European Journal of Marketing*, vol. 16.

Watson, T. J. (1994a) 'Flavours of the Month and the Search for Managerial Control', Labour Process Conference paper, Aston University, 23–25 March.

Watson, T. J. (1994b) *In Search of Management: Culture Chaos and Control in Managerial Work*, London: Routledge.

Watson, T. J. (1995) 'In Search of HRM – Beyond the Rhetoric and Reality Distinction or the Dog that didn't Bark', *Personnel Review*, 24(4), 6–16.

Weatherly, K. A. and Tansik, D. A. (1993) 'Tactics Used by Customer-Contact Workers: Effects of Role Stress, Boundary Spanning and Control', *International Journal of Service Industry Management*, 4(3), 4–17.

Webster, C. (1998) *The National Health Service: A Political History*, Oxford: Oxford University Press.

Weick, K. E. (1987) 'Substitutes for Strategy', in Teece, D. J. (ed.), *The Competitive Challenge*, New York: Ballinger.

Weiss, L. and Hobson, J. (1995) *States and Economic Development*, Oxford: Polity Press.

Wells, W. D. and Gubar, G. (1966) 'The Life Cycle Concept in Marketing Research', *Journal of Marketing Research*, 4, November, 355–63.

Wells, W. D. (1975) 'Psychographics – A Critical Review', *Journal of Marketing Research*, 12, May, 196–213. Reprinted in Annas, B. M. and Cox, K. K. (eds) (1988) *Marketing Classics*, 6th edn, London: Allyn & Bacon.

Wharton, A. S. (1993) 'The Affective Consequences of Service Work: Managing Emotions on the Job', *Work and Occupations*, 20(2), 205–32.

Whipp, R. (1996) 'Creative Deconstruction: Strategy and Organizations', in Clegg *et al*., *op. cit*., 261–75.

Whipp, R., Rosenfeld, R. and Pettigrew, A. (1989) 'Culture and Competitiveness: Evidence from Two Mature UK Industries', *Journal of Management Studies*, 26(6), 561–85.

Whitley, R. D. (1992a) *Business Systems in East Asia*, London: Sage.

Whitley, R. D. (ed.) (1992b) *European Business Systems*, London: Sage.

Whitley, R. D. (1994) 'The Internationalization of Firms and Markets', *Organization*, 1(1), 101–24.

Whitley, R. D. (1994a) 'Dominant Forms of Economic Organization in Market Economies', *Organization Studies*, 15(1), 153–82.

Whitley, R. D. (1995) 'Academic Knowledge and Work Jurisdiction in Management', *Organization Studies*, 16(1), 81–105.

Whitley, R. D. and Kristensen, P. H. (1995) *The Changing Eurpean Firm*, London: Routledge.

Whitley, R. D. and Kristensen P. H. (1997) *Governance at Work*, Oxford: Oxford University Press.

Whittington, R. (1992) 'Putting Giddens Into Action', *Journal of Management Studies*, 29(4), 693–712.

Whittington, R. (1993) *What is Strategy and Does it Matter?*, London: Routledge.

Whittington, R. and Whipp, R. (1992) 'Professional Ideology and Marketing Implementation', *European Journal of Marketing*, 26(1), 52–63.

Whyte, W. (1948) *Human Relations in the Restaurant Industry*, New York: McGraw-Hill.

Wilkinson, A., Godfrey, G. and Marchington, M. (1997) 'Bouquets, Brickbats and Blinkers – TQM and Employee Involvement in Practice', *Organization Studies*, 18(5), 799–819.

Wilkinson, A. and Willmott, H. (eds) (1995) *Making Quality Critical*, London: Routledge.

Wilkinson, B. (1996) 'Culture, Institutions and Business in East Asia', *Organization Studies*, 17(3), 421–47.

Williams, M. J. (1996) 'The Rise of Consultants: External Advisers and Public Policy Since 1979', Working Paper, Politics, No. 4, University of Hertfordshire.

Williamson, O. E. (1975) *Markets and Hierarchies*, New York: Free Press.

Willmott, H. (1992) 'Postmodernism and Excellence: The De-differentiation of Economy and Culture', *Journal of Organizational Change Management*, 5(1), 58–68.

Willmott, H. (1993) 'Strength is Ignorance; Slavery is Freedom: Managing Culture in Modern Organizations', *Journal of Management Studies*, 30(4), 515–52.

Willmott, H. (1995) 'The Odd Couple? Reengineering Business Processes; Managing Human Relations', *New Technology, Work and Employment*, 10(2), 89–99.

Willmott, H. (1997) 'Rethinking Management and Managerial Work – Capitalism, Control and Subjectivity', *Human Relations*, 50(11), 1329–59.

Wilson, D. (1992) *A Strategy of Change*, London: Routledge.

Wilson, D. and Rosenfeld, R. (1998) *Managing Organizations*, 2nd edn, London: McGraw Hill.

Wilson, F. (1996) 'Organization Theory – Blind and Deaf to Gender', *Organization Studies*, 17(5), 825–42.

Wilson, R. M. S. (ed.) (1980) 'The Marketing of Financial Services', *Management Bibliographies and Reviews*, 6(3).

Winward, J. (1994) 'The Organized Consumer', in Keat, R. *et al.* (eds) *op. cit.*

Wood, D. (1983) 'Uses and Abuses of Personnel Consultants', *Personnel Management*, October, 40–44.

Zelizer, V. (1994) *The Social Meaning of Money*, New York: Basic Books.

Zimmeck, M. (1985) 'Gladstone holds his own: the Origins of income tax relief for life insurance policies', *Bulletin of the Institute of Historical Research*, 58, 167–88.

Zollinger, M. (1985) *Marketing Bancaire*, Paris: Bordas.

Zucker, L. (1987) 'Institutional Theories of Organization', *Annual Review of Sociology*, 13, 443–64.

# Index